AF674060

Islamic Fundamentalism

Islamic Fundamentalism

Naseem Akhthar

MD Publications Pvt Ltd
New Delhi
www.mdppl.com

Copyright © 2009 by MD Publications Pvt Ltd.

All rights reserved. No part of this book may be reproduced cr utilized in any form or by any means, electronically or mechanically, including photocopying, recording, or by any information storage and retrieval system, without the prior permission in writing from the publisher.

Published by :

MD Publications Pvt Ltd
"MD House", 11, Darya Ganj,
New Delhi - 110 002
Phone : +91-11-41563325 (Customer Service)
+91-11-41562846 (Editorial)
E-mail (orders): order@mdppl.com
Website: www.mdppl.com

ISBN: 978-81-7533-183-9

Published and Printed by Mr. Pranav Gupta on behalf of **MD Publications Pvt Ltd** at Times Press, New Delhi.

Preface

Increasingly these days, we hear about Islamic fundamentalism from the Western media, the policy makers and many an intellectual. The term has gained so much currency that it deserves some serious scrutiny. It needs our attention especially because it is the Western rendition of Islam, and not an expression which Muslims have anything to do with. Apparently, it seems to imply that there is what you may call fundamentalist Islam as distinct from non-fundamentalist Islam. It seems to emphasize that there are those among Muslims who believe in the basic principles of Islam and there are those who do not.

The premises of Islamic fundamentalism are rooted in an essentialist world view whereby innate qualities and attributes apply to individuals and human societies, irrespective of time, historical change or political circumstances. Hence, an immutable substance governs human existence and determines its outward movement.

One of its most defining features is the "reopening" of the gates of Ijtihad. This distinguishes it as distinct from (but sometimes overlapping with) Islamism, which is the term for a political ideology of Islam, but which may use one of the four preexisting schools of the Shari'ah. Exemplary figures of Islamic fundamentalism who are also termed Islamists are Sayyid Qutb and Abul Ala Mawdudi.

The philosophical roots of Islamic fundamentalism are largely the result of a conscious attempt to revive and restate the theoretical relevance of Islam in the modern world. The writings of three twentieth-century Muslim thinkers and activists - Sayyid Qutb, Ayatollah Ruhollah al-Khumayni and Abu al-'Ala al-Mawdudi - provide authoritative guidelines delineating the philosophical discourse of Islamic fundamentalism. However, whereas al-Khumayni and al-Mawdudi made original contributions towards formulating a new Islamic political theory, it was Qutb who offered a coherent exposition of Islam as a philosophical system.

The movement gained momentum in recent decades within several Muslim nations. Islamic fundamentalists oppose the infiltration of secular and Westernizing influences and seek to institute Islamic law, including strict codes of behavior. They also target political corruption in Muslim nations. Severely repressed by the governments of their own nations, such as Algeria, Egypt, and Saudi Arabia, they nevertheless target the United States as the "Great Satan," chant "Death to America," and provide ready recruits for terrorist networks such as Al Qaeda.

The subject of Islamic fundamentalism attracted a great deal of attention in the West after the Iranian Revolution of 1978–79 — which deposed Iran's ruler, Mohammad Reza Shah Pahlavi (1919–80), and established an Islamic republic — and especially after the September 11 attacks on the United States in 2001 by al-Qaeda, an international Islamist terrorist network. The spectacular nature of these events may have lent plausibility to the common but mistaken belief in the West that Islam and Islamic fundamentalism are closely connected, if not identical. In fact, however, not all Muslims believe that the Qur'an is not the literal and inerrant word of God, nor do all of them believe that Islam requires strict conformity to all the religious and moral precepts in the Qur'an. More important, unlike genuine Islamic fundamentalists, most Muslims are not ideologically committed to the idea of a state and society based on Islamic religious law.

Muslims believe that their religion was revealed by God

(Allah in Arabic) to Muhammad, the Prophet of Islam, the final Prophet delivered by God. However, the Muslims brand of conservatism which is generally termed Islamic fundamentalism encompasses all the beliefs of traditional Muslims that they should restrict themselves to literal interpretations of their sacred texts, the Qur'an and Hadith. This may describe the private religious attitudes of individuals and have no relationship with larger social groups, it describes a variety of religious movements and political parties in Muslim communities and as opposed to the above two usages, in the West "Islamic fundamentalism" is most often used to describe Muslim individuals and groups which advocate Islamism, a political ideology calling for the replacement of state secular laws with Islamic law.

Islamist movements have been politically significant in most Muslim countries primarily because they articulate political and social grievances better than do the established secular parties, some of which (the leftist parties) were discredited following the collapse of communism in eastern Europe and the Soviet Union in 1990–91. Although the governments of Saudi Arabia and other oil-producing countries of the Persian Gulf region have represented themselves as conforming strictly to Islamic law, they continue to face internal opposition from Islamist movements for their pro-Western political and economic policies, the extreme concentration of their countries' wealth in the hands of the ruling families, and, in the Islamists' view, the rulers' immoral lifestyles.

I am very grateful to Mr. Pranav Gupta, Director of MD Publications Pvt Ltd, New Delhi, for his cooperation and support for this book.

Naseem Akhthar

Islam, is he really moving from *islam* to *kufr*? is he really [illegible]

[illegible] from the conflict [illegible] conviction that the message of the Qur'an is based on truth and therefore will prevail [illegible] people for their religion which is described as worse than killing in battle.

[illegible]

[illegible] believing opponents [illegible] do the same.

[illegible] Qur'anic perspective is also shown [illegible] it is stated that the Messenger came not as a watcher over people but only as one who clearly declares the truth: 5:92, 99; 13:40; 16:35, 82; 24:54; [illegible]

Contents

Contents

1

Islamic Fundamentalism

Introduction

Islamic fundamentalism Arabic: *usul*, is a term used to describe religious ideologies seen as advocating a return to the "fundamentals" of Islam, the Quran and the Sunnah. Definitions of the term vary. It is deemed problematic by those who suggest that Islamic belief requires all Muslims to be fundamentalists and by others as a term used by outsiders to describe perceived trends within Islam.

One of its most defining features is the "reopening" of the gates of jihad. This distinguishes it as distinct from (but sometimes overlapping with) Islamism, which is the term for a political ideology of Islam, but which may use one of the four preexisting schools of the Shari'ah. Exemplary figures of Islamic fundamentalism who are also termed Islamists are Sayyid Qutb and Abul Ala Mawdudi.

"The most prolific rhetoric of fundamentalism ... is reserved for Islam, and especially for the depiction of contemporary events in the Middle East." It should be noted up front that many Muslims reject usage of the Western terms "fundamentalism" and "fundamentalist," instead preferring the terms "Islamism" and "Islamists" when speaking of groups advocating Islamic political law. Both the Western roots of "fundamentalist" terminology and the extremist perception associated with the term are reason to resist usage of the term. Nonetheless, "fundamentalism" is now a commonly-used term in describing the ultra-conservative expressions of Islamic, Christian, and Jewish faith groups, among others.

This terminology is useful in that it recognizes, as noted previously, that similarities do exist among ultra-conservative expressions of various faith groups. In addition, the term is employed across faith groups by a growing number of religious scholars' worldwide, scholars who note the differences among faith groups while also recognizing that opposition to modernity is an instrumental, shared element of certain ultra-conservative expressions within a variety of faith groups. Accordingly, for the purposes of this paper, "fundamentalist" terminology will be employed, although with the understanding that it is, in some respects, a contested terminology.

Although Islamic fundamentalism is indeed a modern phenomenon, it cannot be properly understood apart from the larger context of Islamic faith and Muslim history. Ultimately, Islamic fundamentalism is religious in nature, and in approaching the subject one must examine "the dynamics of the expansion of Islam as a world religion of salvation."

Fundamentalist Islamic ideology is based upon two "pillars", the conviction that Islamic law (the *sharia*) is the only valid system for regulating human life (individual, social and political), and the conviction that a true and faithful Muslim society can only be achieved through an Islamic state. The Prophet Muhammad is the founder and central figure of the Islamic faith. In 610 C. E. Muhammad received his first revelation from God. Over time, the Prophet received a number of revelations which were transcribed into the text of the Quran. Received and recorded as God's direct revelation (or Word), the Quran became the written text of Islam and the authoritative source of law. Over the course of ensuing generations, statements and actions attributed to Muhammad and transmitted orally by his followers were compiled and written down into the accepted *hadith* (many sayings and actions attributed to Muhammad were disputed).

The *hadith* revealed the *sunna* (or path) that Muslims should follow in the daily living of their lives. Taken together with the Quran and the consensus of learned scholars within the Muslim community, they eventually formed the *sharia,* Islam's sacred law. Muhammad developed a small following in his hometown of Mecca, but his new religious views eventually put him at odds with city leaders. Forced to flee, Muhammad and his followers settled in the nearby city of Medina in 622. He soon rose to political and military prominence, negotiating a treaty with Mecca in 628, then breaking the treaty and capturing Mecca in 630. For the next two years, Muhammad expanded his power throughout the region of Arabia.

After Muhammad's death in 632 C.E., his followers were left with the task of trying to determine who should succeed the Prophet (Muhammad had left no instructions in terms of successors). Initially, the struggle was of a political nature. Abu Bakr, an early convert to Islam and trusted advisor and close friend of Muhammad, was selected as the first caliph (successor to Muhammad). His selection was controversial and came at a time when the Muslim state was expanding into southern Syria and Iraq. Tribes throughout Arabia openly revolted against Abu Bakr, while proclaiming loyalty to Muhammad.

Near death, Abu Bakr appointed Umar b. al-Khattab as his successor. Umar successfully expanded the Muslim empire, quickly conquering Iraq, Iran, Syria, Palestine, Armenia and Egypt. The conquered peoples were given the status of *dhimi* ("protected peoples") and were treated well. Umar utilized local administrators under the rule of Muslim governors. Umar's assassination in 644 led to the appointment of Uthman b. Affan as the third caliph. Uthman continued Umar's expansionist policies in the midst of growing opposition, at the same time hiring many of his own kin as administrators, to the point of straining the treasury. In addition, he took religious authority upon himself, burning all copies of the Quran other than the one version he deemed the official version.

Uthman was also assassinated, and civil war broke out under his successor Ali b. Abi Talib. Ali, who had been part of the opposition to Uthman, refused to punish Uthman's murderers, in the process alienating supporters of the first three caliphs. In the meantime, Syria appointed a rival caliph, Muawiya, who went to war against Ali and became caliph of the entire empire following Ali's murder, thus ending the original reign of caliphs (all four of whom had been related to Muhammad in some manner) and beginning the reign of the Umayyad dynasty.

Supporters of Ali were Shiite Muslims, who devoted themselves to preserving the house of Ali and seeking to amend the wrong done to him. To the Shiite, the first three caliphs were not legitimate, and the caliphate ended with Ali, as testified by both the end of Muhammad's lineage and the evil acts which took place among the Umayyad dynasty. On the other hand, Sunni Muslims embraced all four caliphs as orthodox, viewing their collective reign as the golden age of Islam, while also recognizing that all the descendants of the Arabian Quraysh tribe (which included the Umayyad clan), despite being marked by some periods of evil, were nonetheless legitimate caliphs.

Shortly after Ali's death, as Arab Muslims sought political organization following decades of expansion, two rebellious movements, the puritanical (Sunni) Kharijism and millenarian Shi'ism, arose advocating Islam as a universal religion of salvation. The Shi'ite millenarian rebellion of the 680s proclaimed a coming messiah (the *Mahdi*), a belief later incorporated into popular Sufism. Kharijism, on the other hand, rejected the present world by separating itself and advocating a rigid application of Islamic law as espoused in the Quran, proclaiming that nominal Muslims were infidels.

The tension between Sunnis and Shiites has remained to the present time. Although the Shiites showed the earliest orthodox tendencies, the vast majority of Muslims today are Sunni, and fundamentalism is more common among Sunnis than Shiites. By the end of the ninth century, Islamic law was in the process of expanding to include not only the Quran, but also the *hadith*. Together, the Quran and the accepted *hadith* came to comprise the authoritative Scripture for the faith community. The establishment of the Sunni Hanbali School of law in the same century, a reaction against rational theology, provided the medieval archetype of later Islamic revivalism. The Hanbalites held to the Quran as the literal, unquestioned, and uncreated Word of God, while affirming the Tradition (or customs) of Muhammad (*Sunna*, and hence *Sunni*) and the consensus of the Muslim community (*jama'a*).

The Hanbalite tradition, in turn, produced the strict Wahhabi tradition in Arabia in the late eighteenth century. The founder of the Wahhabi tradition was Muhammad Ibn 'Abd al-Wahhab, a religious scholar who formed an alliance with Muhammad bin Saud, the first ruler of what would become Saudia Arabia, and who traveled throughout the Muslim world and journeyed to Medina and Mecca. Distraught by the compromises the Islamic faith had made with popular religious practices (as expressed in the mystical faith of Sufism), Ibn 'Abd al-Wahhab, seeking to revive the Islamic faith, taught the transcendent unity of God (*tawhid*) and strict obedience to the Quran.

The Wahhabis, believing that modern Islam had become corrupted and polluted from within, were a revivalist movement which sought to return Islam to its pure roots. In 1766, Wahhab's doctrinal views won recognition among the scholars of Mecca. The Wahhabi movement became very influential, leading to the founding of other similar movements. Properly speaking, the Wahhabi movement was a revivalist movement based on orthodox Islamic law. Ironically, the Wahhabis ideological opposites (the more liberal Sufi expression of the Islamic faith, based on popular spirituality) provided the organizational model for Islamic revivalism. The Wahhabi movement was one of a number of Islamic revival and reform movements in the eighteenth century. In the twentieth century, Wahhabi Islam would provide the theological foundation for a political fundamentalist state.

The 1857 Sepoy uprising in India, in which both Muslims and Hindus revolted against British rule, provided the impetus for the next ideological stepping stone in the history of Islamic fundamentalism. The British reacted to the uprising by persecuting Muslims. In an attempt to prevent suspected Muslim disloyalty from getting out of hand, the British destroyed Muslim holy sites in Delhi. The persecution, in turn, led Muslim *ulama* (theologians) to found private *madrasas* (colleges) over which the British state would have no control. The first such school was located in the town of Deobandi, about 90 miles northeast of Delhi. The Deobandi schools taught adherence to strict interpretations of Islamic law, based on the Quran and the *hadith*.

Intellectually, via publications and debates, the Deobandi scholars sought to establish Islam as the one true faith. Socially, the Deobandi school of thought rejected the shrine elements of Islamic mysticism (Sufism) which had developed in the ninth century as Islam sought to accommodate the faiths of conquered lands.

In the place of mysticism, the Deobandis taught careful personal adherence to morality and piety as spelled out in the Quran and *hadith*. The Deobandi tradition thus served to provide a highly intellectual, socially structured, and overtly evangelical scriptural foundation for an Islamic faith which was facing growing pressure from Western influences. The shift from revivalism to fundamentalism initially took place through the Egyptian Muslim Brotherhood ("The Society of Muslim Brothers") movement in the 1930s. Although originally based in Egypt, the movement has exercised formidable influence throughout the Arab world.

The Muslim Brotherhood, as R. Hrair Dekmejian notes, "More than any other organization, has been the ideological and institutional epicenter of fundamentalism in the Arab sphere and the Islamic world ... it is impossible to comprehend contemporary Sunni Islamism and its Arab manifestations without a firm understanding of the origins and evolution of the brotherhood." Founded in 1929 by Hasan al-Banna, the Muslim Brotherhood tapped into popular unrest against British rule, local political turmoil, and the corrupting influence of the West. Banna, a Sufi spiritualist, Islamic scholar, and activist leader, was the "avatar" of modern Sunni revivalism. His movement, which was more successful than previous revivalist movements, possessed an activist ideology, an organizational structure, charismatic leadership, mass following and a pragmatic orientation.

The movement was based on the Quran and the *hadith*, and translated doctrine into social action at a time when Egypt was in social unrest. Initially espousing non-violence, the Brotherhood quickly became one of Egypt's most powerful organizations. The group was effectively organized, made extensive use of propaganda, and appealed to a cross-section of Egyptian society. However, Banna's efforts to use politics to enact Islamic law in Egypt led to state persecution of the group by the late 1940s, which in turn led to the assassination of the Egyptian monarch by a

Muslim Brother, for which Banna was assassinated in reprisal.

The following decades witnessed escalating clashes between the increasingly violent Brotherhood (as well as the many new fundamentalist groups it spawned) and Islamic secular states. Israel's victory in the 1967 war was a crucial event. Islamic fundamentalists proclaimed that the Arab world lost the war because of a lack of religious faith, and fundamentalist calls for the imposition of *shariah* (Islamic) law found even greater reception in the Arab world. Anwar al-Sadat, who ascended to the Egyptian presidency in 1970, sought to co-opt the rising fundamentalist tide through the 1971 establishment of Islam as the official religion of the Egyptian state, and *sharia* law as a source of legislation (in 1980, *sharia* law was made the main source of legislation).

Nonetheless, Sadat's openness to the West and Israel, as evidenced by the 1979 Camp David Accord with United States President Carter Israeli Prime Minister Begin, resulting in peace with Israel, was scorned by the multiplying Islamic fundamentalist organizations. In September 1981, realizing that he had underestimated Islamic fundamentalists, Sadat led the government in taking direct control of all mosques and arresting thousands of militants. One month later he was dead, assassinated by members of the Islamic fundamentalist group Tanzim al-Jihad. Since Sadat's assassination, a variety of Islamic fundamentalist movements in Egypt have increasingly turned to violence against the state, unacceptable social conduct, and even one another.

A parallel transition from scriptural fundamentalism to political fundamentalism took place in South Asia via the Jama'at-i Islami (Islamic Party), founded by the Deobandi-trained Sayyid Abu'l-A'la Mawdudi (1903-1979) in 1941. Concerned with the decline of Muslim power in India in the early twentieth century, Mawdudi determined that diversity, in the form of interfaith mixing and a growing liberalization of Muslim faith had weakened Islam. The answer was to sever social and political ties with Hindus and other non-Muslims and take up arms against non-Muslims. Mawdudi looked to the Quran for a scriptural rationale for his militant views:

> "Fight in the cause of God those who fight you, but do not transgress limits; for God loveth not transgressors. And slay them wherever ye catch them, and turn them out from where they have turned you out; for tumult and oppression are worse than slaughter; but fight them not at the sacred mosque, unless they (first) fight you there; but if they fight you, slay them. Such is the reward of those who suppress faith. But if they cease, God is Oft-forgiving, most Merciful. And fight them on until there is no more tumult or oppression, and there prevail justice and faith in God; but if they cease, let there be no hostility except to those who practice oppression." (s. 2:190-193)

Mawdudi also found parallel justification in the *Hadith*. The Jama'at-i Islami was thus formed as a political movement to transform society via strict Islamic ideology, considering itself as the "vanguard" of an Islamic revolution. Yet within two decades of its founding, the party became more pragmatic in approach, advocating a constitution for Pakistan that included a commitment to democracy and individual rights. However, faced with Communist encroachments in Pakistan in the late 1960s, the Jama'at-i Islami eventually abandoned cooperative efforts and sought to establish a strict Islamic state identity in opposition to the Bhutto regime. Ultimately failing in this regard, and losing significant grassroots political support in the process, the party fell back to trying to accommodate both ideology and pragmatism. The rebirth of democracy in Pakistan in 1988 has since forced the Jama'at-i Islami to recognize the importance of further compromise if the party is to have a meaningful voice in the political structure of Pakistan.

In short, by the 1980s the legacy of Islamic revivalism, as expressed in Wahabbi Islam and the Deobandi *madrasa* tradition, had found firm fruition in a milieu of political fundamentalist organizations which were actively seeking to impose *sharia* law in states throughout the Arab world and beyond, a subject which will command our later attention. The proliferation of Islamic political fundamentalism, in turn, has been characterized by certain behavioural characteristics, ranging from passive to militant. The following characteristics are indicative of modern Islamic fundamentalism:

Characteristics of Individualistic Passive Fundamentalism:

1. Regular mosque attendance (five times a day).
2. Strict Observance of the Five Pillars of Islam:
    a. Profession of faith (*shahadah*)
    b. Prayers (*salat*)
    c. Fasting (*sawm*)
    d. Almsgiving (*sakat*)
    e. Pilgrimage (*hajj*)
3. Strict adherence to Quranic prohibitions (such as abstaining from alcohol and sexual immorality).
4. Regular religious meditation, reading of the Quran, and reading of other Islamic literature.
5. Participation in religious group activities within and without the mosque.
6. Participation in neighborhood self-help and mutual assistance societies.
7. Growing full beards (lihya) and thin moustaches as a sign of devotion and piety.
8. Wearing distinctive clothing (including a facial and head veil for women).

Characteristics of Individualistic Activist Fundamentalism:

1. Pursuit of passive characteristics listed above with great rigor.
2. Tendency to live together in specific neighborhoods, sometimes in physical and social isolation from passive fundamentalists.
3. Frequenting of specific mosques that cater to activist agendas.
4. Engagement in acts of "purifying" violence directed against sinful institutions, including nightclubs, movie theatres, and governments.

Manifestations of Collective Islamic Fundamentalism:

1. Mosque building (both private and government sponsored).
2. Radio-television programming (provides religious instruction).
3. Observance of holidays (observed with great religious fervor).
4. Mosque attendance (faithful devotion).
5. The press (increase in religious instruction in newspapers).
6. Illumination of mosques (elaborate lighting at nighttime).
7. Religious literature (an unprecedented increase in printing copies of the *Quran* and books on Islamic history and religion.
8. Display of copies of the Quran (in public places).
9. Religious slogans (increasingly displayed in public places).

Finally, terrorist activity against Western government and society has become a vivid expression of Islamic political fundamentalism in recent years. The definition offered by American historian Ira Lapedis distinguishes between mainstream Islamists and Fundamentalists.

Although a fundamentalist may also be an Islamist, a Fundamentalist is "a political individual" in search of a "more original Islam," while the Islamist is pursuing a political agenda.

He notes that Islamic fundamentalism "is at best only an umbrella designation for a very wide variety of movements, some intolerant and exclusivist, some pluralistic; some favourable to science, some anti-scientific; some primarily devotional and some primarily political; some democratic, some authoritarian; some pacific, some violent." Graham Fuller describes it not as distinct from Islamism but as a subset, "the most conservative element among Islamists." Its "strictest form" includes "Wahhabism, sometimes also referred to as salafiyya. For fundamentalists the law is the most essential component of Islam, leading to an overwhelming emphasis upon jurisprudence, usually narrowly conceived."

Another American, Robert Pelletreau, Jr., assistant secretary of state for Near Eastern affairs, believes it the other way around, Islamism being the subset of Muslims "with political goals ... within" the "broader fundamentalist revival". Still another, Martin Kramer, sees little difference between the two terms, "To all intents and purposes, Islamic fundamentalism and Islamism have become synonyms in contemporary American usage."

Author Olivier Roy distinguishes between fundamentalists (or neo-fundamentalists) and Islamists in describing fundamentalists as more passionate in their opposition to the perceived "corrupting influence of Western culture," avoiding Western dress, "neckties, laughter, the use of Western forms of salutation, handshakes, applause." While Islamists like "Maududi didn't hesitate to attend Hindu ceremonies. Khomeini never proposed the status of dhimmi (protected) for Iranian Christians or Jews, as provided for in the sharia: the Armenians in Iran have remained Iranian citizens, are required to perform military service and to pay the same taxes as Muslims, and have the right to vote (with separate electoral colleges). Similarly, the Afghan Jamaat, in its statutes, has declared it legal in the eyes of Islam to employ non-Muslims as experts."

Other distinctions are in Politics and economics. Islamists often talk of "revolution" and believe "that the society will be Islamized only through social and political action, it is necessary to leave the mosque ..." Fundamentalists are uninterested in revolution, less interested in "modernity or by Western models in politics or economics," and less willing to associate with non-Muslims.

- **Sharia.** While both Islamists and fundamentalists are committed to implementing Sharia law, Islamists "tend to consider it more a project than a corpus."
- **Issue of women.** "Islamists generally tend to favour the education of women and their participation in social and political life, the Islamist woman militates, studies, and has the right to work, but in a chador. Islamist groups include women's associations.' While the fundamentalist preaches for women to return to the home, Islamism believes it is sufficient that "the sexes be separated in public."

Controversy

The term Islamic fundamentalism is often criticized. Bernard Lewis, a leading historian of Islam, has had this to say against it:

The use of this term is established and must be accepted, but it remains unfortunate and can be misleading. "Fundamentalist" is a Christian term. It seems to have come into use in the early years of this century, and denotes certain Protestant churches and organizations, more particularly those that maintain the literal divine origin and inerrancy of the Bible. In this they oppose the liberal and modernist theologians, who tend to a more critical, historical view of Scripture. Among Muslim theologians there is as yet no such liberal or modernist approach to the Qur'an, and all Muslims, in their attitude to the text of the Qur'an, are in principle at least fundamentalists. Where the so-called Muslim fundamentalists differ from other Muslims and indeed from Christian fundamentalists is in their scholasticism and their legalism. They base themselves not only on the Qur'an, but also on the Traditions of the Prophet, and on the corpus of transmitted theological and legal learning.

John Esposito has attacked the term for its association "with political activism, extremism, fanaticism, terrorism, and anti-Americanism," saying "I prefer to speak of Islamic revivalism and Islamic activism."

However, in 1988, the University of Chicago, backed by the American Academy of Arts and Sciences, launched "the Fundamentalism Project", devoted to researching fundamentalism in the world's major religions - Christianity, Islam, Judaism, Hinduism, Buddhism, and Confucianism. It defined fundamentalism as "approach, or set of strategies, by which beleaguered believers attempt to preserve their distinctive identity as a people or group ... by a selective retrieval of doctrines, beliefs, and practices from a sacred past."

At least two Muslim academics have defended the use of the phrase. Syrian philosopher Sadik J. al-Azm and Egyptian philosopher Hasan Hanafi surveying the doctrines of the new Islamic movements, Al-Azm found them to consist of "an immediate return to Islamic 'basics' and 'fundamentals.' .... It seems to me quite reasonable that calling these Islamic movements 'Fundamentalist' (and in the strong sense of the term) is adequate, accurate, and correct."

Hasan Hanafi reached the same conclusion, "It is difficult to find a more appropriate term than the one recently used in the West, 'fundamentalism,' to cover the meaning of what we name Islamic awakening or revival."

Interpretation of Texts

Muslims believe that the Qur'an is the unadulterated word of God as revealed to Muhammad through the angel Jibril (Archangel Gabriel). Islamic fundamentalists, or at least "reformist" fundamentalists, believe that Islam is based on the Qur'an, Hadith and Sunnah and "criticize the tradition, the commentaries, popular religious practices (maraboutism, the cult of saints), deviations, and superstitions.

They aim to return to the founding texts." Examples of groups that adhere to this tendency are the 18th century Shah Waliullah in India and Abd al-Wahhab in the Arabian Peninsula. This view is commonly associated with Salafism today.

Social and Political Goals

As with adherents of other fundamentalist movements, Islamic fundamentalists hold that the problems of the world stem from secular influences. Further, the path to peace and justice lies in a return to the original message of Islam combined with a scrupulous rejection of all Bid'ah ("religious innovation") and perceived anti-Islamic traditions.

Some scholars of Islam, such as Bassam Tibi, believe that, contrary to their own message, Islamic fundamentalists are not actually traditionalists. He refers to fatwahs issued by fundamentalists such as "every Muslim who pleads for the suspension of the shari'a is an apostate and can be killed.

The killing of those apostates cannot be prosecuted under Islamic law because this killing is justified" as going beyond, and unsupported by, the Qur'an. Tibi asserts; "The command to slay reasoning Muslims is un-Islamic, an invention of Islamic fundamentalists".

Conflicts with the Secular State

Islamic fundamentalism's push for Sharia and an Islamic State has come into conflict with conceptions of the secular, democratic state, such as the internationally supported Universal Declaration of Human Rights. Among human rights disputed by fundamentalist Muslims are:

- freedom from religious police
- the equality between men and women
- men's responsibility of women
- gross violation of human rights
- slavery of non-muslims, chiefly those who refuse to convert under threat of violence
- the separation of religion and state;
- freedom of religion. Muslims who leave Islam, or criticise it, "should be executed" while the right of non-Muslims to convert to Islam is celebrated.

As a result of this sharp conflict fundamentalist Islam is incompatible with modern liberal democratic states.

Some Major Expressions

As has been noted, Islamic political fundamentalist movements are a twentieth-century development. Not surprisingly, the majority of these movements are of the Sunni variety. Of the 175 Islamic fundamentalist groups (mainly of the political variety) in the Arab world as identified by Dekmejian from 1970-1995, only 32 were Shiite fundamentalists (with an additional four having both Sunni and Shiite followers). Tracing the history of all the various Islamic fundamentalist groups is beyond the purview of this paper. Accordingly, an analysis of a few countries will serve as evidence of the varied manner in which Islamic political fundamentalism has clashed with secular Muslim governments, resulting in mounting tensions, but varying successes, in terms of political involvement.

The ongoing legacy of The Muslim Brotherhood is evidenced in Egypt's central role in Sunni fundamentalism, 40 of the 175 identified Islamic fundamentalist groups are based in Egypt. Of those 40, three are major fundamentalist groups, Hizb al-Tahrir al-Islami (Islamic Liberation Party), Jama'at al-Muslimin (The Society of Muslims; also known as al-Takfir wal-Hijrah) and Tanzim al-Jihad (Jihad Organization). One figure, Sayyid Qutb, is the dominant link between the Brotherhood and all three of these Egyptian-based militant groups. In addition, Qutb links the Brotherhood and Pakistan's Jama'at-i Islami (the two earliest expressions of Islamic political fundamentalism) and is the key to understanding modern expressions of Sunni fundamentalism which originated after his death.

Qutb, an Egyptian government official who was offended by the racism and the openness between sexes he witnessed during a visit to the United States in the late 1940s, became an ideologue and activist, influenced by the radical teachings of Sayyid Abu'l-A'la Mawdudi, founder of the Jama'at i-Islami. Joining the Muslim Brotherhood in 1952, Qutb led the Brotherhood's shift from non-violence to violence. His influence led to the attempted assassination of Nasser in 1954, which in turn led to government suppression of the Brotherhood, including the internment of Qutb and other radical Brotherhood members. Influencing the Brotherhood movement from jail, Qutb garnered support from the military wing of the Brotherhood within and outside of Egypt, while continuing his opposition to Nasser's regime.

By the 1960s, Qutb had formulated a structured, albeit not fully developed, ideology of modern society as evil and ignorant of Islam's divine guidance. The duty of true Muslims was to purify the world by the internal transformation of Islamic society and militant jihad against the non-Islamic world. He published his views in *Milestones* in 1964. Qutb, echoing Mawdudi, called for a "vanguard" of dedicated Muslims to emulate the Prophet in separating themselves from society in order to achieve the ultimate goal of establishing God's sovereignty throughout the earth. The book, along with Qutb's martyrdom in 1966, spurred Islamic fundamentalists to rapid growth and splintering in the 1970s.

The three main Egyptian Islamic fundamentalist groups are all influenced by Qutb and draw support from the midde and lower-middle class (bazaar merchants, clerics, teaches, professionals and burecrats), yet each is distinctive enough to prevent a unified front. Hizb al-Tahrir al-Islami (or ILP) has focused its attacks primarily on government structures, while al-Takfir has charged that all who are not part of the group are unbelievers. Both outsiders, the ILP initially sought to quickly capture political control of Egypt, whereas al-Takfir pursued a long-term policy of political takeover. Both groups were suppressed by the Egyptian government in the late 1970s, although they have not been driven out of existence. Al-Jihad, in contrast, quietly infiltrated military, security services and other governmental institutions. Their power was revealed in the assassination of Anwar Sadat in October, 1981.

The group's leaders cited the disparity between Egypt's laws and Islamic Law, Sadat's peace with Israel, and government persecution against Islamists in September 1981 (part of an effort to counter the growing fundamentalist presence in Egypt) as the rationale for killing Sadat. In the months that followed, the government arrested thousands of Islamic fundamentalists, thus curtailing the group's effectiveness. Today, the Egyptian government continues to suppress militant fundamentalism through government force.

In Syria, the Brotherhood's influence is also drawn from the urban middle to lower-middle classes, comprised of educated small businessmen, professionals and clerics, the segment of the population which has benefited the least from the military and rural oriented Ba'thi party. In addition, the Brotherhood has produced a number of splinter groups. Syrian Islamic fundamentalists became more militant in the 1970s, turning to armed *jihad* by 1976. Numerous attacks on the government structure took place in ensuing years, leading to government efforts to suppress the fundamentalist groups. The Syrian government crushed an uprising of fundamentalists in Hama in 1983, leading to a period of decline for fundamentalists, who were unable to win the Sunni population to their cause. Despite ongoing repression, fundamentalism remains an ongoing threat in Syria.

Algeria has also witnessed the growth of a strong fundamentalist presence. A combination of agricultural crisis, unemployment, rampant inflation, shortages in housing and basic goods, declining revenues from the oil and gas industry, and growing foreign debt led to social unrest and class cleavage. Militant fundamentalist demonstrations resulted, and despite the governments attempt to crack down on fundamentalist groups, mass rioting, led by fundamentalists, took place in 1988. After a bloody government reprisal against the rioters, the Algerian president began a process of democratization.

The fundamentalist Islamic Salvation Front then won major electoral victories in 1990 and 1991, only to have the election results cancelled by the military, and thousands of fundamentalists sent to prison. In the aftermath, the movement went underground. Islamic fundamentalism continues to exist in a variety of sometimes competing movements, and has been responsible, along with the Algerian government, for a period of violent civil war in the past decade. Turkey provides an example of the influence of Islamic fundamentalism in an avowed secular state.

From the 1950s through the 1970s, Turkey was a multi-party state, experiencing military coups in 1960 and 1970. Long-standing political unrest and instability led to a political coup in 1980, with the military regime giving way to a democratic, parliamentary government in 1982. In the ensuing years, the military has remained a powerful force within the parliamentarian structure, as Turkey has continued a program of modernization and remains on friendly terms with the West. Although the democratic political structure and relative freedom within Turkish society has allowed Islamic fundamentalism to flourish, the government and military have kept fundamentalist groups in political check. The main fundamentalist group, Turkish Hezbollah, has been responsible for hundreds of murders in recent decades. In January 2001, the Turkish government raided the organization, arresting scores of militants, and killing the group's leader, Huseyin Velioglu. The raid, which led to the discovery of the corpses of hundreds of Hezbollah victims, dealt a significant setback to the militant group.

Perhaps the most vivid example of Islamic fundamentalism within recent years is that of Afghanistan. In 1978, the People's Democratic Party of Afghanistan (PDPA) seized power in a military coup. Allying with the Soviet Union, the PDPA began shaping Afghanistan along Marxist lines. With Islam thus threatened, the *mujahideen,* a loose alliance of Afghan nationalists, rebelled and took over many of the rural areas of the country. In response, the Soviet Union invaded in 1979 in an effort to shore up the PDPA, a move which swung popular support to the *mujahideen* even as millions of Afghans fled to neighboring Pakistan and Iran. The Pakistan government supported the refugee *mujahideen* with arms and military training, as did many other countries hostile to the Soviet Union, including the United States. Many Islamic fundamentalist groups were among the *mujahideen* factions, including Al Qaeda, led by Osama bin Laden.

When the Soviet Union finally withdrew from Afghanistan in 1989, leaving the PDPA in power, the *mujahideen* did not stop fighting. In 1992 they captured the capital of Kabul and overthrew the PDPA, only to lapse into infighting among the various factions. In 1996 the Taliban, having emerged as the strongest faction, seized control of Kabul. Although initially hailed by both the Afghan populace and the United States hopes for a return of stability to the country, the Taliban, allied with bin Laden, soon forced their concept of Islamic fundamentalism upon Afghanistan. The result was a period of severe oppression as the Taliban, with their religious police, punished citizens who engaged in un-Islamic activities such as television, movies, music, kite-flying and chess. Men were forced to wear beards of proper length, and women were curtailed from public life and were severely punished if not properly clothed or accompanied by a male relative when in public.

Punishment of offenders in the form of death was not uncommon. The reign of the Taliban, however, proved short-lived. On September 11, 2001, Al Qaeda operatives hijacked four U.S. commercial planes, crashing two of them into the Twin Towers of New York City's World Trade Center and one into the U.S. Pentagon. The fourth crashed in rural Pennsylvania as passengers struggled with the hijackers. The attacks killed nearly 3000 people, and the United States quickly launched a counter-attack, invading Afghanistan and installing a new government on December 22, 2001.

Lebanon is another Arab country with a strong opposition fundamentalist presence. Since the 1970s, both Sunni and Shiite fundamentalists (such as the Islamic Unity Movement, the Islamic Association, and Amal and Ummat Hizb Allah) have been competing for political supremacy, fueled by opposition to the West and to Israel, as well as Lebanon's religious establishment and government. Iran provides the sole example of the political triumph of Shiite fundamentalism. The Islamic revolution of 1979, led by the influential Islamic theologian Ayatollah Ruhollah Khomeini and fueled to a significant degree by restless young people, provided a model for how Islamic fundamentalism could takeover government structures. Khomeini's widely disseminated speeches against the Shah and advocating Islamic law helped pave the way for the revolution.

The new regime immediately banned alcohol, repressed women, and implemented the death penalty for adultery, all the while voicing open hatred of the West. By the end of the 1980s, however, revolutionary fervor was waning as Iranian businessman tired of isolation from the West. Although Islamic law yet governs Iran, the country has made various overtures to the West, and the current president of Iran defeated the conservative religious establishment in the last election. Saudi Arabia provides an example of a country governed by Islamic Law (*sharia* law). Long influenced by scriptural fundamentalism of the Wahabbi tradition, the Saudi government in recent decades has nonetheless faced opposition from many Muslims from both the right and left of the political spectrum.

In a country in which women are openly repressed and crimes are dealt with according to a strict interpretation of the Quran, the Saudi ruling royal family has nonetheless maintained ties with the Western world for their own economic benefit and that of the country. Accordingly, many militant fundamentalists (both Shiite and Sunni), opposed to all Western influences, have long agitated for stricter application of Islamic law. The ruling family has responded in recent years by making some concessions to militant fundamentalists, but the Gulf wars have served to heighten the tension between the government and militant fundamentalist factions. Sudan's distinction lies in being the first country to be governed by Muslim Brotherhood Islamic fundamentalism. The Brotherhood pursued a policy of gradualism in the 1970s, while Sudan struggled with socialism.

The gradualist policy paid off in the next decade, leading to a period of significant political influence in the 1980s as

Brotherhood leaders, including Dr. Hasan al-Turabi, formerly imprisoned by the government, were released and given cabinet positions. In 1989 a coup d'etat led to Turabi emerging as Sudan's supreme ideologue and de factor ruler. Shraria law was imposed on the country, and Turabi began an ethnic cleansing campaign against non-Muslims. A strict Islamic state, Sudan's government has been a haven for Islamic terrorists. Many other countries have been dealing with a growing Islamic political fundamentalist presence since the 1970s. Two examples in the non-Arab world are Malaysia and Indonesia. Since the 1980s, Malaysia has become an increasingly Islamic nation as Muslims have proliferated within a society which is open to a variety of beliefs.

Although Islam is now recognized as the official state religion, the state itself is secular, and the constitution provides religious tolerance. Within this political paradigm, the influence of fundamentalist Muslims, initially finding expression in student activists during political and social crisis in the 1970s, is growing in significance. Indonesia, on the other hand, has the largest Muslim population of any country, yet is not an Islamic nation. Islamic fundamentalists, although increasing in influence somewhat, have been hampered by a wide diversity of Islamic faith traditions that are a result of long-standing religious syncretism. The current conflicts in the Arab world are magnifying the Islamic fundamentalist influence throughout the world. As such, a closer examination of Islamic fundamentalist responses to modern science, western society and the secular state is in order.

Responses to Modern Science

As has been noted, modern Islamic political fundamentalism is the product of a desire by some Muslims to return to a pure faith in order to counter and overcome growing pressure from an increasingly westernized world. Identifying and analyzing these pressure points is essential to understanding the rationale behind the often violent expressions of Islamic political fundamentalism whose ultimate purpose is to bring individual, country and world under the sovereign reign of Allah. Islamists view the non-Muslim world, as well as the non-pure Muslim world, as morally evil, a perversion of the one true faith, and an affront to the one true God.

Modernity can be understood in terms of both morality and science. On the one hand, the West, the embodiment of modern morality, is representative of that which is unholy in the world. On the other hand, modernity as symbolized by science and technology is willingly embraced by Islamists. Accordingly, despite the hatred which Islamic fundamentalists harbor towards the West's modern morality, they have displayed a notable tendency to employ scientific instruments and technologies of modernity in their attempts to defeat Westernization and "reclaim" society. Underlying Islamic fundamentalist attitudes towards science are two differing traditions of knowledge, religious sciences and rational sciences (i.e., philosophy and natural sciences).

The former has long been viewed as ultimate truth, while the later has been considered as inferior, foreign, or secular. In short, all Islamic fundamentalists ultimately subordinate the scientific realm to the authority of a sovereign God as revealed in sacred text. In other words, human reason is in the service of revelation. In this context, fundamentalist attitudes toward science are a mixture of both acceptance and rejection, predicated on the religious context of the issue at hand. Sayyid Qutb, considered by many to be the foremost ideological authority among Sunni Muslims, wrote of the concept of a world "split between the domain of the *jahiliyya* ('ignorant') and a domain in which God's method prevails."

Whereas Max Weber determined science to be a product of human reason, Qutb speaks for Islamic fundamentalists in locating science and technology in the Quran. Fundamentalists turn to the Quran for scientific guidance in reaction to nineteenth century Islamic accommodation of Western culture, an integration of faith and Western secularism viewed as a compromise detrimental to true Islam. Ironically, both Islamic modernists (borrowing from Western methodologies) and later fundamentalists (refuting Western influence) have sounded identical themes of Islam rising to repel the West while effecting internal reforms.

In daily practice, Islamic fundamentalist opposition to Westernization has been expressed pragmatically. Whereas modern Western morality is viewed as an evil to be avoided, modern science and technology originating in the West has been absorbed and utilized in politics and society. Accordingly, many products derived from Western science and technologies are readily adopted, while the worldview related to these products is rejected. In essence, in Islamic fundamentalist circles the overarching debate between science and religion is in the determination of "truth," rather than in the usage of products. Not surprisingly, the most common place of contention is in the realm of education.

Modern Islamist fundamentalism is characterized by competing claims for the orientation of Islamic education. One position argues that knowledge comes only from God, and that science and technology are neutral, and thus may be adopted from the non-Muslim world and utilized to benefit Muslims. According to this line of reasoning, the Quran is a "book of orientation" (*kitah hidaya*), including references to science, but not strictly a science textbook itself. As such, adopted innovations must be consistent with the truth of the Quran and its revelations.

A second approach to orienting Islamic education posits that the Quran includes all sciences. Everything from natural sciences to modern medicine must be derived directly from the Quran. Every legitimate scientific achievement is understood to come from the Quran. Little distinction is often made between religious sciences and rational sciences in Islamic history, while European enlightenment (i.e., Descartes and Bacon) is considered to have been influenced by the Quran. As such, by embracing science and technology through the prism of the Quran, modern Muslims are reclaiming their rightful heritage.

A third grouping of fundamentalists asserts the concept of the "Islamization of science." This position affirms the exclusivity of the Quran in terms of science, yet goes further by insisting that Islam is the religion of science, and that to separate the two is a crime. Saudi Wahhabi fundamentalists support this line of reasoning, and have been using their financial resources to teach it throughout the Arab world.

Ultimately, the teaching of an Islamic-centered scientific worldview is imperative in order to conquer and subdue that part of the world (the *jahiliyya*, or ignorant) which is not living under the authority of God and His revelation. To this end, holy war (*jihad*) violence against Western modernity is not merely acceptable, but is in fact necessary. Yet the weapons utilized in this holy war – guns, bombs, dynamite, airplanes, etc. – are themselves the products of western technology. In the end, Islamic fundamentalists' only viable option for fighting Western modernity is to appropriate the very fruit of Western modernity, a tension which is seemingly unrecognized by many adherents.

2

Islamic Terrorism

Religious fundamentalisms arose in the twentieth century and have spilled over into the twenty-first century. By nature, religious fundamentalisms oppose modernity as expressed in contemporary Western morals and social values. Of the various faith groups which contain fundamentalist elements, Islam has provided the most vibrant and politically active expressions. Although originating in the twentieth century, the groundwork for Islamic fundamentalism was established during the course of the previous centuries. The Prophet Muhammad, upon receiving revelations from God which were compiled in the Quran, provided an authoritative perfect text.

In the centuries immediately following Muhammad's death, Muhammad's teachings and actions (as compiled in the *Hadith*) provided authoritative guidance for daily living, while Islamic legal schools established a tradition of strict interpretation of Islamic law. By the 19th century, in the face of pressures from Western civilization and recognized internal weaknesses within Islam, revivalist movements were calling Muslims to return to a pure faith based on strict interpretation and application of Islamic law. The revivalist movements, in turn, led to a focus on the utilization of political force in the twentieth century in ongoing efforts to establish Islamic law at the state level throughout the Middle East, South Asia and North Africa.

Islamic fundamentalism's response to Westernization finds form in a number of expressions. Modernization is embraced even as the West is vilified. Modern science is placed within the context of and subjugated to the Quran. The results of modern science (technology and weapons, for example) are utilized despite their Western origins. Islamic fundamentalists denounce and reject Western society and culture, while simultaneously seeking to purify Muslim society through the forceful implementation of Islamic (*sharia*) law.

Women are the primary targets in fundamentalist's vision of Islamic law, and are subjugated and persecuted in a variety of ways from clothing to appearances in public to roles in public life. In terms of secular states, the ultimate goal of fundamentalist movements is the overthrowing of secular governments and the implementation of theocratic government. The twentieth century to the present has witnessed rising tensions between secularized states and growing fundamentalist movements, as well as varied instances of compromise. In general, tensions continue to increase as the number and intensity of fundamentalist movements has risen sharply in recent decades.

Islamic terrorism (also known as Jihadist terrorism, but not to be confused with Islamist terrorism) is religious terrorism by those whose motivations are rooted in their interpretations of Islam. According to statistics gathered in 2006 by the National Counterterrorism Center of the United States, "Islamic extremism" was responsible for approximately a quarter of all terrorism fatalities worldwide, and a majority of the fatalities for which responsibility could be conclusively determined. Terrorist acts have included airline hijacking, beheading, kidnapping, assassination, roadside bombing, suicide bombing and occasionally, rape.

Perhaps the most resonant, well known, and well documented incident of terrorism was the hijacking of four passenger jets and the destruction of the World Trade Center on the day of September 11 2001, in the United States of

America. Other prominent attacks have occurred in Iraq, Afghanistan, India, Israel, Indonesia, Thailand, Philippines, Britain, Spain, France, Russia and China. These terrorist groups often describe their actions as Islamic jihad (struggle). Self-proclaimed sentences of punishment or death issued publicly as threats often come in the form of fatwas (Islamic legal judgments). Both Muslims and non-Muslims have been among the targets and victims, but threats against Muslims are often issued as takfir (a declaration that a person, group or institution that describes itself as Muslim has in fact left Islam and thus is a traitor). This is an implicit death threat as the punishment for apostasy in Islam is death under Sharia law.

The controversies surrounding the subject include whether the terrorist act is self-defense or aggression, national self-determination or Islamic supremacy; whether Islam can ever condone the targeting of noncombatants; whether some attacks described as Islamic terrorism are merely terrorist acts committed by Muslims or motivated by nationalism; whether the Arab-Israeli Conflict is the root of Islamic terrorism, or simply one cause; how much support there is in the Muslim world for Islamic terrorism and whether support for terror is a temporary phenomenum, a "bubble", now fading away.

Debate over Terminology

"Islamic terrorism" is itself a controversial phrase, although its usage is widespread throughout the English-speaking world. Bernard Lewis believes that the phrase "Islamic terrorism" is apt, because although "Islam, as a religion" is not "particularly conducive to terrorism or even tolerant of terrorism". In his own words:

"Islam has had an essentially political character ... from its very foundation ... to the present day. An intimate association between religion and politics, between power and cult, marks a principal distinction between Islam and other religions. ... In traditional Islam and therefore also in resurgent fundamentalist Islam, God is the sole source of sovereignty. God is the head of the state. The state is God's state. The army is God's army. The treasury is God's treasury, and the enemy, of course, is God's enemy."

This argument is countered by Jamal Nassar and Karim H. Karim, who contend that because there are over a billion adherents of the religion, the phenomenon is more precisely regarded as "Islamist terrorism" or "militant Islamism", because *Islamism* describes political ideologies rooted in interpretations of Islam. In this vein, describing terrorism as "Islamic" may confirm "a prejudicial perspective of all things Islamic".

Karen Armstrong contends that "fundamentalism is often a form of nationalism in religious disguise", and that using the phrase "Muslim terrorism" is dangerously counterproductive, as it suggests those in the west believe that such atrocities are caused by Islam, and hence reinforces the viewpoint of some in the Muslim world that the west is an implacable enemy. Armstrong believes that the terrorists in no way represent mainstream Islam, and suggests the use of other terms such as "Wahhabi terrorism" and "Qutbian terrorism".

According to one source, although Islamic terrorism, at least in the form of suicide attacks - dates back to the Hashshashin sect of the 11th century, "its modern history begins with statements made by Sheik Mohammad Hussein Fadlallah", the spiritual leader of Hezbollah, who said in an interview published in 1983:

"We believe that the future has surprises in store. The jihad is bitter and harsh; it will spring from inside, through effort, patience and sacrifice, and the spirit of readiness for martyrdom."

Organizations and acts

Some prominent Islamic terror groups and incidents include the following:

- Transnational
- Al-Qaeda

Al-Qaeda is a worldwide pan-Islamic terrorist network headed by Osama bin Laden and is most famous for orchestrating the September 11, 2001 attacks against the United States. It now operates in more than 60 countries. Its stated aim is the use of jihad to defend Islam against Zionism, Christianity, the secular West, and Muslim governments such as Saudi Arabia, which it sees as insufficiently Islamic and too closely tied to America.

Formed by bin Laden and Muhammad Atef in the aftermath of the Soviet invasion of Afghanistan in the late 1980s, Al Qaeda called for the use of violence against civilians and military of the United States and any countries that are allied with it. Since its formation Al Qaeda has committed a number of terrorist acts in Africa, the Middle East, Europe, and Asia. Although once supported by the Taliban organization in Afghanistan, the U.S. and British governments never considered the Taliban to have been a terrorist organization.

Europe

Major lethal attacks on civilians in Europe credited to Islamic terrorism include the March 11, 2004 bombings of commuter trains in Madrid, where 191 people were killed and 2,050 wounded, and the 7 July 2005 London bombings, also of public transport, which killed 52 commuters and injured 700.

Russia

Politically-motivated attacks on civilians in Russia have been traced to separatist sentiment among Muslims in its Caucasus region, particularly Chechnya. Russia's two biggest terrorist attacks both came from Muslim groups. In the Nord-Ost incident at a theater in Moscow in October 2002, the Chechnyan separatist "Special Purpose Islamic Regiment" took an estimated 850 people hostage. An estimated 300 Russians died in an attempted rescue. Whether this attack would more properly be called a nationalist rather than an Islamist attack is in question.

In the September 2004 Beslan school hostage crisis 1,200 schoolchildren and adults were taken hostage after "School Number One" secondary school in Beslan, North Ossetia-Alania was overrun by the "Caucasus Caliphate Jihad" led by Shamil Basayev. As many as 500 died, including 186 children. According to the only surviving attacker, Nur-Pashi Kulayev, the choice of a school and the targeting of mothers and young children by the attackers was done in hopes of generating a maximum of outrage and igniting a wider war in the Caucasus with the ultimate goal of establishing an Islamic Emirate across the whole of the North Caucasus.

Turkey

Hezbollah (Turkish)

Unrelated to the more famous Shia Hezbollah of Lebanon, this Sunni terrorist group has been credited with the assassination of Diyarbakir police chief Gaffar Okkan, and the November 2003 bombings of two synagogues, the British consulate in Istanbul and HSBC bank headquarters, killing 58 and wounding several hundred.

Iraq

The area that has seen some of the worst terror attacks in modern history has been Iraq as part of the Iraq War. In 2005, there were 400 incidents of one type of attack (suicide bombing), killing more than 2000 people - many if not most of them civilians. In 2006, almost half of all reported terrorist attacks in the world (6600), and more than half of all terrorist fatalities (13,000), occurred in Iraq, according to the National Counterterrorism Center of the United States. The insurgency in Iraq against the US and Iraqi government combines attacks on "Coalition troops" and the Iraqi security forces, with attacks on civilian contractors, aid workers, and infrastructure.

Along with nationalist Ba'athist groups and criminal, non-political attacks, the insurgency includes Islamist insurgent groups, who favor suicide attacks far more than non-Islamist groups. They include the Abu Musab al-Zarqawi's al-Qaeda affiliate; Al-Faruq Brigades, a militant wing of the Islamic Movement in Iraq (Al-Harakah al-Islamiyyah fi al-arak); Jamaat Ansar al-Sunna; the Mujahideen of the Victorious Sect (Mujahideen al ta'ifa al-Mansoura); the Mujahideen Battalions of the Salafi Group of Iraq (Kata'ib al mujahideen fi al-jama'ah al-salafiyah fi al-'arak); the Jihad Brigades/Cell; "White Flags, Muslim Youth and Army of Mohammed"; Ansar al-Islam, a Taliban-like, jihadist group with ties to Al Qaeda. At least some of the terrorism has a transnational character in that some foreign Islamic jihadists have joined the insurgency.

Lebanon

Fatah al-Islam

Fatah al-Islam is an Islamist group operating out of the Nahr al-Bared refugee camp in northern Lebanon. It was formed in November 2006 by fighters who broke off from the pro-Syrian Fatah al-Intifada, itself a splinter group of Fatah, and is led by a Palestinian fugitive militant named Shaker al-Abssi. The group's members have been described as militant jihadists, and the group itself has been described as a terrorist movement that draws inspiration from al-Qaeda. Its stated goal is to reform the Palestinian refugee camps under Islamic sharia law, and its primary targets are Israel and the United States. Lebanese authorities have accused the organization of being involved in the February 13, 2007 bombing of two minibuses that killed three people, and injured more than 20 others, in Ain Alaq, Lebanon, and identified four of its members as having confessed to the bombing.

Hezbollah

Hezbollah is a Shi'a militia, political party, and social services provider based in Lebanon. Six governments consider it, or a part of it, to be a terrorist group responsible for blowing up the American embassy and later its annex, as well as the barracks of American and French peacekeeping troops and a dozens of kidnappings of foreigners in Beirut. It is also accused of being the recipient of massive aid from Iran, and of serving "Iranian foreign policy calculations and interests," or serving as a "subcontractor of Iranian initiatives" Hezbollah denies any involvement or dependence on Iran.

In the Arab and Muslim worlds, on the other hand, Hezbollah is regarded as a legitimate and successful resistance movement that drove both Western powers and Israel out of Lebanon. In 2005, the Lebanese Prime Minister said of Hezbollah, "it is not a militia. It's a resistance." Hezbollah's simultaneous suicide attacks on US and French barracks in Beirut and the withdrawal of American peacekeeping troops shortly thereafter the bombings prompted is thought to have "made a profound impression on bin Laden."

Israel and the Palestinian Territories

Al-Aqsa Martyrs' Brigades

Hamas

Hamas, ("zeal" in Arabic and an acronym for Harakat al-Muqawama al-Islamiyya), began support for attacks on military and civilian targets in Israel at the beginning of the Intifada in 1987. As the Muslim Brotherhood organization for Palestine its leadership was made up of "intellectuals from the devout middle class,... respectable religious clerics, doctors, chemists, engineers, and teachers.

The 1988 charter of Hamas calls for the destruction of Israel, and it still states its goal to be the elimination of Israel.

Its "military wing" has claimed responsibility for numerous attacks in Israel. Hamas has also been accused of sabotaging the Israeli-Palestine peace process by launching attacks on civilians during Israeli elections to anger Israeli voters and facilitate the election of harder-line Israeli candidates. For example, "a series of spectacular suicide attacks by Palestinians that killed 63 Israelis and led directly to the election victory of Benjamin Netanyahu and his Likud party on May 29, 1996."

Hamas justifies these attacks as necessary in fighting the Israeli occupation of Palestinian territory, and as responses to Israeli attacks on Palestinian targets. The wider movement also serves as a charity organization and provides services to Palestinians.

Hamas has been designated as a terrorist group by the European Union, Canada, the United States, Israel, the United Nations Commission on Human Rights and Human Rights Watch. Opponents of this view claim that Israel is not a legitimate state because of the conditions of its establishment after World War II.

Islamic Jihad

Islamic Jihad is a militant Palestinian group Islamist group based in the Syrian capital, Damascus, and dedicated to waging jihad to eliminate the state of Israel. It was formed by Egyptian Fathi Shaqaqi in the Gaza Strip following the Iranian Revolution which inspired its members. From 1983 onward, it engaged in "a succession of violent, high-profile attacks" on Israeli targets. The intifada which "it eventually sparked" was quickly taken over by much larger the PLO and Hamas. Beginning in September 2000, it started a campaign of suicide bombing attacks against Israelis. It is currently led by Sheikh Abdullah Ramadan. The PIJ's armed wing, the Al-Quds brigades, has claimed responsibility for numerous militant attacks in Israel, including suicide bombings and the group has been designated as a terrorist group by the several countries in the West.

North Africa

Armed Islamic Group

The Armed Islamic Group, active in Algeria between 1992 and 1998, was one of the most violent Islamic terrorist groups, and is thought to have takfired the Muslim population of Algeria. Its campaign to overthrow the Algerian government included civilian massacres, which sometimes wiping out entire villages in its area of operation.

It also targeted foreigners living in Algeria killing more than 100 expatriate men and women in the country. The group's favored technique was the kidnapping of victims and slitting their throats although it also used assassination by gun and bombings, including car bombs. Outside of Algeria, the GIA established a presence in France, Belgium, Britain, Italy and the United States. In recent years it has been eclipsed by a splinter group, The Salafist Group for Preaching and Combat (GSPC), now called Al-Qaeda Organization in the Islamic Maghreb.

South Asia

Lashkar-e-Toiba

Pakistan based Lashkar-e-Toiba is a militant group that seeks the Indian state of Jammu and Kashmir's accession to Pakistan. It has committed mass militant actions against Indian troops and civilian Hindus. The Lashkar leadership describes Indian and Israeli regimes as the main enemies of Islam, claiming India and Israel to be the main enemies of Pakistan. Lashkar-e-Toiba, along with Jaish-e-Mohammed, another militant group active in Kashmir are on the United States' foreign terrorist organizations list. They are also designated as terrorist groups by the United Kingdom, India, Australia and Pakistan.

Jaish-e-Mohammed

Jaish-e-Mohammed (often abbreviated as JEM) is a major Islamic militant organization in South Asia. Jaish-e-Mohammed was formed in 1994 and is based in the Islamic Republic of Pakistan. The group's primary objective is to separate Kashmir from India, and it has carried out a series of attacks all over India.

The group was formed after the supporters of Maulana Masood Azhar split from another Islamic militant organization, Harkut-ul-Mujahideen. It is believed that the group gets considerable funding from Pakistani expatriates in the United Kingdom. The group is regarded as a terrorist organization by several countries including India, United States and United Kingdom. Jaish-e-Mohammed is viewed by some as the "deadliest" and "the principal terrorist organization in Jammu and Kashmir". The group was also implicated in the kidnapping and murder of American journalist Daniel Pearl.

Jamaat-ul-Mujahideen

In Bangladesh the group Jamaat-ul-Mujahideen Bangladesh was formed sometime in 1998 and gained prominence on 20 May 2001 when 25 petrol bombs and documents detailing the activities of the organization were discovered and eight of its members were arrested in Parbatipur in Dinajpur district. The organization was officially banned in February 2005 after attacks on NGOs, but struck back in August when 300 bombs were detonated almost simultaneously throughout Bangladesh. Dhaka international airport, government buildings and major hotels were targeted.

Afghanistan

In Afghanistan, Taliban and Hezb-e-Islami Gulbuddin forces, are reported to have "sharply escalated bombing and other attacks in 2006 and early 2007" against civilians.

During 2006 "at least 669 Afghan civilians were killed in at least 350 armed attacks, most of which appear to have been intentionally launched at civilians or civilian objects. An additional 52 civilians were killed in insurgent attacks in the first two months of 2007."

Southeast Asia

Abu Sayyaf Group

The Abu Sayyaf Group also known as al-Harakat al-Islamiyya is one of several militant Islamist separatist groups based in and around the southern islands of the Philippines, in Bangsamoro (Jolo, Basilan, and Mindanao) where for almost 30 years various Muslim groups have been engaged in an insurgency for a state, independent of the predominantly Christian Philippines. The name of the group is derived from the Arabic, *abu* ("father of") and *sayyaf* ("Swordsmith").

Since its inception in the early 1990s, the group has carried out bombings, assassinations, kidnappings, rapes, and extortion in their fight for an independent Islamic state in western Mindanao and the Sulu Archipelago with the stated goal of creating a pan-Islamic superstate across southeast Asia, spanning from east to west; the island of Mindanao, the Sulu Archipelago, the island of Borneo (Malaysia, Indonesia), the South China Sea, and the Malay Peninsula (Peninsular Malaysia, Thailand and Myanmar). The U.S. Department of State has branded the group a terrorist entity by adding it to the list of Foreign Terrorist Organizations.

Tactics

Some of these groups, such as Hamas and Hezbollah, have limited their acts to localized regions of the Middle East, while others, notably Al-Qaeda, have an international scope for their terrorist activities.

Bombings

An increasingly popular tactic used by terrorists is suicide bombing. This tactic is used against civilians, soldiers, and government officials of the regimes the terrorists oppose. The use of suicide bombers is seen by many Muslims as contradictory to Islam's teachings; however, groups who support its use often refer to such attacks as "martyrdom operations" and the suicide-bombers who commit them as "martyrs" (Arabic: shuhada, plural of "shahid"). The bombers, and their sympathizers often believe that suicide bombers, as martyrs to the cause of jihad against the enemy, will receive the rewards of paradise for their actions.

One source has found interest in new and so far unutilized bombing technique on internet forums used by the Islamic terror group al-Qaeda - the use of "remote-piloted aircraft" and "robot designs," and "training dogs to recognize American troops' uniforms," as a replacement for techniques such as suicide bombing or a detonating planted bombs with a radio-control.

Hijackings

The hijacking of passenger vehicles such as cars, buses, and planes has also become a hallmark of Islamist terrorism, particularly as a result of the simultaneous hijacking of the four passenger jets utilized in the September 11th terrorist attacks as well as the hijacking of a Belgian airlines jet during the 1972 Munich Olympic Massacre.

Kidnappings and Executions

Along with bombings and hijackings, Islamist terrorists have made extensive use of highly-publicised kidnappings and executions, often circulating videos of the acts for use as propaganda. Notable foreign victims include Nick Berg, Daniel Pearl, Paul Marshall Johnson, Jr., Eugene Armstrong, Jack Hensley, Kim Sun-il, Kenneth Bigley, Shosei Koda,

Fabrizio Quattrocchi, Margaret Hassan. One Iraqi victim was Seif Adnan Kanaan. The most frequent form of execution by these groups has been decapitations; often committed while shouting the Islamic chant, "Allahu Akbar" (Arabic for God is greatest). While some targets are military, or seen as supporting the anti-Islamist forces, victims are also as varied as the Red Cross, the Iraqi education ministry, and diplomats.

Motivation, Ideology and Theology

Motivations

To what extent Islamic terrorists are motivated by religious belief is disputed. Robert Pape, has argued that at least terrorists utilizing suicide-homicide attacks – a particularly effective form of terrorist attack – are driven not by Islamism but by "a clear strategic objective to compel modern democracies to withdraw military forces from the territory that the terrorists view as their homeland." However a critic of Pape's theory, Martin Kramer, argues that it does not account for the lack of suicide bombings in the Gaza Strip and the West Bank in Israel for nearly 30 years after the occupation began, for the targeting of native, non-combatant Shia by jihadi bombers in Iraq, the prominence of British-born Pakistanis in bombings in London, or of North Africans, and especially Moroccans, in the second wave of al-Qaeda attackers.

In particular, scholar Scott Atran, points out that the massive increase in suicide bombing has meant most suicide bombings have occurred after Pape's study ended in 2003. "Roughly 600," suicide attacks occurred in just two years, 2004 and 2005, more "than in Pape's entire sample," and the overwhelming majority of these bombers have been motivated by the ideology of Islamist martyrdom.

Some supporters of Palestinian political violence have claimed that citizens of Israel are legitimate military targets because Jewish adolescents are required by law to serve in the country's military. Former CIA analyst Michael Scheuer's states that the Al Qaeda Islamic terror attacks against America are motivated not by a hatred of American culture and religion but by the belief that U.S. foreign policy is a threat to Islam, condensed in the phrase "They hate us for what we do, not who we are." U.S. foreign policy actions Scheuer believes are fueling Islamic terror include

- U.S. troops on Muslim holy ground in Saudi Arabia
- U.S. support for "apostate" police states in Muslim nations such as Saudi Arabia, Egypt, Pakistan, Algeria, Morocco, and Kuwait
- The invasion and occupation of Afghanistan and Iraq
- U.S. support for the creation of the Christian state of East Timor from territory previously held by Muslim Indonesia.
- Perceived U.S. approval or support of counter-insurgency against Muslim insurgents in India, Philippines, Chechnia, Uyghur separatists in western China, Palestine.

Some other academics agree that argues that 'terrorism should be seen as a strategic reaction to American power,' - that America is an empire, and empires provoked resistance in the form of terrorism. The Russian, Ottoman, and Habsburg Empires, for example, all suffered from terrorist attacks and had terrorist organisations - the Black Hand, Young Bosnia, and Narodnaya Volya - spawned from their multiple ethnic, religious, and national peoples (Serb, Macedonian, and Bosnian).

Profiles

Forensic psychiatrist and former Foreign Service officer Marc Sageman, made an "intensive study of biographical data on 172 participants in the jihad," in his book "Understanding Terror Networks". He concluded "social networks", the "tight bonds of family and friendship" rather than behavioural disorders "poverty, trauma, madness, [or] ignorance" inspired alienated young Muslims to join the "jihad" and kill.

Author Lawrence Wright describes the characteristic of "displacement" of members of the most famous Islamic terrorist group, Al-Qaeda.

"What the recruits tended to have in common - besides their urbanity, their cosmopolitan backgrounds, their education, their facility with languages, and their computer skills - was displacement. Most who joined the jihad did so in a country other than the one in which they were reared. They were Algerians living in expatriate enclaves in France, Moroccans in Spain, or Yemenis in Saudi Arabia. Despite their accomplishments, they had little standing in the host societies where they lived. ...."

Scholar Olivier Roy describes the background of the hundreds of *global* (as opposed to local) terrorists who were incarcerated or killed and for whom authorities have records, as being surprising for their Westernized background; for the lack of Palestinians, Iraqis, Afghans "coming to avenge what is going on in their country"; their lack of religiousity before being "born again" in a foreign country; the high percentage of converts to Islam among them; their "de-territorialized backgrounds" - "For instance, they may be born in a country, then educated in another country, then go to fight in a third country and take refuge in a fourth country"; their untraditional belief that jihad is permanent, global, and "not linked with a specific territory."

This profile differs from that found among recent *local* Islamist suicide bombers in Afghanistan, according to a 2007 study of 110 suicide bombers by Afghan pathologist Dr. Yusef Yadgari. Yadgari found that "80%" of the attackers studied had some kind of physical or mental disability. The bombers were also "not celebrated like their counterparts in other Arab nations. Afghan bombers are not featured on posters or in videos as martyrs."

Ideology

Tenets of Qutbism have been summarized by Dale C. Eikmeier as being:

- A belief that Muslims have deviated from true Islam and must return to "pure Islam" as originally practiced during the time of the Prophet.
- The path to "pure Islam" is only through a literal and strict interpretation of the Quran and Hadith, along with implementation of the Prophet's commands.
- Muslims should interpret the original sources individually without being bound to follow the interpretations of Islamic scholars.
- That any interpretation of the Quran from a historical, contextual perspective is a corruption, and that the majority of Islamic history and the classical jurisprudential tradition is mere sophistry.

Transnational Islamist ideology, specifically of the militant Islamists, assert that Western polities and society are actively anti-Islamic, or as it is sometimes described, waging a "war on Islam". Islamists often identify what they see as a historical struggle between Christianity and Islam, dating back as far as the Crusades, among other historical conflicts between practitioners of the two respective religions. Osama bin Laden, for example, almost invariably describes his enemy as aggressive and his call for action against them as defensive.

Defensive jihad differs from offensive jihad in being "fard al-ayn," or a personal obligation of all Muslim, rather than "fard al-kifaya", a communal obligation, which if some Muslims perform it is not required from others. Hence, framing a fight as defensive has the advantage both of appearing to be a victim rather than aggressor, and of giving your struggle the very highest religious priority for all good Muslims.

Many of the violent terrorist groups use the name of Jihad to fight against Christians and Jews. An example is Bin Laden's Al-Qaeda, which is also known as 'International Islamic Front for Jihad Against the Jews and Crusaders'. Most militant Islamists oppose Israel's policies, and often its existence.

The historic rivalry between Hindus and Muslims in the Indian subcontinent has also often been the primary motive behind some of the most deadly terrorist attacks in India. According to a US State Department report, India topped the list of countries worst affected by Islamic terrorism.

In addition, Islamist Jihadis, scholars, and leaders opposed Western society for what they see as immoral secularism. Islamists have claimed that such unrestricted free speech has led to the proliferation of pornography, immorality, secularism, homosexuality, feminism, and many other ideas that Islamists often oppose. Although bin Laden almost always emphasized the alleged oppression of Muslims by America and Jews when talking about them in his messages, in his "Letter to America" he answered the question, "What are we calling you to, and what do we want from you?"

We call you to be a people of manners, principles, honour, and purity; to reject the immoral acts of fornication, homosexuality, intoxicants, gambling's, and trading with interest ... You separate religion from your policies, ... You are the nation that permits Usury, which has been forbidden by all the religions ... You are a nation that permits the production, trading and usage of intoxicants ... You are a nation that permits acts of immorality ... You are a nation that permits gambling in its all forms. ... You use women to serve passengers, visitors, and strangers to increase your profit margins. You then rant that you support the liberation of women.

Given their perceived piety, *The Times* noted the irony when a major investigation by their reporters uncovered a link between Islamic Jihadis and child pornography; a discovery that, according to the London paper, "is expected to improve understanding of the mindsets of both types of criminals and has been hailed as a potentially vital intelligence tool to undermine future terrorist plots."

Accusations of Apostasy

Justification for terrorism against other Muslims by militant Islamists, in particular against Muslim regimes they consider non-Islamic, is often based on the contention that the targets are apostates. Osama Bin Laden, for example, maintains that any Muslim who helps "infidels over Muslims" is no longer a Muslim,

> ... The believer ... should boycott the goods of America and her allies, and he should be very wary that he does not support falsehood, for helping the infidels over Muslims — even with a single word is clear unbelief, as the religious scholars have decreed.

And that Taliban-ruled Afghanistan (deposed in 2001) "is the only Islamic country" in the world. Islamic law traditionally designates death as the penalty for apostasy (converting) from Islam.

Opinions within the Muslim community vary as to the grounds on which an individual may be declared to have apostatized. The most common view among Muslim scholars is that a declaration of takfir (designation of a Muslim as an apostate) can only be made by an established religious authority. Mainstream Muslim scholars usually oppose recourse to *takfir*, except in rare instances. *Takfir* was used as justification for the assassination of Egyptian President Anwar Sadat.

Interpretations of the Qur'an

The role played by the Qur'an, Islam's sacred text, in opposing or in encouraging attacks on civilians is hotly disputed. Mohammed Reza Taheri-azar, an Iranian-born American citizen awaiting trial for nine counts of attempted murder, cited a number of verses from the Qur'an in justifying his attempt to kill civilians, including:

Fighting is prescribed for you, and ye dislike it. But it is possible that ye dislike a thing which is good for you, and that ye love a thing which is bad for you. But Allah knoweth, and ye know not.

The punishment of those who wage war against Allah and His Messenger, and strive with might and main for mischief through the land is, execution, or crucifixion, or the cutting off of hands and feet from opposite sides, or exile from the land, that is their disgrace in this world, and a heavy punishment is theirs in the Hereafter;

But when the forbidden months are past, then fight and slay the Pagans wherever ye find them, and seize them, beleaguer them, and lie in wait for them in every stratagem (of war); but if they repent, and establish regular prayers and practise regular charity, then open the way for them: for Allah is Oft-forgiving, Most Merciful.

Fight those who believe neither in Allah nor the Last Day, nor hold that forbidden which hath been forbidden by Allah and His Messenger, nor acknowledge the religion of Truth, (even if they are) of the People of the Book, until they pay the Jizya with willing submission, and feel themselves subdued. The Jews call 'Uzair a son of Allah and the Christians call Christ the son of Allah. That is a saying from their mouth; (in this) they but imitate what the unbelievers of old used to say. Allah's curse is on them, how they are deluded away from the Truth!

Marmaduke Pickthall, a Western convert to Islam and Islamic scholar commented on verse 2:216, references verse

2:251, and interpreted these particular verses to mean that fighting is not optional when done in defense of the oppressed and the weak.

Pickthall goes on to say that "Nowhere does the Qur'an approve a spirit of revenge" and situates verse 2:194 in the context of a defensive war. Ibn Kathir stated that the Quran clearly commands believers to prefer forgiveness over retaliation wherever possible.

Michael Sells and Jane I. Smith (a Professor of Islamic Studies) write that barring some extremists like Al-Qaeda, most Muslims do not interpret Qura'nic verses as promoting warfare; and that the phenomenon of radical interpretation of scripture by extremist groups is not unique to Islam." According to Sells, "[Most Muslims] no more expect to apply [the verses at issue] to their contemporary non-Muslim friends and neighbors than most Christians and Jews consider themselves commanded by God, like the Biblical Joshua, to exterminate the infidels."

Criticism of Islamic Terrorist Ideology

Although "Islamic" Terrorism is commonly associated with the Salafis or "Wahhabis", the scholars of the group have constantly attributed this association to ignorance, misunderstanding and sometimes insincere research and deliberate misleading by rival groups. Following the September 11, 2001 terrorist attacks in New York, Pennsylvania and Arlington, Shaikh Abdul-Azeez Aal ash-Shaikh (the Grand Mufti of the Kingdom of Saudi Arabia President of the Committee of Major Scholars and centre for Knowledge based research and verdicts) made an official statement that "the Islamic Sharee'ah (legislation) does not sanction" such actions. A Salafi or "Wahhabi" "Committee of Major Scholars" in Saudi Arabia has declared that "Islamic" terrorism, such as the May 2003 bombing in Riyadh, are in violation of Sharia law and aiding the enemies of Islam.

Criticism of Islamic terrorism on Islamic grounds has also been made by anti-terrorist Muslims such as Abdal-Hakim Murad:

Certainly, neither bin Laden nor his principal associate, Ayman al-Zawahiri, are graduates of Islamic universities. And so their proclamations ignore 14 centuries of Muslim scholarship, and instead take the form of lists of anti-American grievances and of Koranic quotations referring to early Muslim wars against Arab idolaters. These are followed by the conclusion that all Americans, civilian and military, are to be wiped off the face of the Earth. All this amounts to an odd and extreme violation of the normal methods of Islamic scholarship. Had the authors of such fatwas followed the norms of their religion, they would have had to acknowledge that no school of mainstream Islam allows the targeting of civilians. An insurrectionist who kills non combatants is guilty of baghy, "armed aggression," a capital offense in Islamic law.

One counter-terrorism scholar, Dale C. Eikmeier, points out the "questionable religious credentials" of many Islamist theorists, or "Qutbists," which can be a "means to discredit them and their message":

With the exception of Abul Ala Maududi and Abdullah Azzam, none of Qutbism's main theoreticians trained at Islam's recognized centers of learning. Although a devout Muslim, Hassan al Banna was a teacher and community activist. Sayyid Qutb was a literary critic. Muhammad Abd al-Salam Faraj was an electrician. Ayman al-Zawahiri is a physician. Osama bin Laden trained to be a businessman.

Yemeni Judge Hamoud Al-Hitar has also attacked the Islamic intellectual basis of terrorism using hujjat or proof "in theological dialogues that challenge and then correct the wayward beliefs" of terrorists or would-be terrorists.

Iranian Ayatollah Ozma Seyyed Yousef Sanei issued a fatwa (ruling) that suicide attacks against civilians are legitimate only in the context of war. The ruling did not say whether other types of attacks against civilians are justified outside of the context of war, nor whether Jihad is included in Sanei's definition of war.

On the other hand, Fethullah Gülen, a prominent Turkish Islamic scholar, has claimed that "a real Muslim," who understood Islam in every aspect, could not be a terrorist. There are many other people with similar points of view such as Karen Armstrong, Prof. Ahmet Akgunduz, and Harun Yahya.

Muslim Attitudes toward Terrorism

Muslim popular opinion on the subject of attacks on civilians by Islamist groups varies. While most Muslims living in the West denounce the September 11th attacks on the US, Hezbollah's rocket attacks against Israeli civilian targets are widely supported in the Muslim world and regarded as defensive Jihad by a legitimate resistance movement rather than terrorism.

A Sunday Times survey taken in UK shortly after the 9/11 attack "revealed that 40% of British Muslims believe Usama bin Laden was right to attack the United States. About the same proportion thinks that British Muslims have a right to fight alongside the Taliban. A radio station serving London's Pakistani community conducted a poll which 98% of London Muslims under 45 said they would not fight for Britain, while 48% said they would fight for bin Laden."

A 2005 Pew Research study that involved 17,000 people in 17 countries showed support for terrorism was declining in the Muslim world along with a growing belief that Islamic extremism represents a threat to those countries. A Daily Telegraph survey showed that 6% of British Muslims fully supported the July 2005 bombings in the London Underground.

A 2004 Pew survey revealed that Osama bin Laden is viewed favorably by large percentages in Pakistan (65%),

Jordan (55%) and Morocco (45%). In Turkey as many as 31% say that suicide attacks against Americans and other Westerners in Iraq are justifiable. The Free Muslims Coalition rallied against terror, stating that they wanted to send "a message to radical Muslims and supporters of terrorism that we reject them and that we will defeat them."

Abdel Rahman al-Rashed, a Muslim and the general manager of Arab news channel, Al-Arabiya has said, "It is a certain fact that not all Muslims are terrorists, but it is equally certain, and exceptionally painful, that almost all terrorists are Muslims." Statistics compiled by the United States government's Counterterrorism Center present a more complicated picture of known and specified terrorist incidents from the beginning of 2004 through the first quarter of 2005, slightly more than half of the fatalities were attributed to Islamic extremists but a majority of over-all incidents were considered of either "unknown/unspecified" or a secular political nature.

The vast majority of the "unknown/unspecified" terrorism fatalities did however happen in Islamic regions such as Iraq and Afghanistan, or in regions where Islam is otherwise involved in conflicts such as the West Bank, the Gaza Strip, southern Thailand and Kashmir. The methodology employed by the Center is sometimes disputed and the center has been accused of responding to political pressure from the Bush administration to show a decline in terrorism.

In 2006, Palestine voters gave the group Hamas - which is designated as a terrorist organization in Israel, United States, Canada, and the European Union - a majority of the seats in its parliament though there is question as to whether the election results represent support for the organization's militia tactics, support for the organization's social programs, or dissatisfaction with the previous government which was widely seen as corrupt and incompetent.

Fred Halliday, a British academic specialist on the Middle East, argues that most Muslims consider these acts to be egregious violations of Islam's laws. Daniel Chirot said "Not many people in the world, either in Islamic countries, or Christian ones, or Hindu, or Buddhist, or anything else, really want to live a life of extreme puritanism, endless hate, and suicidal wars. Extremist leaders can take power, and for a time, be backed by much of their population hoping to redress past grievances and trying to find a new utopia. But as with the most extreme Christian warriors during the European wars of religion, or with the Nazis, or the most committed communist revolutionaries, it eventually turned out that few of their people were willing to go all the way in their struggles if that meant permanent violence, suffering, and death. So it will be with Islamic extremism."

Examples of Attacks

The outer skin of World Trade Center Tower Two that remained standing after an Islamist terrorist attack by Al-Qaeda.

- 4 September 1972 - Munich Olympic Massacre.
- 18 April 1983 - April 1983 U.S. Embassy bombing in Beirut, Lebanon. 63 killed.
- 26 February 1993 - World Trade Center bombing, New York City. 6 killed.
- 13 March 1993 - 1993 Bombay bombings. Mumbai, India. The single-day attacks resulted in over 250 civilian fatalities and 700 injuries.
- 24 December 1994 - Air France Flight 8969 hijacking in Algiers by 3 members of Armed Islamic Group and another terrorist. 7 killed including 4 hijackers.
- 25 June 1996 - Khobar Towers bombing. 20 killed and 372 wounded.
- 14 February 1998. The 1998 Coimbatore bombings occurred in the city of Coimbatore, Tamil Nadu, India.

46 people were killed and over 200 were injured in 13 bomb attacks within a 12 km radius.

- 7 August 1998 - 1998 United States embassy bombings in Tanzania and Kenya. 224 dead and 4000+ injured.
- 12 October 2000 - USS *Cole* bombing. 56 killed.
- 11 September 2001 - September 11, 2001 attacks 4 planes hijacked and crashed into World Trade Center and The Pentagon by 19 hijackers. Nearly 3000 dead.
- 13 December 2001 - Suicide attack on India's parliament in New Delhi. Aimed at eliminating the top leadership of India and causing anarchy in the country. Allegedly done by Pakistan-based Islamist terrorist organizations, Jaish-E-Mohammad and Lashkar-e-Toiba.
- 3 March 2002 - Suicide bomb attack on a Passover Seder in a Hotel in Netanya, Israel. 29 dead and 133 injured.
- 9 March 2002 - Café suicide bombing in Jerusalem. 11 killed and 54 injured.
- 7 May 2002 - Bombing in al-Arbaa, Algeria. 49 dead and 117 injured.
- 24 September 2002 - Machine Gun attack on Hindu temple in Ahmedabad, India. 31 dead and 86 injured.
- 12 October 2002 - Bombing in Bali nightclub. 202 killed and 300 injured.
- 16 May 2004 - Casablanca Attacks - 4 simultaneous attacks in Casablanca killing 33 civilians (mostly Moroccans) carried by Salafaia Jihadia.
- 11 March 2004 - Multiple bombings on trains near Madrid, Spain. 191 killed and 1460 injured. (alleged link to Al-Qaeda).
- 3 September 2004 Approximately 344 civilians including 186 children, are killed during the Beslan school hostage crisis.
- 2 November 2004 - Ritual murder of Theo van Gogh (film director) by Amsterdam-born jihadist Mohammed Bouyeri.

- 4 February 2005 - Muslim militants attacked the Christian community in Demsa, Nigeria, killing 36 people, destroying property and displacing an additional 3000 people.
- 7 July 2005 - Multiple bombings in London Underground. 53 killed by four suicide bombers and nearly 700 injured.
- 23 July 2005 - Bomb attacks at Sharm el-Sheikh, an Egyptian resort city, at least 64 people killed.
- 29 October 2005 - 29 October 2005 Delhi bombings. Over 60 killed and over 180 injured in a series of three attacks in crowded markets and a bus, just 2 days before the Diwali festival.
- 9 November 2005 - 2005 Amman bombings. Over 60 killed and 115 injured, in a series of coordinated suicide attacks on hotels in Amman, Jordan. Four attackers including a husband and wife team were involved.
- 7 March 2006 - 2006 Varanasi bombings. An attack attributed to Lashkar-e-Toiba by Uttar Pradesh government officials, over 28 killed and over 100 injured, in a series of attacks in the Sankath Mochan Hanuman temple and Cantonment Railway Station in the Hindu holy city of Varanasi. Uttar Pradesh government officials.
- 11 July 2006. Mumbai, India. 11 July 2006 Mumbai train bombings were a series of seven bomb blasts that took place over a period of 11 minutes on the Suburban Railway in Mumbai (formerly known as Bombay). 209 people lost their lives and over 700 were injured in the attacks.
- 26 July 2008. Ahmedabad, India. Islamic militants detonate at least 16 explosive devices in the heart of this industrial capital, leaving at least 49 dead and 160 injured. A Muslim group calling itself the Indian Mujahideen claims responsibility. Indian authorities believe that extremists with ties to Pakistan and/or

Bangladesh are likely responsible and are intent on inciting communal violence. Investigation by Indian police led to the eventual arrest of a number of militants suspected of carrying out the blasts, most of who belong to a well-known terrorist group, The Students Islamic Movement of India.

- 26 November 2008. Mumbai, India. Muslim extremists kill at least 174 people and wound numerous others in a serious of coordinated attacks on India's largest city and financial capital. A group calling itself the Deccan Mujaheddin claims responsibility, however, the government of India suspects Islamic militants based in Pakistan are responsible.
- "Religious fundamentalism fits uncomfortably into this world," declares one scholar. To fundamentalists, notes another scholar, "religious enemies are important."
- The twentieth century witnessed the maturing and globalization of the modern Western world. The century, characterized by increasing secularization, large corporations, growing wealth and consumerism, technological progress, military might, and global communications, threatened "traditional" religious views both within and without the Western world. Religious individuals and faith groups responded to and interacted with modernity in a variety of ways, ranging from integration to resistance. During the course of the twentieth century, religious groups and individuals who clung to strict orthodoxy and whose response to modernity was centered in militant resistance became known as "fundamentalists."
- Religious fundamentalists in general have much in common in terms of worldviews. In short, all fundamentalists view modernity as the enemy, that is, the representation of evil. First and foremost, modern Western thought is the embodiment of a secularized and pluralistic mindset, resulting in an intellectual

challenge to traditional religious constructs of a God-centered universe. For all fundamentalists, modernity poses a profound moral crisis of faith, culture and society. Some scholars point to Islamic fundamentalism, in particular, as a revolt of bewildered young people caught between traditional values and complex modern choices. Others note that whereas fundamentalism per se is a reaction to the failures of modernization, the formation of fundamentalist movements has primarily been in response to the failure of political leaders (both religious and political) in dealing with the failures of modernization.

- Secondly, modernity as expressed in society and government is understood to be in active opposition to traditional religious values and structures, thus necessitating a defensive response for the protection of traditional values and structures within an increasingly secular culture. The defense is based on the concept of "enclave," that is, the preservation of the pure faith by harboring it within the protective walls of the true faith community. The enclave, representing God, holds the evil world at bay intellectually and socially.
- Finally, a defensive response is viewed by fundamentalists as only a partial response. Ultimately, the "world" must be conquered (or transformed) by true believers (or by God Himself) and forced to adhere to the one pure faith.
- Before proceeding further, a brief discussion of the actual definition of the term "fundamentalist" is in order. Although characterized by rigid religious beliefs and militant resistance to modern world views, "fundamentalist" is a word which is difficult to precisely define. For example, although all religious fundamentalists are conservatives, not all religious conservatives are fundamentalists. One distinguishing characteristic of religious fundamentalists as opposed

to religious conservatives is the fundamentalist's intolerance of opposing worldviews.

- In addition, although some religious conservatives may join fundamentalists in adhering to an inerrant or perfect text (referred to as the "Word of God"), the reactionary (or militant) manner in which fundamentalists utilize their particular interpretation of the "Word of God" (both within their larger faith group and in relation to society at large) typically sets them apart. Some scholars of religious fundamentalisms oftentimes distinguish between "scriptural" fundamentalism and "political" fundamentalism, particularly in terms of Islamic fundamentalisms. Most scholars of Muslim history, however, reserve the term "fundamentalist" to refer to political movements which seek to establish Islamic law at the state level. Islamic movements which are scripturally strict but avoid politics are viewed as "revivalist" movements.
- Accordingly, for the purposes of this paper, "fundamentalism" (as applied to Islam) will be reserved for the political expression of the Islamic faith which seeks to impose Islamic law upon the state. "Revivalist" will refer to Islamic movements which adhere to a strict interpretation of the Quran, but which are not engaged in politics.
- Historically, religious fundamentalisms as a whole did not emerge from a vacuum. Political, cultural and intellectual pressures in the late nineteenth century created a foundation upon which fundamentalisms would build and develop increasingly organized responses to the pervasive secularization of the twentieth and twenty-first centuries. A brief survey of the rise of Islamic fundamentalism will allow us to place the movement within the larger context of Muslim history.

3

The Label of Islamic Fundamentalism

The Parable

Increasingly these days, we hear about Islamic fundamentalism from the Western media, the policy makers and many an intellectual. The term has gained so much currency that it deserves some serious scrutiny. It needs our attention especially because it is the Western rendition of Islam, and not an expression which Muslims have anything to do with. Apparently, it seems to imply that there is what you may call fundamentalist Islam as distinct from non-fundamentalist Islam. It seems to emphasize that there are those among Muslims who believe in the basic principles of Islam and there are those who do not.

So far, there have been only two sects in Islam - Shia and Sunni. The adherents of both agree that the *Qur'an* is the word of the Almighty as revealed to the Prophet Muhammad. Both share the belief that the Prophet Muhammad was the last of all the prophets. Further, both proclaim that Islam constitutes an ideology which goes far beyond mere praying, and that it provides universal principles for all crucial aspects of social life.

Despite this broad agreement between the two, relationships between the Shias and the Sunnis have been far from easy over the centuries to say the least. Now this interjection of fundamentalist/non-fundamentalist dichotomy might create a four fold sectarianism, the Shia fundamentalists and the Shia non-fundamentalists; the Sunni fundamentalists and the Sunni non-fundamentalists. Should this differentiation be allowed to take root in modern Islam, it would be an artifact of the West and not due to any intrinsic reasons within the community of Islam itself. Naturally, a closer look at this new expression is in order. What does fundamentalism mean and why is it being used in the context of Islam by the Western media and the policy makers? We shall address ourselves to these questions in this chapter.

Fundamentalism Defined

Every ideology, whether economic, political, familial or religious, is based on certain characterizing features or the least common denominators so to speak. These features of a given ideology are its fundamental principles. Logically, then, fundamentalism would mean an attitude, an effort or a movement which adheres to or tries to promote these fundamentals. For instance, when we speak of a free market economy and private ownership of property, we describe the fundamentals of modern capitalism; and those who conduct their economic affairs accordingly may aptly be called capitalists.

When we talk of the government of the people, for the people and by the people, we point out the fundamental principles of modern Western democracy; and those who practice and promote this form of polity may be called democratic people or nations. Also, when some believe in the principle of Trinity and the Gospel as the inspired word of God, they are declaring the fundamental principles of Christianity and are known as Christians. Likewise, there are certain essentials that characterize Islam and differentiate it from other systems or ideologies of the past and the present. Those who believe in these as inviolable aspects of Islam are the ones called Muslims. Described in these terms fundamentalisms means the core of all what the adherents of an ideology believe and are expected to practice.

However, what appears to be surprising is that we never hear of democratic fundamentalism, capitalist fundamentalism, socialist fundamentalism or secularist fundamentalism. The term fundamentalism is almost exclusively used in the context of religion. What is disturbing is that whenever used, fundamentalism is spoken of in a highly value laden manner almost invariably with negative connotations - some thing highly dogmatic, something that does not belong in the modern world, and something that has to be reckoned with. To the sensitive Muslim audience, then, the term Islamic fundamentalism seems to carry a message, loud and clear; Believe in Islam if you will; just so not practice it!

Christian Fundamentalism

A more general reason for this negative approach toward religion is Western secularism, which, by the way, has its own fundamentalism. More specifically, the term fundamentalism and secular negativism toward it dates back to the latter part of the 19th century. Even until the late 1850's, the dominant trend, especially in North America was to emphasize the uncritical authority of the Bible. But, soon the parishioners as well as a number of church leaders started demanding a more liberal understanding of the Bible in the light of historical and scientific information. The controversy became so acute that in 1878 a Bible conference was convened in Niagara Falls, New York. This conference was most notably attended by the leaders of the Baptist, Presbyterian and the Disciples of Christ churches. The conference laid down nine fundamental principles.

The signatories of this declaration named themselves fundamentalists and called their challengers heretics.

Among others, these principles included infallibility of the Bible, Trinity, eternal sinfulness of man, the atonement of Jesus for the sin of man, and his imminent return to a reign of one thousand years. With time, the fundamentalist movement gained strength. In 1893, it ousted Charles A. Briggs, one of the most outstanding figures among the Presbyterians. A high point of the movement was reached in 1925 at the famous Scopes trial in Dayton, Tennessee, whereby teaching the theory of biological evolution was prohibited in the state subsidized schools.

Because of the Great Depression and World War II, the movement declined considerably during the decade of the 1930's. It began to regain momentum in the 1940's with the formation of the American Council of Christian churches in 1941 and the much larger National Council of the Evangelists in 1942. Beginning in the 1950's and the 60's, these evangelists discovered the media and used it to their advantage. Especially very graphic pictures on the TV screen - of the blind being able to see again and the lepers being healed - were meant to impress and attract larger audience most of whom were (are) uneducated, undereducated, simple country folks. Never mind if later on some investigative reporters found these demonstrations to be dirty tricks.

Understandably, other more liberal churches do not favor fundamentalism. It is also in disfavor with the liberals of the media, the universities, and the polity in America. It is not favored for at least four major reasons. First is the very dogmatic approach of the fundamentalists. While most Christians including the secular liberals would not question the principle of Trinity, they are more cautious when talking about the eternal sinfulness of man and the atonement of Jesus for the sins of man; and while they entertain serious reservations about liberal application of the Bible in everyday life, most of them are wary of the fundamentalist claim regarding the imminent return of Jesus to a reign of one thousand years.

Secondly, although frequently used, there is little room for the label of heresy in Christianity. Over the years, Christianity has left its door ajar for sectarian, even individual interpretation of its fundamental message. There is no equivalent of heresy in Islam, although *Bida'* may come close. But, whereas in Islam *Bida'* may still not be *Kufr*, heresy in Christianity is only a shade away from *Kufr*. Naturally, no Christian, no matter whatever his or her persuasion, would like to be called a heretic. These nine fundamental principles of Christianity notwithstanding, there are disputes over as to the range of what else could be added (or subtracted).

For instance, the fundamentals of Eastern Orthodox, Roman Catholic, Protestant, Jehovah's Witness and the Mormon religions have irreconcilable differences among them. Even among the fundamentalists themselves, there is scant unity. Consequently, Christianity has become, perhaps, the most sect infested religion in the world today. Christians in America in particular have thoroughly personalized their faith. In this situation, calling some one a heretic is like denying him the 1st Amendment. Thirdly, fundamentalists, like others, raise funds in order to preach. Some of them, using the media, have mastered the art almost to perfection. However, in doing this, they seem to have confused means with ends. Preaching fundamentalism has become big business in America.

Though not on Wall Street yet, Evangelism seems to have all the trappings of modern multinationals - extraordinary large capital, large investments, complex bureaucracy, large "cuts" for the senior executives, a jet set life style, large domestic and an expanding overseas clientele, and an increasing political clout. In a primarily business oriented society like America, none would call this material success of the fundamentalists heresy. However, to make questionable presentations in order to lure the clientele is like passing an adulterated product in the market. Fundamentalist preachers have not been sued in court for such acts yet, which may be because of their local and national political clout. But this does not stop the liberals from talking.

Fourthly, fundamentalism was shocked to the core and its membership plummeted in the recent past as incidences of sexual and financial scandals came to the surface in the early 90's, involving some of the most prominent fundamentalist ministers. Court convictions and a series of libel suits and counter suits that followed did not help the cause to say the least. In short, fundamentalism in America has lately developed a serious image problem presumably even among some of its traditional followers and contributors. Liberal church leaders as well as secular opinion makers look down upon the fundamentalists as being dogmatic, conservative, arrogant and corrupt. Although weakened, fundamentalism possesses amazing resilience. It is still very much alive and has a large following, especially in the American South, where, once its dirty linen is washed, its appeal may quickly translate into political power - a nightmare of the secular institutions in American centers of power.

Evidently, fundamentalism in America has a history and a character of its own but, when secular media pundits and the power elites who are wary of fundamentalism in their own midst, speak of Islamic fundamentalism, it makes one wonder. A survey of the Muslim world, past and present, would show that among Muslims there is not and there has not been a group or a sect which called itself fundamentalist. We do not know of any Muslim group or sect which called some other group by this name. Nor do we know of any Muslim sect or school of thought which even remotely resembles American Christian fundamentalism. Lastly, we are not aware of any Muslim party or a movement which is in cahoot with the American fundamentalist movement.

Apparently, American secular leaders, now readily followed by the European leaders in general, have come to look at Islam or some Muslim groups in the image of their fundamentalists. It has not been necessary for some Muslim groups to congregate at some lakeside resort and pronounce themselves Islamic fundamentalists. Western secularists chose to assume this responsibility themselves. In doing this, they picked a bewildering array of a wide range of ideological, narrowly nationalistic and even revengeful groups in the disparate Muslim world suffering from a lack of communication, coordination and a sense of unity.

Those who have been labelled as Islamic funda-mentalists include the Sunni Ikhwan al Muslimoon (Muslim Brotherhood) of Egypt, the Shia government of post revolution Iran, the Sunni Jamaat Islami (Islamic Party) of Pakistan, the Shia activists of southern Lebanon, and the Sunni Afghan Mujahideen. Not to mention those convicted of bombing the World Trade Center in 1993 or the rock throwing children in Palestine; even such apolitical groups as the Jamaat Tabligh of Pakistan and the Salafi factions in Saudi Arabia are not spared of this label. It seems that whosoever in the Muslim world evokes the name of Islam outside of the mosques is liable to be called Islamic fundamentalist.

Consequently, whenever and wherever a Muslim group is fighting for its survival or its constitutional and basic human rights, whether in Algeria, in Egypt, in Palestine, in Kashmir, in Mindanao or in Bosnia, has been called Islamic fundamentalist - even by Radovan Karadizc, the now notoriously famous mass murderer and ethnic cleanser of Bosnia and Hertzegovina.

Why, one wonders, is there such an elevated level of concern in the West approaching paranoia about Islam? Why this excitement about Islam at this juncture in history, some of these movements being more than fifty years old or even older? It may be easier to answer the latter question, which may also at least partly explain the first. Heightened concern in the West about the Muslim world coincides with the demise in the mid 1980's of the Soviet Union, the socialist giant which remained a bogy for the Western powers for almost fifty years in the 20th century.

With the socialist specter out of the way, it seems that the Western elite must before too long find another demon to exorcise; and what could be a better target than the good old sick genie of Islam, which, far from refusing to die, shows disturbing signs of life every now and then. Before the exit of the Soviet Union from the international scene, developments in the Muslim world, such as the overthrow of the "Friendly Tyrants" in Egypt, in Syria, in Iraq, and to cap all that, in Iran in 1979, did sometimes create serious concerns among Western policy makers who, however, found themselves without any well thought out or united policy to deal with these "delinquents," all their energies having been spent on containing the Soviet Union.

Not any more. Beware Muslim activists. Or, as Avineri (1993:167) put it:

> A specter is haunting Europe - and the world in general, the specter of Islamic fundamentalism. All the world powers have entered into a holy alliance to exorcise this specter, the pope and the President of Russia, Helmet Kohl and Francois Mitterrand, French radicals and German police agents, and of course the CIA and right-wing Israeli politicians.

It is in the light of this observation that one may understand what looked like utter hypocrisy on the part of the European powers who, while shedding crocodile tears nonetheless allowed the events of mass murder, "strategic rape" and Muslim ethnic cleansing to go on unabated in Bosnia through four tortuous winters of 1992, 1993, 1994 and 1995. This may also explain why when after their liberation from the socialist regime, people are redecorating and making new churches all over Eastern Europe as well as in Russia, such acts are hailed as being the signs of resilience of Orthodox religion; and yet when the newly independent Tadjiks, who after centuries long extremely oppressive rule of the Czars and the Soviets, now want to rebuild their old mosques, once famous centers of learning, they are labeled as Islamic fundamentalists and massacred in thousands by the heavily equipped Russian troops, who do not have any sovereignty over the region any more - an incident that not even the nosiest Western reporter cared to report. Why, one may ask, it did not make a ripple in Washington, London or Paris or Bonn after the Islamic Democratic party of Algeria was nipped by the military brass after it won the first ever nationwide democratic election by a land slide in 1992.

How is it that the Muslim genocide in Kashmir at the hands of the highly trained and very well equipped Indian army has been only whispered about but never brought to public attention by the Western elites of the media and public policy? Why this a West paranoia about Islamic revival? Is it a danger to world stability and Western civilization? "And should one look under every bed for Muslim fundamentalists the way some people (sometimes the same people) used to look for communists in the good old bad days of the evil empire?"

With millions of Muslims living in the West as citizens these days, are we about to see yet another love affair with McCarthyism? Outside of Christianity and Judaism, Islam is the most known religion in the West. It is also, perhaps, the most misunderstood religion in the West. This is so because most Western students of Islam, with a few exceptions, have tried to understand it in terms of their own historical, moral and ideological biases. First, even if we forget about ancient problems between the Levant and Europe, there exists a deep rooted suspicion of Islam dating back to the shocks that Europe received at the hands of early Islamic armies in the 7th century; and especially to the encounters during the Crusades which generated voluminous literature about Islam and Muslims. This literature and this lore with few exceptions, has been mostly critical, often negatively biased and sometimes even obscenely against Islam. So writes Armstrong (1992:11).

Even when Europe recovered from the Dark Ages and established its own great civilization, the old fear of the ever-expanding Muslim empire remained. Europe could make no impression on this powerful and dynamic culture, the Crusading project of twelfth and thirteenth centuries eventually failed........This fear made it impossible for Western Christians to be rational or objective about the Muslim faith. At the same time that they were weaving fearful fantasies about Jews, they were also evolving a distorted image of Islam, which reflected their own buried anxieties. Western scholars denounced Islam as a blasphemous faith and its Prophet Muhammad the great pretender...In Mummers' plays he was presented as the enemy of Western civilization, who fought our own brave St George.

This inaccurate image of Islam became one of the received ideas of Europe and continues to affect our perception of the Muslim world. Although present generations in the West hardly remember or even care about the Crusades, negative images of Islam and Muslims persist in the Western culture, many a text book, and even in the works of the Middle East "experts". Some time ago, a professor at a college run by a fundamentalist church wrote to this author that Muslims worship *Hajre Aswad* - the piece of the black rock in the side of the *Ka'bah* - and sprinkle holy water (*Zam Zam*) as a part of the *Hajj* ceremonies. There are even more serious accusations against Islam that need not be repeated here. Suffice it to say that even some pagan and animistic religions receive a much better treatment than Islam in the West today.

Secondly, the crusades also created a specter of the Muslims rallying in the name of Islam. Ever since Salahuddin Ayyubi (Saladdin) defeated the forces of King Richard of England toward the end of the long fought

Crusades, Islam and politics have been seen as being a wrong combination for those who would be contemplating colonizing or extending their hegemony over the Middle East region. Because politics is not beyond the pale of Islam, outsiders as well as power mongering insiders in the Muslim community generally remain hostile toward Islamic movements unless they openly disavow any political involvement.

Thirdly, although Western colonialism is fast becoming history, its legacy persists in the minds of many a Western policy maker and even the intellegentia in the form of a patronizing big brother-like attitude toward the "natives" who better listen to and follow the big brother if they want to make any progress.

Fourthly, secularism has a built-in bias against religion in general. From this perspective, not only Islam, but also religion is outdated. It does not belong in modern discourse. A sympathetic critic of this author once wrote that the very term religious or Islamic sociology may alienate Western sociologists. Thus, as Western Christianity is fading out, Western secularism is emerging as a new enemy of Islam. It is strange that when Christianity was the major mode of thinking in the West, Islam was being attacked as being blasphemy. Now that secularism is the guiding principle, Islam is being looked at in the image of Christianity. According to Avineri.

The underlying assumption has always been that Islam - as a culture and not only a religious creed - was primitive, underdeveloped, retrograde, at best stuck in the memory hole of a medieval splendor out of which it could not disentangle itself without a radical transformation; and this could only be based on Western, "rational", "progressive" values.

In short, men and women of influence and power in the West seem to harbor deep seated complexes and anxieties with respect to the efforts at rejuvenating Islam. In trying to achieve their modernist goals, their experience with their own dominant religion has not been very encouraging. However, looking at Islam and all other religions for that matter, in the image of Christianity seems to create a tunnel vision, developing a "trained incapacity" to understand Islam.

The Return to Islam

Sometimes there is a tendency, especially in the Western media, to lump acts of extremism, sabotage or even airplane hijacking on the part of some splinter groups in the Muslim world with movements of Islamic revival. Even such sympathetic writers on Islam as Armstrong (1992:12) seem to have fallen in this trap. Following this reasoning, might one point out that Gush Amunim and Rabbi Mier Kahane, or Dr. Goldstein, the murderer of scores of innocent Muslim worshippers in a Hebron mosque in the fasting month of *Ramadhan* of 1994, represent Zionism! Although they are a part of the general history of Zionism as it is unfolding before our eyes, are these groups or individuals to be equated with Zionism per se?

Likewise, the movement to return to Islam must not be confused with airplane hijacking, the bombing of the World Trade Center, or even the Palestinian *Intifidah* of rock throwing children. In fact, the two largest movements espousing a return to Islam in modern times - *Ikhwan al Muslimoon* (Muslim brotherhood) of Egypt and the *Jamaat-i-Islami* (Islamic party) of Pakistan - are avowed constitutionalists who, for over fifty years and much to the displeasure of other splinters with similar objectives, have made it their explicit goal to establish Islam through peaceful means. In order to highlight how these movements have functioned over the past half a century in the Muslim world, we present an excerpt from a policy speech given to his party workers by late Abul Ala Moududi (1951), the founder of the *Jamat-i-Islami* (Islamic Party) and "fundamentalist" *par excellance* in Pakistan.

We may participate in them directly or indirectly, but we can not divorce ourselves from the electoral processes, although how we would participate in them should be left up to the Shura (executive) board of the party.

In order to keep the electoral process in perspective, we should be cognizant of three major facts. First, in order to establish the Islamic way of life in this country, it is inevitable to change its political leadership.

Secondly, in this country we have a functioning constitutional democracy; and there is only one way to change its leadership - through elections.

Thirdly, it is not permissible (by the Islamic Shariah) to try to remove the existing constitutional government through unconstitutional means.

Moududi's perhaps, the strongest statement to date disavowing any violent action aimed at overthrowing the constitutional government. Evidently, he was of the opinion that the electoral process is basic to Islamic polity, especially in regards to bringing about political change. What is true of the *Jamaat* in Pakistan has been true also of the *Ikhwan al Muslimoon* (Muslim brotherhood) of Egypt. These parties and similar movements elsewhere in the Muslim world have in general functioned by extending basic social services like food, clothing, education and even medical help to the needy, participating in local and national elections, and quite significantly by providing the only voice of opposition.

Despite their lack of success over past several decades, these movements are emulated in several distant places. The Algerian Islamic Democratic Party which was deprived of its landslide success at the polls in 1992 is an example. That these movements have been continuously given a bad coverage means that either they are confused as being "terrorists" or that their ultimate objective - a return to Islam - is not appreciated in the West. We have already discussed reasons for this Western ambivalence in the above.

Although still subscribed to by a minority in the Muslim world, if the voices of these two and similar movements are being heard more attentively and more extensively now than before, it is because, most significantly, during the past fifty years, the Muslim population has more than doubled itself, making itself much younger than before; and as more educated youth are entering the job market, they quickly develop an acute feeling of what has come to be known as "relative deprivation" (Staufer,1955) because the Muslim power elite has almost invariably failed in solving the problem of a increasingly restive society. According to Armstrong (1992), Islamic revivalism is, by far, the movement of the young, the educated and the disenchanted.

Another reason as pointed out by some (for instance, Avineri, 1993) is that the Muslim intellectuals, politicians as well as the military rulers have tried just about every Western ideology in the book - from republicanism and constitutionalism to different forms of socialism and even shades of fascism - but to no avail. With the exception of few oil rich sheikdoms, the Muslim world at large remains afflicted with widespread under nutrition, substandard positions, very low literacy and inevitable anger aimed at their elites and those powers that continue to support these elites.

Those who think that the "Muslim society looks profoundly repulsive.....It looks repulsive because it is repulsive", and that "the [Muslim] sickness gets worse the more the [Islamic] remedy is taken", ought to be informed that, of late, the sick Muslim has tried just about every remedy in the book except Islam. Maybe he continues to remain "repulsively sick" because he has been denied the right medicine. In this sense, as Khan (1994) pointed out, the return to Islam is, in fact, a postmodern phenomenon - a response to peculiar strains and stresses of the late-twentieth-century national and global developments.

At least this is what an increasing number of Muslim intellectuals, many of them former *communisants* and liberal intellectuals in the Muslim world are beginning to think these days. They are rediscovering that far from being merely a worshipping formula, Islam encompasses rules of societal institutions which may work where modern ideologies have failed them; and which have great appeal for the Muslim sense of justice, equality and compassion for all. Western secular elite do not necessarily have to agree with all things Islamic. No two culture areas are completely congruent.

"But, per contra, it is simplistic Western cultural imperialism - be it liberal or Marxist - to think that the West, with its own internal, modern and postmodern problems, can give adequate answers to Islamic societies. Two centuries of *HUBRIS* ought to disprove the proposition that all the Islamic East needs is an injection of Western Christian or post-Christian values and institutions... Terrorism inspired by Islamic fanatics should be fought tooth and nail...But Western intellectuals and statesmen should not mount a new crusade against Islam wrong enemy and wrong-headed thinking.

Dimensions of Islamic Ideology

All human beings have two major needs. First, they have to have food, clothing and shelter. These are known as economic needs. To these, we humans at different times and places have also added other things considered to be essential for life (means of communication and transportation, leisure and amusement, cooking and heating, etc.). Secondly, as we grow up, we develop sexual and reproductive needs. As basic as they are, these needs can not be satisfied without us interacting with, cooperating with and living with other human beings.

However, paradoxically, these very demands also have the potential of great discord and dispute in the presence of others unless we develop some measure of normative control. Polity or the exercise of power, then, is the third major element that we humans need while living a plural life. Lastly, but not least, we human beings have also shown a great need for the super natural and some way of communicating with Him - individually and collectively.

All societies, however primitive or modern, see to it that these four human needs are satisfied through highly regulated patterns of interaction. Sociologists call these patterns of interaction institutions - of economy, family, polity, and worship. Without first three of this human society is unthinkable. Without all four of them, human society has not existed historically. Together, norms governing these social institutions describe most essential ingredients of social life universally. As dissimilar as these institutional patterns of interaction are, ideally or from culture relativity point of view, they must be interdependent and mutually reinforcing.

However, in reality except for the very primitive societies, this is hardly the case. In fact, we may safely hypothesize that as a society becomes more complex, indeed with every new development, its institutions tend to exert centrifugal pressure upon one another. Last in the succession of divinely revealed religions of the world, Islam came at the threshold of accelerating societal complexity. Human population was increasingly becoming sedentary. As horticulture was widely replaced by irrigation based civilizations, animal husbandry and nomadism was giving way to agricultural and international commercial settlements while gold standard was already giving rise to a monetary economy almost world wide.

At this juncture in human history, Islam came with full compliment of social institutions essential for human society. We do not know of any other "ism", ideology, or religion which deals with these four indispensable aspects of human life at once - as manifestations of the same source which provides them with organic unity. A common ideological root in Islam, obviously, is meant to keep the increasingly complex society of man from coming apart at its institutional seams. This claim stands in defiance to all other ideologies of the past and the present which have failed to provide a singular design of institutional unity for human society.

When practiced in its totality, Islam aims at creating what the *Qur'an* calls the "Middle Nation" as against all other "oscillating cultures" which only take extreme positions. The centralizing tendency in Islam has the potential of negotiating ideological extremes and providing them a common ground. For instance, in its economic aspects, although Islam respects private property and favors an open market system, yet it discourages excessive capital accumulation by prohibiting interest, gambling, profiteering and hoarding. Far from creating a socialistic economy, it ordains transfer of substantial amount of resource from the very rich to the very poor and the needy who are encouraged to seek work and discouraged to subsist on charity. Thus, Islamic economy has a built-in motivation for the individual initiative while commanding dispersion far in excess of what capitalism would tolerate but far below the level that socialism could tolerate.

In short, Islam allows capitalism minus material obsession. While defying any socialistic solutions, however, it attacks the very roots of exploitation in a free market economy. Traditionally, human family has functioned on the basis of extended kinship. It is mainly since the advent of industrialization that the family has become increasingly marriage based and modern nuclear family. Islam does not commit itself to either form. While there may be few precious tears to be shed on the passing of tribal or clan system, Islam is aimed at creating a web of relationships in which the family of orientation (birth) plays a major role in shaping, accommodating and sustaining the family of procreation (wife and children). Even if arranged marriage is a norm among Muslims, Marriage in Islam can not be solemnized without an explicit consent on the part of the marrying partners in the presence of adult and sane Muslims.

Not being a sacrament, marriage in Islam is strictly a civil contract requiring a declaration, witnessing and documentation if possible. In this respect alone, Islamic marriage has preempted modern marriage by more than thirteen hundred years. Having rejected priesthood, Islam leaves no room for theocracy. By the Divine decree in the *Qur'an* and according to the *Sunnah* of the Prophet (p), *Shura* is the fundamental principle of polity in Islam. Roughly translated as consultation in English language, however, *Shura* does not mean an advice that could be rejected later. The structure of the *Khilafah* following the *Sunnah* of the Prophet (p) shows that *Shura* constitutes consultation that culminates in binding decisions.

This puts Islamic polity squarely between democracy and authoritarianism. After all *Shura* has its roots in the *Qur'an* and the *Sunnah* of the Prophet (p). Consequently, Islamic polity may elect the rulers who institute laws, make any policies, and introduce any programs as they deem fit only so long as they do not transgress the authoritative limits as laid down in the *Qur'an* and the *Sunnah*. In short, the *Qur'an* and the *Sunnah* describe constitutional limits of Islamic polity. But, then, who is going to decide whether or not those in authority in Islam acted according to the *Qur'an* and the *Sunnah*? The answer is that the *Qadi* or the judge does this for you. An independent judiciary specializing in the *Shariah*, then, is a necessary condition of the process of *Shura*.

Evidently, this system is not theocracy. Obviously, it does not accommodate monarchy either. Finally, worship in Islam has broader as well as more specific meanings. In a broader sense, worship or *Ibadah* in Islam literally means obedience to all the commandments as laid down in the *Qur'an* and the *Sunnah* including all institutional as well as extra-institutional rules of conduct. Thus, when a person avoids interest or extramarital involvement, preaches Islam, or participates in and promotes Islamic polity, he or she is worshipping. Likewise, when a Muslim develops his personal character according to the *Qur'anic* commandments, he or she is engaging worship. In a more general sense, then, worship in Islam means obedience to the Divine commandments.

In a more limited sense, as in its dictionary meanings these days, worship in Islam means observations of the "Five Pillars" - the proclamation of faith or the *Shahadah*, praying five times a day or the *Salat*, giving poor due or the *Zakat*, fasting from dawn to dusk for the whole lunar month of *Ramadhan* or *Saum*, and pilgrimage at Makkah at least once in life time or *Hajj*. These "Five Pillars of Islam" must not be considered to be mere supplications. They are duties imposed on Muslims by their Creator. They are not left at the convenience or whims and wishes of the believer. These duties are to be performed conscienciously at their proper times as practiced and instructed by the Prophet (p).

What is emphasized here is that this is not God who needs man's worship and sacrifices. It is man who needs to worship Him in order to strengthen his own moral fiber and personal commitment (*Taqwa*) to obey the commandments of his Creator. Because both aspects of worship in Islam belong to the same generic root i.e. the *Qur'an*, relationship between the two is close and reciprocal. While worship in terms of the Five Pillars is necessary for committing a Muslim personally to the practice of the Islamic institutional order, this commitment or *Taqwa* itself needs Islamic institutional environment in which to nourish and sustain it. There is little doubt that without personal commitment or *Taqwa*, the institutional order of Islam would not last very long.

It is equally true that without an Islamic institutional environment, *Taqwa* would be rendered useless, goalless, and meaningless. Personal worship in terms of the rituals, even if performed collectively or in congregations, is characteristic of all religions in which its function is to inculcate in the worshipper personal piety aimed mainly at developing a commitment to do well to others and avoid harming them. But, these religions do not generally go any further than that; and because they do not do so, they do not provide personal piety an appropriate environment which it may promote and in which it may rejuvenate itself. Indeed, in most societies these days personal piety of the worshipper is becoming increasingly irrelevant because contemporary social institutions of modern societies do not have any generic relationship with and, indeed, go against the very spirit of personal piety.

In Islam, as must be evident from the above, personal worship and abidance by the Islamic laws governing other institutions are two sides of the same coin. One can not be without the other. This broadening of the meanings of worship in Islam is unique to it. Above all, what it means is that for all or most Muslims to become pious, personal ritualistic worship at home or in the mosque must be reinforced by the Islamic economy, the Islamic family and the Islamic polity. Thus, those who are afraid of the spread of "Muslim extremism", must understand that peaceful Muslim can be found only in a functioning Islamic order. This is the message that the "Islamic fundamentalists" are trying to convey to their rulers, and to those who are leading the non-Muslim world.

In this we have tried to show that expression Islamic fundamentalism which is increasingly gaining currency especially among Western policy makers, intellectuals and the media is not only misleading, it may also be counterproductive. The term is misleading because its vocabulary and its imagery is borrowed primarily from

Christian fundamentalist movement of the American South. American fundamentalists proclaim a number of dogmas which are not welcome among American liberal church leaders as well as secular elites in the media, politics and the universities.

But, to be scared of the fundamentalist movement in their back yard is one thing. It is quite another to look at Islam in the image of their garden variety. There is no and there has never been any fundamentalist/non-fundamentalist differentiation in Islam during the past fourteen centuries.

As used by American, and now increasingly also by other Western elites, the expression *Islamic fundamentalism,* and the very negative connotations that go with it, may also be counter-productive. This is because to many a sensitive Muslim ear, it may sound like a deliberate effort to create a new rift in the already fractionated world of Islam. May be most Western elites do not even know that they are victims of the medieval anti-Islamic biases of their forefathers. May be they are falsely afraid of something which may surprise them only if they set their ethnocentrism aside. Even so, during these closing years of the 20th century, the world is waking up to the fact that one does not have to harbor Western values in order to outperform the West.

Every ideology, whether religious, economic, political or otherwise, is based on certain fundamental principles. So does Islam. The question is, are Islamic fundamentals dogmatic in the same sense as those of Christianity? A closer look shows Islam to be a surprisingly integrated ideology which has pre-empted modern socioeconomic ideologies by quite a few centuries. Only, Islam does not leave its institutions at the mercy of self-centered and materialistic pragmatism. More seriously, it must not be overlooked that the primary responsibility of the misperception of Islam in the West and among other non-Muslims lies on none other than the Muslim elites - political, educational, economic and those in the media - of the past and the present.

No teachings of Islam can be equal to experiencing Islam as a living society. However, since deviance from Islam has increasingly become a norm among those who have taken upon themselves to lead the Muslim masses, Islamic norms are becoming deviant in Muslim societies. Consequently, those who call for and are active in trying to reestablish the Islamic institutional order, draw the wrath of the Muslim elites in several different ways - ridiculed in media presentations, criticized in academic and educational publications, ignored in national and international business dealings, and often severely punished by those in control of political power. Compared to the treatment the Islamic activists receive from leaders of their own societies, being labeled as Islamic fundamentalists by the Western elites, may look awfully benign indeed.

However, in the long run existing Western attitude toward Islam is definitely more harmful than any atrocities committed by the Muslim elites. Existing Muslim elites, with a few exceptions, are either dependent on the West for their own claim to power; or they are superficially Westernized to one degree or another, perhaps, less in their convictions than in their action. In either case, most Muslim leaders these days tow the Western line voluntarily or otherwise. Thus, as long as the Muslim elites are able to keep the Islamic activists under control, say, in Algeria, in Egypt, in Pakistan and in the oil rich sheikdoms, Western powers do not have to intervene with force directly. However, sustained Islamic revivalist activity or assumption of power by the Islamic activists (like in Iran in 1978 or in the Sudan in 1992) apparently gives rise to an ancient anti-Western specter in the minds of the Western elites.

Now that the Soviet Union, the arch rival of the West for the most part in the 20th century, is gone for good, full attention is being given to Islam - the fallen "enemy" that is trying to resurrect itself. "Islamic fundamentalism" is only relatively a milder expression, which betrays the same old Western antipathy toward Islam. It must be noted here that any direct Western intervention in the Muslim countries - even at the behest of the government in power - invariably creates an hostile reaction among the masses boosting the appeal of the Islamic revivalist movements - most often the only voice of political dissent in the Muslim world. This is how the West has been contributing to the appeal of the call for return to Islam. There is hardly any empirical data available on the subject, but it is quite plausible to believe that the Western posture toward revolutionary Shia Iran has contributed tremendously to the Islamic call in Sunni Muslim countries.

Likewise, the Soviet invasion of Afghanistan on Christmas eve in 1979, created an anti-socialist backlash even among leftist intellectuals in Pakistan, in Algeria and even in such avowedly Marxist countries like Southern Yemen (Ahmed, 1981). Besides, the chronic problem of Palestine, and now Bosnia and the Muslim states under former Soviet Union (Tadjikistan, Chachnia) have undoubtedly been tremendous contributing factors in this direction. But, under the setting sun of the 20th century two momentous developments are taking place, one of them in the Muslim world and the other in the West. First, the Islamic revivalism is fast taking root in the newly independent Muslim countries especially among the intellegentia many of whom received their higher education in some of the most renowned seats of learning in North America and Europe.

Toward the end of the first half of the 20th century, there was only one visible Islamic revivalist movement in the Muslim world - Jamaate Islami of Pakistan. The Ikhwan al Muslimoon of Egypt was already in ruins and scattered at the behest of the British in 1948. At that time undoubtedly there were many in the Muslim world who would subscribe to the views of these two movements. However, by 1950, Jamaaat was the only organized movement of its kind left in the Muslim world. But, toward the end of the second half of the 20th century, today nearly all major Muslim countries from Indonesia and Malaysia to Pakistan, Iraq, Syria, Turkey and nearly all of North African countries have active Islamic movements. Additionally, Iran (a Shia state) and Sudan (a Sunni state) are already functioning Islamic states. Algeria, Egypt, and Yemen seem to be next in line. Should this happen, other Muslim states may not necessarily fall like the dominoes.

Which and how many other Muslim states will adopt Islamic polity shall to a great extent depend upon how already Islamicized states behave and are allowed to survive. In any case, in as much as the West stricken Muslim political elites have so far spectacularly failed in seeking solutions to the chronic problems of their respective societies, Islamic revivalists armed with most advanced education and training that the modern world can offer, seem to be the most formidable and able adversaries to their brittle regimes. Last forty years saw the emergence of two Islamic states (Sudan and Iran), and two (Algeria and Afghanistan) nearly succeeded in doing so. Next forty years may see the emergence of four or five more such states. It means that by the 2030's, there may be six or seven functioning Islamic states in the world.

Two patterns of international relations may be predicated regarding this development. First, provided Western ambivalence toward Islam is not abated, these Islamic states, like Shia Iran and Sunni Sudan today, would go out of their way to cooperate among themselves and support one another politically, economically and otherwise, notwithstanding their sectarian differences. Secondly, despite Iran's hostility toward the West which is more situational than ideological, these Islamic states would love to create a happy symbiosis with the West (as well as with others) i.e. unless others continue to attack and subverse Islamic revivalism. None of the Islamic revivalist movements, not even the hated Ikhwan of Egypt and the Jamaat of Pakistan have been inherently anti-Western in the same sense as the socialist ideology or the Soviet Union was.

Second event of great significance that is going on at the time of this writing is the transformation of the Western religious landscape. With a world wide migratory movement from technologically less developed countries of the so-called Third World toward industrially developed nations of the West, both Europe and North America are homes not merely to the Christians and the Jews. They are also now hosting Islam, Hinduism, Buddhism, Sikhism and scores of other large and small belief systems. Of these, Islam undoubtedly is the fastest growing community. This growth of Islam in the West is not due to immigration alone. In significant respects, it is also because of DAWAH (invitation to Islam) and conversion to Islam.

Future of this community in the West on the one hand, and quite significantly, the nature of the relationship between the West and the future Islamic states on the other hand, shall to one degree or the other depend on the resourcefulness, organization and political and social savy with which Muslims in the West compose themselves. With their high level of education, professionalism, and income especially in America and Canada what is needed is unity in organization, resource mobilization and social and political policy before they would be perceived as "model minorities" recreating the correct image of Islam, making their presence felt and wisely exercising their political clout. In short, given the disgraceful attitude toward Islam and Muslims especially on the part of many a Western policy and opinion maker, some one has to take an initiative to correct the situation. While Islamic revivalists are doing their share in the Muslim world, Muslims in the West especially those in North America have to do their share in this endeavor. That their potential to do so is increasing by the day, there is little doubt about it.

Model for Countering Islamist Extremism

Essentialism and Dualism

Paganism (*jahiliyya*) is the generic designation given to all systems of thought other than Islam, both ancient and modern. According to Islamic fundamentalism, since the dawn of history human society has been a battleground between belief and unbelief, right and wrong, religious faith and idolatry. Individuals and their beliefs may carry different names in different ages, but this duality remains essentially the same.

The definition of paganism is thus stretched to encompass Greek philosophy in the ancient world as well as utilitarianism and existentialism in the modern age. To Sayyid Qutb, for example, paganism is deemed to be present wherever 'people's hearts are devoid of a divine doctrine that governs their thought and concomitant legal rules to regulate their lives'. Moreover, although outward manifestations may differ from age to age, the nature and attributes of paganism remain permanent. On the other hand, religion operates throughout the ages within constant perimeters, rotating around a fixed axis. Furthermore, religion and the cosmic order reflect God's will in its harmonious design.

In this scheme of things, human nature and the cosmos are substances which retain their identities while undergoing change. A substance generates properties and assigns them a function peculiar to their qualities. Properties inhere in substances and are dependent for their existence and persistence on them. Such properties are not incidental, but form an identifiable structure quite distinct from other structures. These properties are therefore not transferable, in that once transferred they lose their function or significance.

According to Islamic fundamentalism, the essential nature of human beings is religious and atheism is an aberration. Throughout human history there have been only two methods of organizing human life, one that declares God to be the sole sovereign and source of legislation, and another that rejects God, either as a force in the universe or as the lord and administrator of society. These two methods are irreconcilable, the first denotes Islam, the second paganism. Once human beings accept legislation to be dependent on the will of an individual, a minority or a majority, and not as the prerogative of God alone, they lapse into a type of paganism, be it a dictatorship, capitalism, theocracy or communism.

However, human history is an emanation of a doctrinal concept that is implanted by God in human beings in their capacity as his designated lieutenants on this earth. The lieutenancy (*khilafa*) of a human being is to carry out the commands of God. According to this line of reasoning, most human societies in the twentieth century resemble in their way of life the state of affairs that existed before the rise of Islam. In order to re-establish Islam as a system of government, it is thus of primary importance to discover anew the fundamental constituents of its doctrine. Such an honourable task falls to a well-disciplined group of believers. These pioneers, dubbed 'the vanguard' by Qutb, 'the Revolutionary Party' by Abu al-'Ala al-Mawdudi and 'the holy warriors' by Ayatollah Ruhollah al-Khumayni, are called upon to undertake the reinstatement of Islam in both its doctrinal and political dimensions. The method of struggle is often referred to as *jihad,* or holy war launched in the path of God.

The Fundamental Principles of Islam

The fundamental principles of Islam and the injunctions of its laws are one seamless garment woven by God for his creatures. Whereas Greek thought, particularly Aristotelian thought, asserted that we are political animals by nature, Islamic fundamentalism contends that the basic instinct of human beings is intrinsically religious. Religion is understood in this context to be Islam itself. Islam has its own constant, immutable and clearly defined nature. Its underlying aim is to change the process of history and create a new human being, unfettered by subservience to other human beings or institutions. To be a Muslim is to believe in the fundamental principles of Islam in their entirety.

Moreover, the doctrinal principles of Islam are not to be studied theologically, metaphysically or philosophically. Their study is primarily a practical endeavour aimed at discovering the base on which an all-embracing system is to be erected for the benefit of humanity. Theory and praxis go hand in hand; knowledge is simply a prelude to social action and political engagement. For Qutb, al-Mawdudi and al-Khumayni, the doctrine of Islam forms an organic unity. A description of its constituent parts is therefore a mere analytical device, which should under all circumstances indicate the interdependence and complementarity of these parts. Once a part is detached and treated on its own it loses its significance, depriving the harmonious totality of its beauty and truth. The true nature of divinity, for example, cannot be understood apart from its direct efficacy in regulating the movement of the universe and in all its physical and spiritual connotations.

Thus God's divinity ensures the harmonious essence of cosmic laws: God sustains, guards and regulates the universe according to fixed laws. Nevertheless, his absolute will fashions every movement or event without being bound by them. These laws are not self-regulatory in that they persist as a result of the immediate act of God, and are thus created anew every moment. The world was created in time, a fact denoting a temporal beginning rather than an eternal existence. In classical Islam, God's attributes were enumerated and discussed by a number of theologians and philosophers, but his essence was deemed to lie beyond human knowledge. Islamic fundamentalism, as represented by Qutb's system, shifted the debate to Islam's essence and attributes. Hence the fundamental principles of Islam were considered by Qutb to consist in their delineation of God's divinity as well as human servitude in carrying out the tenets of the message as handed down to the seal of the prophets, Muhammad.

These fundamentals spell out God's divinity (*uluhiyya*) and the servitude of animate and inanimate objects to God (*'ubudiyya*), in addition to the true essence of the cosmos, life and humanity. Moreover, the visible and invisible worlds are both an integral part of this doctrine and should be present in treating the vicissitudes of human existence. These fundamentals are not the result of an exertion by the human mind. Rather, the human mind receives them in their entirety once it is freed of its *a priori* conceptions. One does so by adhering to the sound linguistic or conventional meaning of the text in which such principles are propounded. The human mind has no function other than to understand the exact meaning of the text, irrespective of its conformity to the axioms of reason. Hence, one must accept the existence of angels, *jinns,* resurrection, hell and paradise without equivocation.

According to Qutb, the principle of divinity is the primary and most efficacious essence in the formation of the Islamic doctrine. The existence of such an essence, being absolute and eternal, does not stand in need of external evidence. The innate nature of human beings recognizes this existence, unless it is encumbered by corrupt beliefs that render it incapable of receiving this single fact. Furthermore, the methodology of the Qur'an itself is not concerned with affirming the existence of divine power. Rather, it concentrates on describing its true quality in order to rectify the distorted views of other creeds. This rectification is not confined to distortions which prevailed before the rise of Islam; its scope covers all deviant beliefs down to the present.

It thus shows the aberrance or the negativity of Aristotle's God, that of Plato's Forms and their adoption in Schopenhauer's unconscious will, and the series of emanations elaborated by Plotinus and taken over by so-called Islamic philosophy. It also rectifies the dualism of Descartes as well as Bergson's vital power, in addition to the materialism of Parmenides in the ancient world and that of Karl Marx in our modern period. The Qur'anic methodology is first and foremost concerned with the question of monotheism rather than existence. Its main aim is to show the simple, indivisible and unique essence of God; it also asserts the attributes of God in their utter uniqueness and splendour.

Islam's Attributes

Whereas orthodox Islamic philosophy and theology (*'ilm al-kalam*) were largely concerned with defining and elabourating God's attributes, Islamic fundamentalism shifted its focus to the attributes of Islam itself. In other words, Islam became a substantive quality with certain characteristics which could rival in their structures and functions other modern ideologies, such as fascism and Marxism. This is not to say that the divine attributes were ignored, but their significance was made a function of the predicative characteristics of a new Islamic theory.

It is well known that in mainstream Islamic theology, as propounded in the tenth century AD by Abu al-Hasan al-Ash'ari, only those attributes denoting God's acts are considered to lie within human knowledge. These acts were held by al-Ash'ari to be seven in number. It is in this context that Qutb's doctrinal work, Khasa'is al-tasawwur al-islami (The Characteristics of the Islamic Conception), gains in significance. Although Qutb contended that Islamic theology and philosophy were outdated modes of knowledge, tainted by their reliance on categories derived from classical Greek thought, he aspired to inaugurate a new Islamic vision using an amalgamation of ancient and modern ideas. He claimed, for example, that his new interpretation consisted of a direct act of understanding the Qur'an. This receptivity is said to be unmediated and based on an immediate grasp of Qur'anic verses.

However, Qutb's binary division of Islam into 'characteristics' and 'fundamentals' is reminiscent of orthodox debates on the essence and attributes of God. It is also worth mentioning that in enumerating the characteristics of Islam, Qutb devised a new list which nevertheless, in a manner reminiscent of al-Ash'ari, included seven attributes: lordship, constancy, comprehensiveness, balance, positivity, realism and absolute unity or monotheism. These attributes of Islam emanate from God's will and specify certain rules and modes of behaviour incumbent on all believers.

Knowledge, Causation and Faith

In Islamic fundamentalism, the affinity between philosophy and natural science, an axiom of classical and medieval thought, is ruptured and deemed to be unwarranted. Scientific knowledge is then confined to technical details and superficial alterations, a fact that renders its concepts temporary, relative and liable to change. Science is linked with experimental knowledge rather than the discovery of underlying principles. Islam continues to be credited with stimulating the promotion of experimental methodologies that were appropriated by European scholars after the Renaissance. Nevertheless, Islamic fundamentalism, while placing the Qur'an outside the scope of modern science and philosophical debates, persists in alluding to the shortcomings of Western theories and trends of thought. Qutb, for example, highlights the fact that life itself is not inherent in the nature of matter or the universe; rather, it was infused by God into dead substances.

This statement allows him to refute Darwin's theory of evolution in so far as it leaves aside supernatural factors in explaining the emergence of living beings. He also calls Karl Marx's interpretation of social progress by means of purely economic laws an arbitrary idea; so also is Bergson's concept of life as a willed or vital creation. While Islamic fundamentalism rejects the atomist theory of orthodox Muslim theologians, it retains the idea of God as the real cause of events. Thus the connection between a cause and its effect is assumed to be the result of God's action.

The metaphor used by al-Ghazali to show that combustibility, in the case of a flame coming into contact with a piece of cotton, has no other cause but God, is reiterated by Qutb. A piece of cotton is not set alight because of an act performed by a flame, but as a result of God's will to render the piece of cotton combustible. Moreover, God may decide to suspend the common course of nature, and miracles occur as an indication of the divine interruption of fixed laws. Such a miracle, Qutb points out, is mentioned in the Qur'an in relation to Abraham when a burning flame failed to set him alight. It is for this reason that the use of empirical evidence in order to demonstrate causality becomes an arbitrary human construct.

4

Theology and Philosophy in Islam

Science and Metaphysics

The Muslim inspiration for the study of nature comes straight from the Qur'an. The Qur'an specifically and repeatedly asks Muslims to investigate systematically natural phenomena, not simply as a vehicle for understanding nature but also as a means for getting close to God. In Surah 10, for example, we read:

> He it is who has made the sun a [source of] radiant light and the moon a light [reflected], and has determined for it phases so that you might know how to compute years and to measure [time]...in the alternative of night and day, and in all that God has created in the heavens and on earth, there are messages indeed for people who are conscious of Him.

The Qur'an also devotes about one-third of its verses to describing the virtues of reason. Scientific inquiry, based on reason, is thus seen in Islam as a form of worship. Reason and revelation are complementary and integrated methods for the pursuit of truth.

The philosophy of science in classical Islam is a product of the fusion of this metaphysics with Greek philosophy.

Nowhere is this more apparent than in Ibn Sina's theory of human knowledge which, following al-Farabi, transfers the Qur'anic scheme of revelation to Greek philosophy. In the Qur'an, the Creator addresses one man - the Prophet - through the agency of the archangel Gabriel; in Ibn Sina's Neoplatonic scheme, the divine word is transmitted through reason and understanding to any, and every, person who cares to listen. The result is an amalgam of rationalism and ethics.

For Muslim scholars and scientists, values are objective and good and evil are descriptive characteristics of reality which are no less 'there' in things than are their other qualities, such as shape and size. In this framework, all knowledge, including the knowledge of God, can be acquired by reason alone. Humanity has power to know as well as to act and is thus responsible for its just and unjust actions. What this philosophy entailed both in terms of the study of nature and shaping human behaviour was illustrated by Ibn Tufayl in his intellectual novel, Hayy ibn Yaqzan. Hayy is a spontaneously generated human who is isolated on an island. Through his power of observations and the use of his intellect, Hayy discovers general and particular facts about the structure of the material and spiritual universe, deduces the existence of God and arrives at a theological and political system.

While Mu'tazilite scholars had serious philosophic differences with their main opponents, the Ash'arite theologians, both schools agreed on the rational study of nature. In his *al-Tamhid,* Abu Bakr al-Baqillani defines science as 'the knowledge of the object, as it really is'. While reacting to the Mu'tazilite infringement on the domains of faith, the Ash'arites conceded the need for objective and systematic study of nature. Indeed, some of the greatest scientists in Islam, such as Ibn al-Haytham, who discovered the basic laws of optics, and al-Biruni, who measured the circumference of the earth and discussed the rotation of the earth on its axis, were supporters of Ash'arite theology.

The overall concern of Muslim scientists was the delineation of truth. As Ibn al-Haytham declared, 'truth is sought for its own sake', and al-Biruni confirmed in the introduction to his *al-Qanun al-mas'udi*, 'I do not shun the truth from whatever source it comes.' However, there were disputes about the best way to rational truth. For Ibn Sina, general and universal questions came first and led to experimental work. He begins his *al-Qanun fi'l-tibb*, which was a standard text in the West up to the eighteenth century, with a general discussion on the theory of drugs. For al-Biruni, however, universals came out of practical, experimental work; theories are formulated after discoveries. But either way, criticism was the key to progress towards truth. As Ibn al-Haytham wrote, 'it is natural to everyone to regard scientists favourably.... God, however, has not preserved the scientist from error and has not safeguarded science from shortcomings and faults'. This is why scientists so often disagree amongst themselves. Those concerned with science and truth, Ibn al-Haytham continued, 'should turn themselves into hostile critics' and should criticize 'from every point of view and in all aspects'. In particular, the flaws in the work of one's predecessors should be ruthlessly exposed. The ideas of Ibn al-Haytham, al-Biruni and Ibn Sina, along with numerous other Muslim scientists, laid the foundations of the 'scientific spirit' as we have come to know it.

The 'scientific method', as it is understood today, was first developed by the Muslim scientists. Supporters of both Mu'tazilism and Ash'arism placed a great deal of emphasis on systematic observation and experimentation. The insistence on accurate observation is amply demonstrated in the *zij*, the literature of astronomical handbooks and tables. These were constantly updated, with scientists checking and correcting the work of previous scholars. In medicine, Abu Bakr Muhammad al-Razi's detailed and highly accurate clinical observations in the early third century ah (ninth century ad) provide us with a universal model. Al-Razi was the first to observe accurately the symptoms of smallpox and described many 'new' syndromes. However, it was not just accurate observation that was important; equally significant was the clarity and precision by which the observations are described, as was demonstrated by Ibn Sina in his writings.

The emphasis on model construction and theory building can be seen in the category of Islamic astronomical literature known as *'ilm al-haya*, or 'science of the structure (of the universe)', which consists of general exposition of principles underlying astronomical theory. It was on the strength of both accurate observation and model construction that Islamic astronomy launched a rigorous attack on what was perceived to be a set of imperfections in Ptolemaic astronomy. Ibn al-Haytham was the first to declare categorically that the arrangements proposed for planetary motions in the *Almagest* were 'false'. Ibn Shatir and the astronomers at the famous observatory in Maragha, Adharbayjan, built in the thirteenth century by Nasir al-Din al-Tusi, developed the Tusi couple and a theorem for the transformation of eccentric models into epicyclic ones.

It was this mathematical model that Copernicus used to develop his notion of heliocentricity, which played an important part in the European 'scientific revolution'. Apart from the exact sciences, the most appropriate and interesting area in which theoretical work played an essential role was medicine. Muslim physicians attempted to improve the quality of *materia medica* and their therapeutic uses through continued theoretical development. Emphasis was also placed on developing a precise terminology and ensuring the purity of drugs, a concern that led to a number of early chemical and physical procedures. Since Muslim writers were excellent organizers of knowledge, their purely pharmacological texts were themselves a source for the development of theories. Evolution of theories and discovery of new drugs linked the growth of Islamic medicine to chemistry, botany, zoology, geology and law, and led to extensive elabourations of Greek classifications. Pharmacological knowledge thus became more diversified, and produced new types of pharmacological literature.

As this literature considered its subject from a number of different disciplinary perspectives and a great variety of new directions, there developed new ways of looking at pharmacology; new areas were opened up for further exploration and more detailed investigation. Paper-making made publication more extensive and cheaper than use of parchment and papyrus, and this in turn made scientific knowledge much more accessible to students. While Muslim scientists placed considerable faith in scientific method, they were also aware of its limitations. Even a strong believer in mathematical realism such as al-Biruni argued that the method of inquiry was a function of the nature of investigation, different methods, all equally valid, were required to answer different types of questions. Al-Biruni himself had recourse to a number of methods.

In his treatise on mineralogy, *Kitab al-jamahir (Book of Precious Stones)*, he is the most exact of experimental scientists. However, in the introduction to his ground-breaking study India he declares that 'to execute our project, it has not been possible to follow the geometric method'; he therefore resorts to comparative sociology. The work of a scholar of the calibre and prolificity of al-Biruni inevitably defies simple classification. He wrote on mineralogy, geography, medicine, astrology and a whole range of topics which dealt with the dating of Islamic festivals. Al-Biruni is a specific product of a philosophy of science that integrates metaphysics with physics, does not attribute to either a superior or inferior position, and insists that both are worthy of study and equally valid.

Moreover, the methods of studying the vast creation of God - from the movement of the stars and planets to the nature of diseases, the sting of an ant, the character of madness, the beauty of justice, the spiritual yearning of humanity, the ecstasy of a mystic - are all equally valid and shape understanding in their respective areas of inquiry. In both its philosophy and methodology, Islam has sought a complete synthesis of science and religion. Polymaths such as al-Biruni, al-Jahiz, al-Kindi, Abu Bakr Muhammad al-Razi, Ibn Sina, al-Idrisi, Ibn Bajja, Omar Khayyam, Ibn Zuhr, Ibn Tufayl, Ibn Rushd, al-Suyuti and thousands of other scholars are not an exception but the general rule in Muslim civilization. The Islamic civilization of the classical period was remarkable for the number of polymaths it produced. This is seen as a testimony to the homogeneity of Islamic philosophy of science and its emphasis on synthesis, interdisciplinary investigations and multiplicity of methods.

Revival Attempts

At the end of the twentieth century, scholars, scientists and philosophers throughout the Muslim world are trying to formulate a contemporary version of the Islamic philosophy of science. Two dominant movements have emerged. The first draws its inspiration from Sufi mysticism and argues that the notions of 'tradition' and the 'sacred' should constitute the core of Islamic approach to science. The second argues that issues of science and values in Islam must be treated within a framework of concepts that shape the goals of a Muslim society.

Ten fundamental Islamic concepts are identified as constituting the framework within which scientific inquiry should be carried out, four standing alone and three opposing pairs: *tawhid* (unity), *khilafa* (trusteeship), *'ibada* (worship), *'ilm* (knowledge), *halal* (praiseworthy) and *haram* (blameworthy), *'adl* (justice) and *zulm* (tyranny), and *istisla* (public interest) and *dhiya* (waste). It is argued that, when translated into values, this system of Islamic concepts embraces the nature of scientific inquiry in its totality; it integrates facts and values and institutionalizes a system of knowing that is based on accountability and social responsibility. It is too early to say whether either of these movements will bear any real fruit.

The Pre-Mu'tazilite Groups

The term *kalam* has usually been translated as 'word' or 'speech', but a more appropriate rendering in this context would be 'discussion', 'argument' or 'debate'. Those who engaged in these discussions or debates were referred to as *mutakallimun* (those who practise *kalam* or debate). The term has special significance in that traditionalists disapproved of these discussions, arguing that the early Muslims were not known to have indulged in them. Those who dabbled in such debates were said to have 'spoken about' or 'discussed' (*takallma fi*) 'forbidden' topics. The proponents of *kalam* also liked to refer to it as *'ilm al-usul* (the science of basic principles) or *'ilm al-tawhid* (the science of [affirming God's] unity), and it is under this latter name that some of its topics continue to be taught and discussed in Muslim educational institutions today.

The rise of *'ilm al-kalam* was a result of the many controversies that had divided the Muslim community in its early years. Although the emergence of Islam was characterized by polemics with polytheists and followers of earlier revelations, controversies over fundamental religious questions were deemed irreverent by early Muslims, especially during the lifetime of the Prophet. However, disputes (mainly political) broke out immediately following the death of the Prophet, and again following the tragic events that led to the murder of the third Caliph Othman in AH 35/AD 656, this time heralding the breakdown of the political system established after the Prophet's death.

In a community that defined itself in terms of its religious identity, political disputes inevitably turned into theological ones. The political struggles over who should lead the Muslim community gave rise to three major competing groups, the Khawarij, who opposed the fourth Caliph 'Ali and rejected the compromises he made with his opponents; the Shi'a, who supported 'Ali; and the Murjiya, who tried to remain neutral. These groups attempted to influence a wider Muslim community dominated by a loose grouping of mainstream schools, mainly conservative or traditionalist, known collectively as *ahl al-sunna wa'l-jama'a* (the proponents of the [Prophet's] traditions and consensus).

The term *khawarij* (literally 'rebels') first referred to a group of dissidents who rebelled against the leadership of 'Ali following the inconclusive battle of Siffin (AH 37/AD 658) between 'Ali and his challenger, Mu'awiya, and later evolved into a distinct antiestablishment tendency. The Khawarij had neither a unified leadership nor a settled doctrine, and was primarily a militant political tendency with an uncompromising attitude. The core of their views revolved around the nature of legitimate leadership and the conditions for salvation. Although the Khawarij's uncompromising views condemned them to a marginal existence, their impact on the general body of the Muslim community was significant.

Most of the major schools of thought that emerged did so in response to one or other of their assertions, especially on the issues of leadership and the 'status of sinners' and at the opposite pole stood the Shi'a (party) of Ali. Unlike the Khawarij, who defied all authority, the Shi'a believed in the undisputed authority of the divinely ordained *imam* (leader). The position of 'Ali as *imam* and successor to the Prophet was vouchsafed by revelation only and not a matter of opinion. Each *imam* would then designate his successor by virtue of the divine authority vested in him. In theory, Shi'ism should not have encouraged much theological speculation, since it sought to perpetuate and reproduce the authority of the Prophet and vest it in the person of the living *imam*, who had direct access to the divine truth.

Policy in the 21st Century

Politicians and pundits often erroneously compare the current, but poorly named, "Global War on Terror," to the ideological struggles against fascism and communism that defined the World War II and Cold War eras. Admittedly, the fight against extremism is likely to be as prolonged as these contests and will require a comparable mobilization of resources if it to be successful, but it is important not to overstate the comparison. Today's 'war' against terror lacks several characteristics that defined the generational struggles of the twentieth century. For example, the "front lines" are no longer well defined.

The enemy uses unorthodox weapons and tactics, and does not recognize standard rules of engagement. Nor is the distinction between civilians and enemy combatants as clear as it once was. Indeed, the global Islamist movement lacks a traditional army, and is instead staffed by a highly dynamic and transnational collection of decentralized non-state actors who attempt to blend into society and hide the militant religious ideals that motivate them. In short, the challenge posed by Islamists extremism is fundamentally different from the state-centric threats that defined the security paradigm of the twentieth century.

Therefore, in order to combat this new peril, it is necessary to modify and supplement the traditional toolbox of national security responses, because it was designed to confront the enemies of another era. Counterterrorism efforts need to begin to emphasize techniques and analytic methodologies that acknowledge the unconventional and transnational attributes of Islamist extremism. This chapter argues that viewing religious terrorism through the lens of epidemiology is an alternative that offers such benefits. However, because Islamist extremism remains poorly understood, this chapter will first lay-out a different way of thinking about the current threat, before fully describing this alternate approach to counterterrorism.

The New Strategic Challenge

The complete lack of consensus about how to describe the current strategic threat reveals that we are still struggling to grasp its nature, let alone to determine an effective way to combat it. Is the threat "global terrorism," "Islamic terrorism," "al Qaeda and its affiliates," "Sunni jihadists," "Islamist radicals," or "terrorist extremism"? This is more than just a semantics issue, because without clarity on who, precisely, is our adversary, we are unlikely to ever develop a clear and comprehensive understanding of the enemy's objectives, strategy, and operational character. And, failing to understand these vital characteristics make it difficult, if not impossible, to conceive of an effective and sustainable response. Our preference is to classify this broader challenge as "Islamist militancy."

Like the 9/11 Commission, we feel it important to use the modifier "Islamist"—a politicoreligious movement within the Muslim world—rather than "Islamic"—the culture and religion of Islam. Unlike the 9/11 Commission, however, we prefer the simpler, less loaded term "militancy" to "terrorism." Using the term "militants" to refer to those who either employ or espouse violent means in pursuit of political ends not only avoids the notoriously slippery definitional problems associated with terrorism, but also serves to underscore that the challenge is both multi-dimensional and broad based. The militancy involves more individuals than just those actors who actually carry out terrorist attacks. Indeed, Islamist militancy has three main constituent groups whose memberships are constantly evolving and overlap in significant ways.

There are, first, the transnational jihadist groups that have a global agenda (principally al Qaeda and its affiliates); second, the nationalist insurgent groups that have essentially a local agenda (e.g., Hamas, Hezbollah, and some of the Kashmiri groups); and, third, the miscellaneous organizations and networks that directly and indirectly support these militant groups. Distinctions among these groups are increasingly difficult to discern as a growing plethora or organizations, which share traits common to more than one classification, have begun to emerge. Although far from an exhaustive illustration of the threat's components, it provides a general snapshot of the principal actors within Islamist militancy in 2006.

Most observers accept that Islamist militancy does not represent a conventional national security threat, but it is also useful to differentiate this phenomenon from conventional terrorism. Unlike Islamist militancy, traditional terror groups typically have a distinctive, often singular, identity and a well-defined organizational structure. They normally espouse reasonably clear political objectives, and take actions to attempt to implement these goals within as specified, and relatively narrow, area of operations. Therefore, conventional counterterrorist responses, which emphasize apprehending an organization's leaders and rolling-up networks of supporters through improved intelligence gathering and information sharing, are usually effective against traditional groups.

Although such methods remain just as necessary to any campaign against Islamist militancy, it is also becoming clear that they will not be sufficient because Islamist militancy includes a unique component absent from earlier terrorist campaigns: self-organization. Prominent recent attacks, including the bombing of London's mass-transportation system (July 2005) and the bombing of Madrid's Atocha railway station (March 2004), were conducted by small local groups, which adhered to the ideology of Islamist militancy, but lacked operational connections to established groups, such as Al Qaeda. Conventional counterterrorism responses cannot address such adversaries because these groups lacked both formal leadership and hierarchy.

Because this type of emergent behaviour is becoming increasingly common, a growing number of experts now advocate drawing on the strategies and tactics of unconventional, or "irregular," warfare to meet the challenge. They portray the threat as a global insurgency that requires a commensurate global counterinsurgency (COIN) campaign. There is some logic to this as elements of the challenge reflect characteristics of a classic insurgency. Certainly, al Qaeda's stated goal of expelling "Jews and crusaders" from the Muslim world and cleansing it of apostate regimes in order to reestablish a purified caliphate can be viewed as an insurgency of sorts. However, this paradigm has severe limitations. Describing the threat as a global insurgency dangerously exaggerates the degree of organization and unity among its various actors.

To borrow COIN's own military lexicon, there are no clearly established lines of command and control operating between established extremist groups, much less between these organizations and the sorts of self-organizing adherents described in the previous paragraph. The COIN approach also risks conflating many kinds of Islamist struggles and perversely even serving to legitimize them. Unless suitably adapted, the standard COIN framework, with its simplistic distinctions between "enemies," "friends," and "uncommitted," could make matters worse especially if military or "kinetic" responses come to domi-nate. With these concerns in mind, we propose an alternative strategy, counterterrorism efforts should view the challenge of Islamist militancy as one would a global public health threat.

The conceptual leap required of this approach is not as far as it first appears. Social scientists increasingly have looked to epidemiology to understand a variety of social contagions, and here Islamist militancy is no different. Specifically, our approach draws on the scientific principles and practices of epidemiology as well as the insights from a growing body of research on "social contagion phenomena" such as fashions, fads, rumors, civil violence, and revolutionary ideas. Comments by U.S. officials and other commentators, who frequently make use of disease metaphors to describe Islamist militancy, also support the validity of this approach. References to terrorism being a "virus" or to al Qaeda "mutating" or "metastasizing" are common.

Similarly, pundits often invoke the image of madrassas and mosques as "incubators" of a "virulent ideology." Such metaphors have a visceral appeal in that they help to convey a dangerous and darkly insidious threat. For some, the disease metaphor also sets—implicitly, at least—a more realistic goal for what counterterrorism efforts can achieve. Just as modern medicine has completely eradicated very few diseases; it remains unlikely that any efforts to combat Islamist militancy will find complete success. The best that can be hoped for is for it to transform the threat into a manageable, low-probability, albeit sometimes deadly, nuisance much likes many other social ills.

Beyond its metaphorical appeal there are more practical attractions to an epidemiological/public health approach. Three stand out:

- First, epidemiologists observe rigorous standards of inquiry and analysis to understand the derivation, dynamics, and propagation of a specific disease. In particular, they seek clarity on the origins and geographical and social contours of an outbreak: where the disease is concentrated, how it is transmitted, who is most at risk or "susceptible" to infection, and why some portions of society may be less susceptible, or, for all intents and purposes, immune. Applying the same methodological approach to mapping and understanding Islamist militancy can yield immediately useful guidance on where and how to counter it.
- Second, epidemiologists recognize that diseases neither arise nor spread in a vacuum. They emerge and evolve as a result of a complex dynamic interactive process

between people, pathogens, and the environment in which they live. Indeed, the epidemiologic concept of "cause" is rarely if ever singular or linear but is more akin to a "web" of direct and indirect factors that play a lesser or greater role in differing circumstances. To make sense of this complexity, epidemiologists typically employ a standard analytical device that "deconstructs" the key constituent elements of a disease. This model helps not only to understand the phenomenon in its entirety but also to anticipate how it might evolve in the future. As will be discussed, the same systemic conception of disease can be adapted to understand the constituent elements of Islamist militancy and their evolution.

- Third, just as epidemiologists view disease as a complex, multifaceted phenomenon, so public health officials have come to recognize that success in controlling and rolling back an epidemic typically results from a carefully orchestrated, systematic, prioritized, multipronged effort to address each of its constituent elements.

At the same time, however, it is also recognized that significant progress or major advances can sometimes be precipitated by relatively minor interventions—or "tipping points." Again, there are lessons and insights to be learned here for orchestrating a global counterterrorism campaign. Before turning to what such a campaign to defeat Islamist militancy might look like were it to follow a public health or counterepidemic approach, it is necessary to understand how epidemiologists typically try to understand disease and how this can help us understand the challenge we face.

The Epidemic Model

As indicated, epidemiologists employ a standard approach, or model, to study epidemics that deconstruct an outbreak into four key components, recognizing that in reality they are all dynamically interconnected. In simple terms, the agent refers to the pathogen (e.g., a virus or bacterium) that causes disease. The host is the person infected by the disease—called the "infective" in epidemiological jargon—while the environment refers to a variety of external factors that affect both agent and host. At the center of the triad are the vectors, which serve as conduits and key pathways that help the disease to propagate. However, the epidemiological metaphor is imperfect because Islamist militancy lacks the clinical features of a biological disease. Individuals who contract illnesses are typically passive and unwitting receptors of a harmful pathogen, while adherents to extremism make a conscious decision to play an active role in terror.

Yet, Islamists' actions are clearly driven by a core set of ideas and beliefs that has an "infectious" appeal, granting these ideology epidemic-like qualities. It, too, therefore, can be deconstructed using the classic epidemic model. Thus, according to this framework, militant Islamist ideology plays the role of "agent". Specifically, two primary "strains" can be identified, a transnational Salafist/jihadist ideology as espoused by al Qaeda and a nationalist/insurgent Islamist militant ideology as espoused by groups such as Hezbollah, Hamas, and some of the militant Kashmiri groups.

A specific set of underlying assumptions, motivations, and goals characterizes each of these ideological strains. The host is the group or person "infected" by the agent—in other words, all those who become adherents of militant Islamist ideology. As defined, Islamist militants are those who employ or espouse the use of violence in pursuit of political goals. Although a subtle distinction, it is worth noting that this definition includes rabble-rousers who disseminate violent Islamist propaganda, as well as individuals who conduct attacks.

The environment refers to key factors specific to the Muslim world that promote exposure to Islamist militancy—conflict, political repression, economic stagnation, and social alienation being the leading influences. In this case, the term "vectors" refers to a variety of known conduits that are used to propagate the ideology and associated action agendas, such as mosques, prisons, madrassas, the Internet, satellite television, and diasporic networks. However, it is important not to overstate the virulence of Islamist militancy.

The vast majority of Muslims find the core elements of the Jihadist ideology both aberrant and abhorrent. To extend the epidemiological metaphor, they are effectively "immunized" to the appeal of extremism. Nevertheless, some unknown, yet critical, proportion of the Muslim population clearly remains "susceptible" to becoming not only an adherent of the ideology but actively motivated by it. Conceptualizing Islamist militancy according to the terms of an epidemiological model provides several policy-relevant benefits.

First, this notion captures the key elements of the challenge in a *systemic* manner, rather than in the disaggregated, unconnected way that so often bedevils analysis and understanding, but is, nonetheless, commonly found in both the intelligence community and academia. Second, the epidemiological model is *dynamic*; it acknowledges that extremism is not a static phenomenon, but, instead, a constantly evolving threat. New strains, new hosts, new vectors, and changing environmental conditions continually emerge.

Third, this model presages the potential future evolution of Islamist militancy. However, the specific repercussions of this coming evolution remain difficult to ascertain, because unlike with an outbreak of disease, in which those infected typically (though not always) have substantial motivations to report their condition and to seek treatment, new adherents to Islamist militancy have every incentive to keep their ideological affiliation clandestine, making it incredibly challenging to assess both the size and spread of the extremist phenomenon.

A combination of indicators (e.g., the number of attacks conducted or thwarted and militants killed or incarcerated, the influence of Jihadist Web sites, the dissemination of training materials, etc.) suggests that Islamist militancy is expanding and mutating in the ways indicated earlier. Surveys taken within the Muslim world of people's attitudes toward the United States and the West also suggest that the pool of "susceptibles," those at risk for becoming Islamist militants, is large and expanding in certain countries.

The Counterepidemic Approach

Faced with the outbreak of an infectious disease, public health officials typically employ a three-pronged strategy to counter the threat. The first step is to *contain* the most threatening outbreaks to prevent them from gaining enough mass and momentum to overwhelm public health responders and threaten public order. Standard measures include quarantining specific areas to contain the movement of infectious individuals, eliminating or decontaminating identifiable vectors of transmission, and, if an antidote exists, treating and rehabilitating individuals who have succumbed to the disease.

Although such successes are rare, efforts to containing and contract the number of infective can sometimes effectively eradicate the pathogen. Public health officials' second measure is to *protect* the high-risk groups, who are most vulnerable to the disease, as well as high-value groups, who are most critical to a functioning society. Targeted immunization programs are typically the most effective countermeasure. Interestingly, not everyone needs to be inoculated to achieve what is known as "herd immunity"—essentially, the level at which the probability of an infected person being in contact with a nonimmunized person is very low, if not zero.

If an effective vaccine is not available, public health officials employ other protective strategies, including encouraging "safe practices" through public education to reduce the probability of exposure and the rate of new infection. The third and final step in public health campaigns against epidemics is to *remedy* the environmental conditions that fostered the emergence of the disease in specific areas and its subsequent spread. Many types of interventions are conceivable, from the local to the global, depending on the nature of the threat. Adapting the same basic strategic imperatives of a counterepidemic campaign to the threat posed by Islamist militancy would immediately translate into the following operational priorities:

- Containing and contracting the activities of the most "virulent" Islamist militant organizations, namely the transnational Jihadist groups with global reach and apocalyptic agendas, as well as those who could gain a meaningful operational presence in areas of significant strategic interest. These areas would include most notably Iraq, Pakistan, Afghanistan, Saudi Arabia, Egypt, Palestine, the Caucasus, and the Muslim diaspora communities of Western Europe, as well as areas in the vicinity of key global financial/economic infrastructure assets.
- Protecting the high-risk/high-value communities of the Muslim world. According to unclassified open-source accounts, a disproportionate number of the officers and foot soldiers in the transnational Jihadist cause come from a few countries—Saudi Arabia, Egypt, Morocco, Algeria, Yemen, Pakistan—and from the European diaspora communities. The high-value communities consist of the educational, religious, political, and security sectors of countries where Islamist militant organizations could make the greatest inroads and the growing number of transnational cultural, business, and media networks that affect the lives of many

millions of Muslims throughout the larger *Ummah* (Islamic community).

- Remedying the key environmental factors that foster Islamist militancy. The most important would appear to be the ongoing conflicts or insurgencies involving Muslims and non-Muslims that help validate the central Jihadist argument that Islam is under attack and that also serve as recruiting magnets and training grounds—notably, Iraq, Palestine, Kashmir, Afghanistan, Chechnya, and several smaller conflicts in Central and Southeast Asia. Social alienation within the European diaspora communities and public corruption, political repression, and economic stagnation in key areas of the Muslim world are widely viewed as additional factors. These strategic imperatives can be further translated into specific containment, protective, and remedial programs or initiatives that, again, draw on the principles and practices of a counterepidemic campaign.

Containment Measures

In addition to limiting the operational reach and capabilities of the most threatening Islamist militant organizations by using standard counterterrorism measures and discrete special intelligence/military operations, containment initiatives would extend to placing greater emphasis on disrupting and restricting the untrammeled use of key vectors—the Internet, satellite TV, prisons, schools, mosques, and so on—by Islamist militant organizations. Some vectors can be physically shut down, others "decontaminated" of unwanted infectious agents. Containment measures appear to be a largely haphazard, after-the-fact effort at the present, rather than a systematically planned, internationally executed campaign. As the importance of civil liberties trumps counterterrorism in an open society, there are obvious limitations to vector containment initiatives.

Therefore, greater attention should be given to nurturing and propagating "ideological antidotes" to the key tenets of Islamist militant ideology. A key component of any such measure involves the mobilization of moderate religious figures, who are inclined to issue fatwas that condemn the extremist ideology, denounce Jihadist propaganda, and disallow specific practices, such as beheading innocent civilians. In addition to these broad-based initiatives, efforts should include more discrete efforts aimed toward a specific group or community. The former includes encouraging key opinion makers, cultural leaders, and mass media figures to second the edicts of moderate religious leaders. Such efforts have been made, but apparently not in an extensive or concerted way.

More targeted activities include exploiting the ideological contradictions or schisms within the transnational jihadist movement to foment internal dissension and possible defection. There are reports, for example, of successful counterideological efforts in Yemen that in turn yielded operational success in rolling-up a local al Qaeda network. Although many Islamist militants are beyond such intellectual suasion, this may not be the case with some groups and organizations. Local national-insurgent movements, in particular, may be susceptible to an approach that approximates health care's attempts at treatment and rehabilitation of the infirmed.

The evolving role of groups such as Hamas and Hezbollah, for example, suggests the possibility of their integration into their respective political systems, encouraging them to abandon armed struggle in much the same way as other former terrorist organizations. The provision of amnesties to insurgents willing to lay down arms, as in Afghanistan, constitutes another element of rehabilitation. And in Iraq, reports suggest a growing rift between the nationalist Iraqi elements of the insurgency and foreign Jihadists, in part as a result of the latter's indiscriminate targeting of civilians.

Protective Measures

Whereas the containment measures are directed primarily at those already infected, protective measures are aimed at those who are most at risk and those who play important societal functions. It is conceivable that with better understanding of why certain groups and individuals progress along a continuum that begins with a sympathetic conception of Islamist militancy, then evolves into tangential support of the cause, and culminates in active participation in terror, counterterrorism efforts could design targeted programs to effectively immunize at-risk groups. There are many cases where key populations have been targeted in ways designed to turn off their receptiveness to specific ideas, messages, and unhealthy or antisocial practices, including by appealing to people's common sense, their personal safety, their peer group standing, religious edicts, and societal norms, among other approaches.

In some cases the tactics used are not unlike real vaccination programs that work on the principle of exposing uninfected populations to a weakened or attenuated version of the virus so that the body learns to identify and reject the real thing. Political campaigns, for example, often expose key undecided voters to the arguments of opposing candidates, in some cases to ridicule the candidates, but more often to "arm" the voters with convincing reasons to be skeptical when they hear the same arguments from those candidates. Similar public programs aimed at undermining the appeal of militant Islamist ideology could be designed and implemented in many different arenas, from schools to mosques to mass media outlets.

Unless they are undertaken in the Muslim communities of Western Europe, however, these are clearly not initiatives that the United States (and the West more generally) should lead or be openly associated with. Western states can, however, prod allies and partners in the Muslim world and provide discreet assistance. Ideally, such "ideological immunization" efforts aimed at high-risk communities should offer a positive and compelling alternative vision for the future, instead of simply providing a negative image of militant Islamism. Indeed, efforts to undermine militant Islamism and provide a positive counterideology can be mutually reinforcing. Because schools, mosques, mass media outlets, and other conduits have a critical role to play in both efforts, attempts to strengthen moderate voices are an indispensable component of the overall campaign.

Remedial Measures

If parallel efforts are not also taken to remedy some of the key environmental conditions that promote Islamist militancy in the Muslim world, many of the previous initiatives will be harder to accomplish or will likely fail. For reasons discussed earlier, an intensified effort should be made to resolve or at least tamp down the violent conflicts that have a particularly strong resonance within the Muslim world. Indeed, successful conflict management and prevention strategies will play a key role in impeding the spread of Islamist militancy. Conflict resolution efforts will not only mitigate the direct role that violent conflict plays in Jiahdist recruitment and training, but will also invalidate extremist propaganda, thereby buttressing moderate support.

The implementation of political reforms focused on good governance, particularly greater transparency, accountability, and the rule of law, will also play a key role in neutralizing Islamist militant ideology that calls for the overthrow of corrupt regimes. Likewise, greater civil liberties, including broader freedoms of assembly and expression as well as the freedom to form political parties and other associations, will help to level the political playing field and allow "healthy" outlets for dissent. Particular emphasis should be placed on institution building, in order to prevent autocratic regimes from undermining democratic gains or exploiting non-democratic opposition forces. Facilitating the political participation of peaceful, moderate Islamists can also help to develop an effective counterweight to Islamist militants and their violent tactics.

The implementation of economic reforms designed to spur growth and bolster job creation will likewise help to ease popular disaffection, particularly among the Middle East's disproportionately young population. In addition, economic reforms that create an environment that is more appealing to foreign investors will help the Muslim world to integrate more effectively into the broader global economic system and help bridge the gap in relative performance between the Muslim world, particularly the Arab world, and the global economy. Over time, the combined effect of these containment, protective, and remedial measures will be to reverse young Muslims' growing disenfranchisement and the increasing appeal of extremism. The effect will be to divide, isolate, and weaken the Islamist militant organizations and marginalize their operational impact.

The pool of susceptibles will also shrink in relation to the rest of the Muslim world, which through the various remedial efforts; will become a more "healthy" and integrated part of the larger, globalizing world. As with a global health campaign, success in countering the challenge of Islamist militancy will depend on a sustained commitment over many years, if not decades, by a broad coalition of like-minded states acting in partnership with a multitude of nongovernmental actors. Simply stated, there is no single or easy cure. In fundamental respects, the counterepidemic approach to Islamist militancy follows the basic tenets of effective conflict prevention and management. Using common admonitions from the world of public health care, these tenets can be summarized as follows:

- *Prevention is better than cure.* Reducing the momentum of a conflict, is clearly more difficult than taking early preventive measures to forestall violence, positions harden, options narrow, and the costs rise after passions have become inflamed and blood has been spilt. Early warning and early response can, therefore, make all the difference.
- *Diagnose before treating.* Knowing thy ailment is just as important as knowing thy enemy. While it doesn't guarantee success, understanding clearly the source(s) and dynamics of a conflict before taking action obviously improves the chances of a positive outcome because it allows counterterrorism officials to apply the right tools in the right place at the right time.
- *Do no harm.* The Hippocratic Oath is as relevant to conflict management as it is to medicine. As countless examples attest, poorly timed or calibrated interventions can make a problem worse, not better. Knowing what to do and when to do it in conflict management is as much an art as a science, but again, experience provides a rich set of guidelines, particularly when it comes to balancing incentives with disincentives, and force with diplomacy.
- *Address the source, not the symptoms.* Resolving the root cause of a conflict typically raises the bar in terms of what is required to secure peace, but as many long-festering disputes attest, the "Band-Aid" approaches to conflict management at best delays and in many instances complicates the task of finding a sustainable solution.
- *Palliate what you cannot cure.* Unfortunately, effective solutions sometimes remain beyond practical reach. Just as some diseases are— at least for the time being,— incurable, so some conflicts become, for all intents and purposes, intractable. Under such circumstances the best that can be achieved is to limit the consequences and not make a bad situation worse.

As indicated at the outset, however, the task of conflict prevention and management must adapt to the emerging realities of the twenty-first century. As a consequence of globalization, the world has become a smaller, more interconnected place. Threats to international peace and stability that were once considered distant and inconsequential now resonate more widely, more quickly, and with greater impact. Nonstate actors have been able to capitalize on the opportunities presented by this new interconnected world; they can now wield unprecedented power for good and bad because they have much greater latitude to operate across borders, as al Qaeda and numerous warlords around the world have demonstrated.

At the same time, states seeking to prevent and manage conflict, whether it be within their borders or in areas both adjacent and distant, find themselves in a changed operating environment. Besides the interdependencies of a globalized world, emerging legal rules and norms affect their freedom much more than was ever previously the case. Their actions, furthermore, are subject to greater scrutiny and accountability by virtue of not only the constant 24/7 gaze of the global media, but also an expanding network of intergovernmental and nongovernmental organizations. As a consequence of these new realities, states can rarely, if ever, address threats to peace and stability as singular actors. The task is likely to be too big to solve alone.

Important advantages—not least in terms of generating international legitimacy—can be derived from acting collectively. This imperative to cooperate may seem too high a price to pay to those concerned about national sovereignty, but such concerns are arguably becoming redundant in an increasingly interdependent world, if they haven't already become so. Indeed, giving up some de jure sovereignty may be the only way for states to regain some de facto sovereignty, especially when it comes to non-state threats such as transnational terrorism. The growing imperative to cooperate internationally is matched by the comparable need for states to partner with nongovernmental actors and civil society in general. The benefits are mutual.

States need the cooperation of NGOs to manage those who would exploit the business and commerce sectors, among others, for nefarious ends. NGOs likewise need the support of governments to operate effectively and relatively freely. Again, such partnerships can confer legitimacy on both sides. Finally, states must adapt their internal political and bureaucratic structures and processes to these new imperatives. What were largely vestiges of the Cold War and earlier eras have to be reformed or replaced with new mechanisms for governmental decision making, coordination, and implementation. Without such changes, effective conflict prevention and management will only become more difficult to achieve.

Islam on Religious Freedom

Freedom of belief is enshrined in the Koran - the foremost textual authority in laying down the principles of Islamic law. But there is disagreement among Muslim scholars as to the limits of that freedom.

"There is no compulsion in religion" (al-Baqarah, 256); is one of the most quoted phrases from the Koran to back up freedom of belief. There is no clear-cut text in the Koran, however, that calls for the killing of apostates. But those who call for the execution of Muslims who abandon their faith base their judgement primarily on the sayings of the Prophet Muhammad, also known as the hadith.

These constitute a secondary textual authority - albeit weaker than the Koran itself - used in formulating Islamic law, or Sharia. Abdelsabour Shahin, an Islamist writer and academic at Cairo University, told the BBC that although Islam in principle enshrined freedom of belief, there were severe restrictions on that freedom.

"If someone changes from Islam to kufr (unbelief), that has to remain a personal matter, and he should not make it public," he said. In other words, an apostate in a Muslim society, according to this view, forfeits his freedom of expression. If he goes public he should be executed, says Dr Shahin.

But if the Koran has not stipulated the killing of apostates, how does Dr Shahin come to this judgement? He says there is an authoritative and unambiguous hadith (saying of the prophet) which calls for the killing of the apostate - "He who changes his religion should be killed", says Dr Shahin, quoting from the sayings of the prophet.

Professor Abdelmouti Bayoumi of the Islamic Research Academy in Cairo told the BBC that the generality of the aforementioned hadith has been restricted by another hadith from the prophet. Dr Bayoumi says that according to that hadith changing one's religion alone is not enough for applying capital punishment. He says the apostate has also to be found working against the interests of the Muslim society or nation - only then should he be executed.

Interests of the State

Dr Bayoumi's stance is a good example of modernisers, who try to reconcile between Islamic tradition and modern practice. An apostate in this perspective is a traitor. He is punished, not for what he believes in, but for what he does and which could be harmful to the interests of the state.

But Dr Shahin says the mere fact that someone goes public with his apostasy "amounts to fitna (sedition, or civil strife), he is thus like someone fighting Islam, and should therefore be killed." Writers like Dr Shahin derive their position from the interpretations of classical scholars, all of whom have endorsed the principle of capital punishment for apostates. The question is, how have they adopted this stance in the face of abundant evidence from the Koran itself in favour of freedom of belief?

Gamal al-Banna - an Islamic thinker and brother of the founder of the Egyptian Muslim Brotherhood - says the reason for that is political and has nothing to do with the Koran itself. Mr al-Banna says the classical interpretations are more than 1,000 years old, and were formulated at a time of state building where conformity and social cohesion were deemed more important than personal freedom.

He adds that "each and every individual has the right to change his religion without any conditions whatsoever."That person has also the right to campaign for his views, provided he does so peacefully," he told the BBC.

Before discussing the question of punishment of apostasy, it is well to define what apostasy is. A person commits apostasy (*irtidad*) or becomes an apostate (*murtadd*) if he describes himself a Muslim and then at a later time takes one of the following actions in a public way:

1. Converts to another religion, e.g. becomes a Christian or Buddhist or Baha'i etc.
2. Rejects a part of the Qur'an after recognizing it to be a part of the Qur'an. For example, all those "Muslims" who opposed the Shari'ah-based arbitration in family and business disputes in Ontario have become apostates if they knew well that a great part of the Shari'ah that they opposed is based on the Qur'an. May Allah guide them back to Islam.
3. In some cases when the whole ummah agrees that a certain interpretation of some Qur'anic verses or ahadith is unacceptable, and then the person who holds such an interpretation may become an apostate by a decision of the ummah. For example, Ahmadis insist on being called Muslims and they indeed profess and practice much of Islam like most Sunni Muslims. But they believe that Mirza Ghulam Ahmad of Qadiyan in the British colonial India was a prophet and in order to

prepare room for this belief they interpret *khatm nubuwwah* in a way different from the rest of the ummah. The ummah has rejected their interpretation of *khatm nubuwwah* and Mirza's claims for which this interpretation is devised. The ummah has also declared this group as non-Muslims and banned their entry into Makkah. Finally, the falsehood of Mirza's claims has been proved by history. Consequently, all converts from Islam to Ahmadism are apostates.

Normally, however, having an interpretation of a part of the Hadith or Qur'an, the different from the one held by other Muslims does not result in apostasy. For example, if the people who rejected Shari'ah-based arbitration in Ontario would have said that the way rules of Shari'ah are interpreted and applied is not faithful to the teachings of God and his Messenger and argued for more discussion about correcting the interpretation and the application before adopting Shari'ah-based arbitration, they would not have committed apostasy. But they opposed Shari'ah as such and for this reason they should be considered apostates.

An apostate is different from a hypocrite (*munafiq*). A hypocrite is a person who is outwardly willing to say/do what a Muslim says/does but in his heart has decided not to believe in Islam. An apostate, in contrast, is someone who openly and knowingly does or says something that makes him a non-Muslim after he had called himself a Muslim. It also needs to be pointed out that we should distinguish apostasy from a state of *kufr* that many Muslims may privately pass through during the process of their growth towards the state of *iman*.

In most Muslim families we have some members who express disbelief about the existence of God or about divine revelations or about the hereafter. Muslims have wisely and correctly tolerated such disbelief because they recognize that the way to *iman* is not always smooth and may pass through doubts and confusion (cf. Qur'an 6:76-79, 93:7). However, if a Muslim expresses his disbelief in the form of a declared position and insists on its truth publicly, then he will be considered an apostate.

It is a significant fact that the Book of God does not prescribe any punishment for apostasy. Many Muslims would immediately say, The Qur'an does not tell us everything. We need to go to the Hadith to find guidance on matters not touched by the Qur'an. But while this is true of matters of detail, this is not true of fundamental issues. God knew that while the Qur'an would be preserved faithfully, the authenticity of ahadith will remain subject to doubts in most cases. Therefore, he would make sure that all the basic teachings would be included in the Qur'an while leaving some details to ahadith so that the size of the Qur'anic text remains manageable for memorization. Looked in this way the absence in the Qur'an of any punishment for apostasy becomes very significant.

The punishment for apostasy is not a detail that we can expect God to leave for ahadith, especially if that punishment is death, since taking the life of a person, if done without a just cause, is regarded by the Qur'an as tantamount to killing all human beings (5:32). Even lesser penalties for theft (cutting of hands, 5:38), illicit sexual intercourse (100 lashes, 24:2), and unsubstantiated accusation of adultery (80 lashes, 24.4) were not considered by God as matters of details to be left to the ahadith. Therefore there is no reason why God would consider the more serious penalty of death for a more serious sin of apostasy as a matter of detail to be left to ahadith.

It is also significant that the Qur'an refers to apostasy several times (2:217, 3:86-90, 4:137, 9:66, 9:74, 16:106-109, 4:88-91, 47:25-27) and yet does not prescribe any punishment for it. Had the Qur'an not mentioned apostasy at all, we could have perhaps argued that there was no occasion for the Qur'anic revelation to deal with this subject and it was therefore left for the Holy Prophet to deal with. It may also be noted that almost all the verses that refer to apostasy are found in surahs said to be belonging to the Madinan period when the Islamic state had been established and penalties for crimes could be prescribed and applied. Only 16:106-109 appears in a surah identified as Makkan. It is thus a natural conclusion to draw that the absence of any legal penalty for apostasy in the Qur'an means that God never intended any such penalty to become part of Islamic Shari'ah.

The Death Penalty

The evidence against any legally prescribed penalty for apostasy in Islam does not rest only on the fact that the Qur'an does not prescribe any such penalty while referring to the subject of apostasy many times. We can go further and state that:

a. There is no mandatory death penalty in the Qur'an for any crime.
b. The death penalty for apostasy in fact conflicts with the Qur'an.

The truth of the above statements can be seen by examining the verses: 5:32-33, 45, 2:178 and 4:88-91.

Qur'an 5:32-33, 45, 2:178

In 5:32, after relating the story of the murder of *Habil* by his brother *Qabil*, God says:

On that account we ordained for the Children of Israel that if any one slew a person - unless it be for murder or for spreading mischief in the land - it would be as if he slew the whole humanity: and if any one saved a life, it would be as if he saved the whole humanity. Then although there came to them Our Messengers with clear (guidance), yet, even after that, many of them continued to commit excesses in the land. (5:32)

In the context of an emphasis on preserving the life of each and every individual the above verse mentions only two crimes for which a person can be killed:

1. Murdering another human being;
2. Spreading mischief (*fasad*) in the land.

Nowhere else the Qur'an mentions any other crime for which the death penalty is considered. There are, of course, verses that mention killing during a war in the way of God. But that is different from killing as a penalty for a crime. Moreover, in the Qur'anic understanding the objective of even killing in a war is to stop or punish crimes similar to the two mentioned in the above verse — violence and mischief — when committed in an organized way by a tribe or nation (2:191-193, 2:217, 4:88-91 etc).

Hence the above-mentioned two crimes exhaust all possible cases for which the Qur'an considers the death penalty. And in both of these cases, the death penalty is not mandatory in the Qur'an. In case of spreading mischief in the land, the Qur'an says in the next verse:

The recompense for those who wage war against God and his Messenger, and strive with might and main for mischief through the land is: execution, or crucifixion, or the cutting off of hands and feet from opposite sides, or exile from the land. That is their disgrace in this world, and for them in the hereafter is a severe punishment. (5:33)

There is no prescribed mandatory death penalty here. Even when the person wages war against God and his Messenger along with striving in the land for mischief, death is considered only one of several options, starting from exile. If such is the case with persons who wage war against God and his Messenger and actively seek to spread mischief in the land, then the question of death as a prescribed penalty for an apostate who continues to lead a peaceful life after his sin of apostasy can hardly arise within a Qur'anic perspective.

A little later in the same surah, al-Ma'idah, the Qur'an deals with the other crime – murdering another human being — for which death penalty can be applied:

And we ordained for them in [the Torah]: "Person for person, eye for eye, nose for nose, ear for ear, tooth for tooth, and wounds equal for equal." But if anyone remits the retaliation as charity, it shall be expiation for him. And whoever does not judge by what God has sent down, such are the transgressors (*zalimun*). (5:45)

The above verse refers to what God commanded the Jews through the Torah, but in the following verse the Qur'an gives a more balanced law to the Muslims:

O you who believe! Retaliation is prescribed for you in the matter of the slain, the free for the free, and the slave for the slave, and the female for the female. But if one (who killed) is forgiven by the brother of (the one killed) against ransom, there should be follow up in fairness and payment to the heir in handsome gratitude. This is a concession from your Lord and a mercy (from him). Then whoever exceeds the limit (of the ransom agreement) after this he shall have a painful chastisement. (2:178)

Again there is no mandatory death penalty. If the relatives of the murdered person accept ransom, the death penalty can be removed. Hence: a) there is no mandatory death penalty in the Qur'an for any crime; and b) since the Qur'an does not prescribe the death penalty even for crimes more serious than simple apostasy, death penalty for apostasy as such has no place within the Qur'anic perspective.

Qur'an 4:88-91

The four verses, 4:88-91, when carefully examined, also show that the Qur'anic perspective conflicts with the death penalty for apostasy. The first two verses state:

Then what is the matter with you that you are divided into two groups regarding the hypocrites? God has cast them backward (*arkasa*) because of what they have earned. Do you want to guide him whom God has made to go astray? And he whom God has made to go astray, you will not find for him any way. They wish that you reject faith as they have done, so that you all become the same. So take not protectors/friends from them till they emigrate in the way of God. But if they turn away, seize them and kill them wherever you find them, and take neither protectors/ friends from them or helpers. (4:88-89)

This passage begins by talking about hypocrites, that is, people who had declared themselves Muslims but in their hearts had decided not to believe in the teachings of Islam. The demand that they should do *hijrah fi sabil Allah* (emigrate for the sake of God) shows that they are not the hypocrites of Madinah but are living among non-Muslims in Makkah and possibly elsewhere. Verse 98 of the same surah shows that these people were not doing *hijrah* despite the fact that they were able to. The reason for their not doing *hijrah* was their hypocrisy. Makkan non-believers who had persecuted Muslims for years, would not have tolerated in their midst any true Muslims. They would have accepted among them only those "Muslims" who had stopped taking their "islam" seriously and felt more comfortable among non-believers, hostile to Islam, than among Muslims.

These hypocrites pretended to be Muslims because they wanted to be secure from both sides. And Makkan non-believers did not force them to publicly renounce their "islam" because they found them useful for gathering information about Muslims or for some other subversive actions against the ummah. In order to defeat these hypocrites in their game and force them to clearly choose between Islam and *kufr*, God commanded them to do *hijrah*. Their obedience to this command meant that they had chosen Islam and their disobedience meant that they had chosen *kufr*. Those who chose *kufr* in this way became apostates, since previously they called themselves Muslims. Thus the verses are a source of guidance for us regarding the way the apostates are to be treated.

At first sight the words "seize them and kill them wherever you find them" would suggest that they are to be killed. But this is quickly seen to be wrong if we read the next two verses:

> Except those who join a group between you and whom there is a (peace-) treaty or those who approach you with their hearts restraining them from fighting you or fighting their own people? Had God willed he would have given them power over you and they would have fought you. So if they withdraw from you and do not fight you but give you (guarantees of) peace, then God has opened no way for you against them.
>
> You will find others that wish to gain your confidence as well as that of their people. Every time they are sent back to temptation they give in to it. If they do not withdraw from you nor give you (guarantees) of peace, nor restrain their hands, seize them and kill them, wherever you find them. In their case we have provided you with a clear warrant against them (4:90-91) and these verses clarify the command "seizes them and kills them". The apostates who rejected Islam by failing to emigrate as commanded by God are divided into three categories:

1. Those that ally themselves with a group with whom Muslims have a peace treaty;
2. Those who want to keep neutrality, committing themselves to peace with both the Muslims and their own people who had not accepted Islam;
3. Those that provide no real guarantee of peace to Muslims and by all indications ally themselves with non-believers engaged in hostilities towards Islam.

The first two types of apostates are to be left in peace while the third one is to be treated like any non-believers in a state of war, they are to be seized and killed wherever they are found. Notice that the Qur'an uses the words "God has opened no way for you against them" in connection with the apostates of the first two types. This means that the Qur'an actually prohibits killing those apostates who want to live in peaceful terms with the Muslims. Thus according to the Qur'an the apostates are to be treated like other *kuffar*, If they want to live in peace with the Muslims, they are to be left in peace and if they assume a hostile attitude, then they are to be treated accordingly.

Additional Evidence

There are some other Qur'anic verses that, although not as conclusive as those discussed above, nevertheless reveal a perspective that is at odds with a legal penalty for apostasy. Thus the Qur'an is very emphatic that victory belongs to truth. It says:

"Truth has come and falsehood has vanished. Surely, falsehood was bound to vanish" (17:81)

"Nay, we fling the truth against falsehood and it destroys it and behold it then vanishes" (21:18)

In other passages it predicts the victory of Islam because it is the religion of truth:

He it is who has sent his Messenger with guidance and the religion of truth that he may make it prevail over all (corrupted expressions of) religion.

These verses show that the Qur'an was founded on a complete confidence in the validity of the following three principles:

1. Truth is bound to win over falsehood.
2. Islam is founded on truth.
3. Islam will therefore prevail.

Within this perspective Islam has no need for keeping people under its fold at pain of death. Such measures befit those systems that are essentially built on falsehood because that is the only way their followers can hope to slow down their inevitable march to defeat and disappearance. For a "religion of truth" it is more advantageous if people are free to examine ideas and then choose the religion or ideology or system they want. This is why the Qur`an establishes the following famous principle:

There is no compulsion in religion. Right has become distinct from wrong. So whoever rejects evil and puts faith in God has grasped the most trustworthy hand-hold that never breaks. And God is hearing, knowing. (2:256)

This verse is usually understood to mean that people cannot be compelled to become Muslims but they can be compelled to stay Muslims. But the words, "no compulsion in religion" are very general. They should apply equally to entering or leaving any religion, including Islam. One may try to argue against this general understanding of the verse as follows:

A person cannot be compelled to enter Islam but a person who is a Muslim is subject to the laws of Islam and those laws require death for leaving Islam. This argument would have had force only if we are able to establish that the Qur'an prescribes the death penalty for apostasy like it prescribes penalties for theft, *zina'* etc. But in the absence of any such prescription, we must take the words "no compulsion in religion" in their general sense and understand them to be applicable for both entering and leaving Islam.

Moreover, apostasy is a move from *Islam* to *kufr*. But what if we cannot establish the *Islam* of a person? For example, consider a person born in a Muslim family who at one point described him as a Muslim according to custom but him never really believed in Islam. If he then renounces

Islam, is he really moving from *Islam* to *kufr*? Is he really bound by the laws of Islam considering that he never really made a choice to live by them?

From the confident conviction that the message of the Qur'an is based on truth and therefore will prevail, comes also the Qur'anic condemnation of *fitnah,* persecuting people for their religion, which is described as worse than killing in battle:

> And fight in the way of God those who fight you but do not transgress due limits ... *al-fitnah* is worse than killing (in battle). ... Fight them till there is no *fitnah* and the religion is for God (alone).

These verses refer to the fighting that the non-believers were waging against the Prophet and his followers. This fighting was part of their *fitnah* or persecution of Muslims, aimed at suppressing the Islamic movement. The verses commanded the Muslims to fight back because *fitnah* is worse than killing in battle and so they should choose the lesser of the two evils. The fighting should continue till there is no more *fitnah* and the religion is for God. The words "the religion is for God (alone)" are closely related to "there is no more *fitnah*" and mean that the choice of religion is a matter between a person and God and not to be determined by force. Contrary to what some commentators suggest the words do not mean, "till everyone accepts Islam" because it is definitely known that the Prophet made peace with many tribes even though they had not accepted Islam and because the Qur`an explicitly states that when the non-believing opponents incline to peace the Prophet should do the same (8:61).

That the death penalty for apostasy conflicts with the Qur'anic perspective is also shown by those verses in which it is stated that the Messenger came not as a watcher over people but only as one who clearly declares the truth: 5:92, 99, 13:40, 16:35, 82, 24:54, 29:18, 36:17, 42:48, 64:12.

Significantly, the first of these verses is addressed to the believers, since it is after explicitly addressing the believers and giving to them some laws (5:90-91) that the verse says:

"And obey God and obey the Messenger and beware (and fear God). Then if you turn away, know that our Messenger's duty is to simply convey (the message) clearly. (5:92)

The Qur'an then continues addressing believers, giving some further regulations, and then says again:

On our Messenger there is no obligation but conveying (the message). And God knows what you reveal and what you conceal (5:99)

In 5:92 and 99 the Muslims are not told that if you turn away then death penalty awaits you but rather they are told that the Messenger has done his duty by conveying the message to you and now it is up to you whether you want to stay faithful to him or whether you want to turn away from him.

Dealing with Apostasy

As observed above the Qur'an expects us to deal with apostates like other *kuffar*. Therefore the Qur'anic guidance for dealing with the apostates is essentially the same as its guidance for dealing with other *kuffar*. Briefly, this guidance is that we should treat them according to the degree of friendship or hostility they show to Islam and Muslims. To translate this into more specific guidance we can divide apostates in three categories and see how each category is to be treated:

1. An apostate leaves Islam because of ignorance of Islam or some confusion that leads him to think that his new religion or way is truer and better. Such a person will be willing to listen to the Muslims if they want to show him that he has made a mistake. The Muslims should treat him kindly and argue with him in the best

possible way. (60:8, 16:125). But Muslims should be careful not to show him more kindness than they show to other Muslims, for, otherwise the apostate may be encouraged to stay an apostate.

2. An apostate leaves Islam, not out of a belief that he is moving to something truer and better, but to satisfy some of his worldly desires, e. g., to get greater importance or more comfortable life or greater acceptance of his lifestyle such as homosexual lifestyle. A sign of such an apostate is that he shows little inclination to listen to any reasoning. If such an apostate does not engage in any hostile activity against Islam and Muslims, he should not be subjected to any active hostility (4:90). But since he has clearly preferred *kufr* over *iman* the following commandment of God will apply:

O you who believe! Do not take for friends and allies (even) your fathers and your brothers if they love disbelief more than faith, if any of you do so, they are the wrong doers. (9:23)

According to some traditions "this *ayah* was revealed concerning those nine men who after apostasy went to Makkah". (Panipati, *Tafsir Mazhari*)

Beyond avoiding friendship and alliance with apostates of this second type, the Muslims can impose boycott against them, since such boycott was imposed by the Prophet on the three Companions mentioned in 9:118. These three Companions did not commit apostasy but simply failed to join the Muslims in jihad without a good reason.

3. The third type of apostate is one who leaves Islam and then engages in hostile actions against Islam and Muslims, e.g. knowingly engages in propaganda against Islam and Muslims blatantly ignoring facts that he is expected to know well, passes secrets to the enemy, and takes part in fighting against the Muslims. Such an apostate can be punished by anything from exile to death.

5

Fundamentalists or Islamists

No one who reads or writes about events in the Muslim world can avoid the question of how to label those Muslims who invoke Islam as the source of authority for all political and social action. Should they be labeled Islamic (or Muslim) fundamentalists? Or are they better described as Islamists?

The issue has been the subject of a heated debate for two decades. For a while, both general and scholarly usage in America accepted fundamentalism. Islamism emerged in the late 1980s in French academe and then crossed into English, where it eventually displaced Islamic fundamentalism in specialized contexts. More recently, the term Islamism has gained even wider currency, and since September 11, 2001, it may even have established itself as the preferred American usage. Still newer terminology may lie over the horizon.

Behind the battle over usage lies another struggle, over the nature of the phenomenon itself. In fact, the two contests, over English usage and analytical understanding, are inseparable. Nor are they free of associations left by past usages. Here follows a short history of changing usage—itself a history of changing Western perceptions of Muslim reality.

The Debut of Islamism

The term Islamism first appeared in French in the mid-eighteenth century. But it did not refer to the modern ideological use of Islam, which had not yet come into being. Rather, it was a synonym for the religion of the Muslims, which was then known in French as *mahométisme,* the religion professed and taught by the Prophet Muhammad.

This usage dated to the early seventeenth century. It reflected a new willingness, born of the Renaissance, to recognize Islam as a religious system with a founder, like Christianity. But it rested upon the erroneous presumption that Muhammad stood in relation to Islam as Christ stood in relation to Christianity. Nevertheless, the usage became pervasive across Europe. In 1734, George Sale, whose English translation of the Qur'an set a new standard, wrote: "It is certainly one of the most convincing proofs that Mohammedism was no other than a human invention, that it owed its progress and establishment almost entirely to the sword."

Even a century later, when attitudes to Islam had changed dramatically, it was still common to call the faith after the Prophet. In 1833, the French poet Alphonse de Lamartine demonstrated the change in European attitudes, even as he employed the old usage, "*Mahométisme* could effortlessly and painlessly accommodate a system based on religious and civil liberty ... by nature; it is moral, forbearing, uncomplaining, charitable and tolerant." In the eighteenth century, the Western study of Islam made enormous strides, and polemical denigration no longer informed every Western pronouncement.

The thinkers of the Enlightenment knew perfectly well that Muslims called their faith Islam. They searched for a way to reflect that understanding through usage and thus classify Islam as a religion appreciated in its own terms. It was the French philosopher Voltaire who found the solution, when he coined the term *islamisme.* Voltaire had an abiding interest in Islam, and wrote extensively about it, comparing it to other faiths, sometimes favorably.

He also understood the role of Muhammad in Islam, leading him to correct his readers: "This religion," he wrote, "is called *islamisme*." Not only did his usage depart from Sale's, but so did his conclusion, "It was not by force of arms that *islamisme* established itself over more than half of our hemisphere. It was by enthusiasm and persuasion." The great nineteenth-century French dictionary by Littré quoted just this passage from Voltaire's *Essai sur les mœurs* when it defined *islamisme* as "the religion of Mahomet."

In the course of the nineteenth century, this usage gained ground throughout Europe. Alexis de Tocqueville, writing in 1838, found the "root of *islamisme* in Judaism." In 1883, Ernest Renan, pioneer of philology, published an influential essay entitled *L'Islamisme et la science*. As the French historian note the Renan's use of *islamisme* "did not have the present-day sense of the political utilization of Islam." Rather, he meant Islam. It is in this sense, too, that Islamism appeared in the *New English Dictionary* in a fascicle published in 1900. It defined Islamism as "the religious system of the Moslems; Mohammedanism."

Even the word Islamist appeared there, defined as "an orthodox Mohammedan," and the entry included this example from a magazine article published in 1895, "Judgment should not be pronounced against Islam and Islamists on rancorous and partisan statements." There are two points worth noting about the use of Islamism and *islamisme* in the nineteenth century. First, while it reflected a more accurate understanding of Islam's doctrine, it did not exclude critical interpretations of Islam's character.

In a dispatch of 1873, a British consul wrote of "the inherent characteristics of Islamism," which he called "deficient in vitality," "aggressive," and "carrying in its bosom the seeds of decay." The French Orientalist, Baron Bernard Carra de Vaux, wrote in 1901, "*Islamisme* is a spent religion." In both cases, the reference is to the religion of Islam per se—and in both cases, it is clearly derogatory.

The second point is that Islamism and *islamisme* did not completely displace Mohammedanism and *mahométisme*, even in scholarship. In 1890, Ignaz Goldziher, the Hungarian-Jewish Orientalist regarded as the founder of modern Islamic studies, published his two-volume study of the Muslim oral tradition (*hadith*) under the title *Muhammedanische Studien*. Other notable instances of its continued use in book titles include D. S. Margoliouth's *Mohammedanism* (1911), A.A. Fyzee's *Outlines of Muhammadan Law* (1949), and Joseph Schacht's *Origins of Muhammadan Jurisprudence* (1950).

Only at mid-century did this usage expire, primarily because Western writers realized that they also had Muslim readers, who resented it. In 1946, the British Orientalist H.A.R. Gibb wrote an introduction to Islam in the same series that had included Margoliouth's *Mohammedanism* thirty-five years earlier. The publisher wished to keep the same title. Gibb assented, but he was quick to disavow the title on the very first page, "Modern Muslims dislike the terms Mohammedan and Mohammedanism, which seem to them to carry the implication of worship of Mohammed, as Christian and Christianity imply the worship of Christ." In the text that followed, Gibb referred to the believers as Muslims and to the faith as Islam.

But Islamism also began to disappear from the lexicon from about the turn of the twentieth century. Many scholars simply preferred the shorter and purely Arabic term, Islam. In 1913, Orientalists from many countries joined together to produce the *Encyclopaedia of Islam*. By the date of its completion in 1938, Islamism had all but disappeared from usage, replaced simply by Islam.

In summation, the term Islamism enjoyed its first run, lasting from Voltaire to the First World War, as a synonym for Islam. Enlightened scholars and writers generally preferred it to Mohammedanism. Eventually both terms yielded to Islam, the Arabic name of the faith, and a word free of either pejorative or comparative associations. There was no need for any other term, until the rise of an ideological and political interpretation of Islam challenged scholars and commentators to come up with an alternative, to distinguish Islam as modern ideology from Islam as a faith.

Fundamentalism and Islam

The term fundamentalism originated in America in the 1920s. As the pace of social change accelerated, Protestant Christians felt threatened by the higher criticism of the Bible and the spread of philosophical skepticism. They sought to reaffirm their belief in the literal text of the Bible and the "fundamentals" of Christian belief, including creationism. These Christians called themselves fundamentalists, a term that gained wide currency at the time of the Scopes ("Monkey") trial in 1925. At the time, it acquired a strongly pejorative association in the minds of liberals and modernists.

In the subsequent few decades, odd references to Islamic fundamentalism appeared in print, but they were rare and inconsistent in their meanings. "If you looked in the right places," wrote the British historian Arnold Toynbee in 1929, "you could doubtless find some old fashioned Islamic fundamentalists still lingering on. You would also find that their influence was negligible." From the context, it is obvious that by fundamentalists, Toynbee meant Muslim traditionalists and not the new activists who, that same year, founded the Society of the Muslim Brethren in Egypt.

Only fifty years later did Islamic fundamentalism come into widespread usage, thanks in large measure to media coverage of Iran's revolution? Journalists, ever on the lookout for a shorthand way to reference things new and unfamiliar, gravitated toward the term fundamentalism. It was American English; it was already in *Webster's Dictionary*, and it evoked the anti-modernism that Ayatollah Khomeini seemed to personify. The use of fundamentalism in connection with Islam spread rapidly—so much so that by 1990; the *Concise Oxford English Dictionary* defined it not only as "the strict maintenance of traditional Protestant beliefs," but also as "the strict maintenance of ancient or fundamental doctrines of any religion, especially Islam." By sheer dint of usage, Islamic fundamentalism had become *the* most cited fundamentalism of all.

Yet the more popular Islamic fundamentalism became in the media, the more scholars of Islam recoiled from it. The reasons varied. Some thought that the term fundamentalism failed to capture the methodology and style of Iran's revolution and comparable Muslim movements. Bernard Lewis, preeminent historian of Islam, made this case against it:

The use of this term is established and must be accepted, but it remains unfortunate and can be misleading. "Fundamentalist" is a Christian term. It seems to have come into use in the early years of this century, and denotes certain Protestant churches and organizations, more particularly those that maintain the literal divine origin and inerrancy of the Bible. In this they oppose the liberal and modernist theologians, who tend to a more critical, historical view of Scripture. Among Muslim theologians there is as yet no such liberal or modernist approach to the Qur'an, and all Muslims, in their attitude to the text of the Qur'an, are in principle at least fundamentalists. Where the so-called Muslim fundamentalists differ from other Muslims and indeed from Christian fundamentalists is in their scholasticism and their legalism. They base themselves not only on the Qur'an, but also on the Traditions of the Prophet, and on the corpus of transmitted theological and legal learning.

Other scholars, particularly those who sympathized with the new Muslim movements, protested that the label of fundamentalist unfairly stigmatized forward-thinking Muslims. John Esposito, America's foremost apologist for Islam-driven movements, made this argument against using fundamentalism in an Islamic context:

> For many liberal or mainline Christians, "fundamentalist" is pejorative or derogatory, being applied rather indiscriminately to all those who advocate a literalist biblical position and thus are regarded as static, retrogressive, and extremist. As a result, fundamentalism often has been regarded popularly as referring to those who are literalists and wish to return to and replicate the past. In fact, few individuals or organizations in the Middle East fit such a stereotype. Indeed, many fundamentalist leaders have had the best education, enjoy responsible positions in society, and are adept at harnessing the latest technology to propagate their views and create viable modern institutions such as schools, hospitals, and social service agencies.

Esposito added that fundamentalism "is often equated with political activism, extremism, fanaticism, terrorism, and anti-Americanism," a prejudgment by label. Unlike Lewis, who was prepared to make a concession to widespread usage (it "must be accepted"), Esposito balked, "I prefer to speak of Islamic revivalism and Islamic activism rather than of Islamic fundamentalism."

Edward Said, defender of Palestine and critic of Western representations of Islam, also weighed in. He did not so much object to the term (if it were properly defined) as to the way it had come to be employed *against* Islam:

> Instead of scholarship, we often find only journalists making extravagant statements, which are instantly picked up and further dramatized by the media. Looming over

their work is the slippery concept, to which they constantly allude, of "*fundamentalism*," a word that has come to be associated almost automatically with Islam, although it has a flourishing, usually elided relationship with Christianity, Judaism, and Hinduism. The deliberately created associations between Islam and fundamentalism ensure that the average reader comes to see Islam and fundamentalism as essentially the same thing.

In this usage, claimed Said, "fundamentalism equals Islam equals everything-we-must-now-fight-against, as we did with communism during the Cold War."

The term fundamentalism did have a few academic defenders. In 1988, the University of Chicago, backed by the American Academy of Arts and Sciences, launched the Fundamentalism Project, devoted to comparing trends in Christianity, Islam, Judaism, Hinduism, Buddhism, and even Confucianism. The project began with the hypothesis that the acceleration of modernity was forcing the faithful of all religions into a reactive (and sometimes violent) mode. Its organizers defined fundamentalism as "a strategy, or set of strategies, by which beleaguered believers attempt to preserve their distinctive identity as a people or group ... by a selective retrieval of doctrines, beliefs, and practices from a sacred past." Some 150 experts on diverse religious traditions contributed to the project, and their papers appeared in five hefty volumes, bearing titles like *Fundamentalisms Observed* and *Fundamentalisms and the State*.

The Fundamentalism Project was the most sustained effort to legitimize the term as a tool of comparison across religions. Yet its impact remained limited, perhaps because it never generated a single, powerful statement of its case. Quite often, the organizers and participants hedged their own use of the term with a thicket of reservations and disclaimers. Sadik J. al-Azm, the Syrian philosopher, provided perhaps the strongest intellectual defense of the use of fundamentalism in an Islamic context. Al-Azm, an iconoclast famous for his past clashes with religious authorities, surveyed the doctrines of the new Islamic movements, and found them to consist of "an immediate return to Islamic 'basics' and 'fundamentals.'" Arab Muslims themselves, he added, had resorted to the Arabic neologism *usuli* (from *usul*, the "fundamentals"), as a calque for fundamentalism.

"It seems to me quite reasonable," he concluded, "that calling these Islamic movements 'Fundamentalist' (and in the strong sense of the term) is adequate, accurate, and correct." The Egyptian philosopher Hasan Hanafi performed the same analysis and reached the same conclusion, "It is difficult to find a more appropriate term than the one recently used in the West, 'fundamentalism,' to cover the meaning of what we name Islamic awakening or revival."

The Dutch Islamicist J.J.G. Jansen reinforced this argument with a practical one. The term was convenient. "In a way the discussion of the word 'fundamentalism' echoes the discussion once caused by the invention of the telephone," he wrote. "Would not the term 'telephone' be much too simplistic? Would it do justice to the beauty and the many possibilities of the device? How about 'speaking telegraph' or 'electrical speaking telephone'?" Jansen spoofed those who proposed elaborate alternatives like "revolutionary extremist neotraditionalist ultra-Islamic radicalism." The definitions of these far-fetched creations usually were not much different from what people meant by fundamentalism.

But the strongest argument for fundamentalism was its sheer ubiquity. In an entry entitled "Fundamentalism," published in the *Oxford Encyclopedia of the Modern Islamic World* in 1995, historian John Voll enumerated the most common objections to the term and made a list of alternatives. These included Islamism, integrism, neo-normative Islam, neo-traditional Islam, Islamic revivalism, and Islamic nativism. "However," he added with a hint of resignation, "'fundamentalism' remains the most commonly utilized identification of the various revivalist impulses among Muslims. More technically accurate terms and neologisms have not gained wide acceptance."

The Islamist Alternative

The resurrection and redefinition of Islamism, like its birth, took place in France. In the late 1970s, the French grappled with the problem of how to describe the new Islamic movements that had moved to the fore. *Islamisme* appealed to French scholars for two reasons. First, it had a venerable French pedigree going back to Voltaire. *Fondamentalisme,* the loan word from American English, had none. Second, there was a certain reluctance to deploy the only French alternative, *intégrisme,* because it remained too embedded in its original Catholic context and too implicated in ongoing debates about authority in the church. *Islamisme* in any case had been retired from daily use as a synonym for Islam. Why not impart new meaning to the term? Soon *islamisme* was cropping up in the titles of articles and books.

The retrieval of *islamisme* and its deployment to describe the new movements did not pass without criticism, most notably by Maxime Rodinson, the greatest living French historian of Islam. "In the dictionary, *islamisme* is given as a synonym for Islam," Rodinson reminded his colleagues. "If one chooses this term, the reader may become confused between an excited extremist who wishes to kill everyone and a reasonable person who believes in God in the Muslim manner, something perfectly respectable." For this reason, Rodinson preferred *intégrisme,* which he found perfectly serviceable provided it was carefully defined. But his objections did not persuade younger French scholars, who did not feel bound by entries in old dictionaries. By the mid-1980s, *islamisme* was no longer simply, or even primarily, a synonym for the religion of Islam in contemporary French usage. Increasingly, it was understood to mean only one thing, Islam as a modern ideology and a political program.

It is possible to date almost precisely when the term made the crossing from French to English. In 1983, it had not yet arrived. That year, Georgetown University's Center for Contemporary Arab Studies organized its annual conference on "New Perspectives on Islam and Politics in the Middle East." Bruce Lawrence, a professor of religious studies, opened with an exhaustive survey of the pros and cons of the term Islamic fundamentalism, as well as its alternatives, but made no mention of Islamism. Neither did any other conference participant. A year later, in 1984, the French sociologist of Islam, Gilles Kepel, published an influential book with the subtitle *Les mouvements islamistes dans l'Egypte contemporaine*.

In 1985, it appeared in English translation as *Muslim Extremism in Egypt*. The English translator had difficulty with Kepel's extensive use of *islamiste* and translated it as "Islamicist." A footnote in the translation made this apology: "The term 'Islamicist' is used throughout to render the French 'islamiste'. The loan word 'Islamist' did not gain currency until after this translation had been completed." By about 1985, then, the French seed had been planted in English (though not much before that). Initially, the term encountered some principled resistance. The American anthropologist Henry Munson, Jr., in a book published in 1988, listed the disadvantages of fundamentalism, but decided to retain it anyway, "I cannot think of an adequate alternative term to characterize those Muslims who advocate a strictly Islamic policy. The term *Islamist* strikes me as a clumsy neologism."

Clumsy or not, however, Islamism began to displace fundamentalism in specialized usage. It particularly appealed to scholars who disliked the supposedly pejorative associations of fundamentalism. Graham Fuller, a RAND analyst and enthusiast for the new Islamic movements, made an early statement in its favor. Fundamentalism, he determined in 1991, "is an unsatisfactory term, suggesting as it does a strict reversion to the institutions of a medieval or even early Islamic state. This more recent phenomenon is better termed *Islamism,* suggesting not so much theology as an ideology whose implications are not at all old-fashioned, but thoroughly modern." In 1993, the political scientist Louis Cantori likewise argued that fundamentalism conveys a sense of extremism and dismissal. In reference to Islam, in the world of scholarship, and now internally within U.S. agencies, it is being abandoned as being prejudicial and polemical.

Instead, the term Islamism is used increasingly to denote the political manifestation of the religion of Islam. "Islamism" permits one to more dispassionately make distinctions between extremist and mainstream Islam. Cantori still noted that Islamism had not carried the day in the media, "Unfortunately, journalists especially still use the term fundamentalism and, in the process, fail to recognize and appreciate the moderation of the Islamic revival's mainstream." But Cantori left no doubt that the term Islamism was gaining ground in academe and in Washington. In this early stage, the use of Islamism was also a marker for scholars more likely to sympathize with the new Islamic movements.

In Washington, Islamism did gain at the expense of fundamentalism. The term made a few cameo appearances in policy statements, and then received an official definition from Robert Pelletreau, Jr., assistant secretary of state for Near Eastern affairs, in remarks made in 1994. Pelletreau warned that "Islamic fundamentalism" had to be used "with requisite caution," and only to refer to the broad revival of Islam. Within that broad revival, there were subdivisions.

In the foreign affairs community, we often use the term "Political Islam" to refer to the movements and groups within the broader fundamentalist revival with a specific political agenda. "Islamists" are Muslims with political goals. We view these terms as analytical, not normative. They do not refer to phenomena that are necessarily sinister, there are many legitimate, socially responsible Muslim groups with political goals. However, there are also Islamists who operate outside the law. Groups or individuals who operate outside the law—who espouse violence to achieve their aims—are properly called extremists.

Here, then, was a three-tiered division, there were fundamentalists; some of these were Islamists; and some of these were extremists. Only the last constituted a threat. This statement was pregnant with its own analytical contradictions. For example, did a decision by a Middle Eastern government to put a movement outside the law automatically render it extremist? Or did only espousal of violence do so? What about movements that employed both bullets and ballots simultaneously?

But despite the statement's logical lacunae, it established Islamism in the official lexicon as a synonym for politicized and ideological Islam. By 1996, Pelletreau had devised a full-blown definition of Islamism, firmly establishing the term's privileged status:

We normally use the term "Islamist" to refer to Muslims who draw upon the belief, symbols, and language of Islam to inspire, shape, and animate political activity. We do not automatically seek to exclude moderate, tolerant, peaceful Islamists who seek to apply their religious values to domestic political problems and foreign policy. We do, however, object strongly to Islamists who preach intolerance and espouse violence in the domestic and international arenas.

The shift in preferences could be measured by running terms against one another on Internet search engines. In a

Google search early in 2003, the exact phrases "Muslim fundamentalists" and "Islamic fundamentalists" together returned 45,300 results; "Islamists" returned 82,100. The exact phrases "Islamic fundamentalism" and "Muslim fundamentalism" still returned more results than "Islamism," 58,280 compared to 23,900. But it was probable that the growth lay in the use of the term Islamism. The clear preference for "Islamists," and the strong showing of "Islamism," was especially remarkable given that the major print media outlet in the United States, *The New York Times*, uses neither Islamism nor Islamists.

But the very success of these neologisms undermined the intent of those who had imported them from France. They had hoped that the term Islamist, used in place of fundamentalist, would dispel prejudice. But militant Muslims continued, as before, to commit or justify highly publicized acts of violence. As Islamism gained currency, it too became associated with benighted extremism, from the Taliban to the Algerian Armed Islamic Group, culminating in the mega-terror of Usama bin Ladin. Critics of Islamism found it easy to add Islamism to the list of dangerous twentieth century "isms" that had defied the liberal West and gone down to defeat.

"Islamism Is Fascism"—thus ran the headline of an interview with analyst Daniel Pipes. "Islamism Is the New Bolshevism"—thus went the headline of an op-ed column by former British Prime Minister Margaret Thatcher. The entry of Islamism into common English usage had not improved the image of these movements and paradoxically made it easier to categorize them as threats of the first order. As fundamentalists, these Muslims might have claimed some affinity to Christian and Jewish fundamentalists, who were generally tolerated. As the Muslim equivalent of fascists or bolshevists, they were clearly marked as the enemies of democracy and freedom. Ultimately, of course, the problem of these movements was not what they were called. It was what they did. And as long as these movements continued to spawn, nurture, or tolerate the most violent forces in contemporary Islam, they would bring stigma to whatever term was applied to them.

Muslim Responses

On the whole, the debate over usage in the West bore little relationship to the parallel debate in the Muslim world over what to call the new Islamic movements. The arguments on behalf of various Arabic, Persian, and Urdu terms are a topic that deserves its own treatment, based on other sources. But from time to time, Muslims expressed opinions over what terms Westerners should use. Leaders of the new movements generally followed the lead of their Western sympathizers in rejecting the use of "fundamentalism." Rashid al-Ghannushi, the former leader of Tunisia's An-Nahda party, gave a speech in London in 1992 in which he "emphatically" rejected the term fundamentalism "insofar as it reflects the negative connotations implied by Western usage."

The same year, the head of the National Islamic Front in Sudan, Hasan at-Turabi, told a U.S. congressional committee that fundamentalism was "a misleading term in the sense that it describes a phenomenon which is very liberal, very progressive, and forward-looking, rather than a movement which is dogmatic, conservative, if not reactionary." If fundamentalism was unacceptable, then what term did these Muslims recommend to Westerners? In 1988, the French academic Francois Burgat published *L'Islamisme au Maghreb*, a landmark book very sympathetic to the new movements. Nonetheless, Abbassi Madani, the leader of the Algerian Islamic Salvation Front (FIS), reprimanded him, "In your book, you must first of all change the title! Why 'Islamism'? It is Islam that is at work in Algeria, nothing but Islam. We are Muslims!" From Madani's point of view, any label but Muslim was pejorative by definition.

Ayatollah Muhammad Hussein Fadlallah, the spiritual mentor of Hizbullah, was asked by an English-language periodical in 1992 whether he thought fundamentalist or Islamist was more appropriate. Like Ghannushi and Turabi, Fadlallah rejected fundamentalist because of its "violent" associations. But like Madani, he also found Islamist unacceptable. It was a term "used by outsiders to denote a strand of activity which they think justifies their misconception of Islam as something rigid and immobile, a mere tribal affiliation." And his conclusion was identical to Madani's, "Having thought a good deal about this matter, I am satisfied to use the word 'Muslim,' which includes all the activities carried on within the scope and fold of Islam."

Fadlallah later revised his position, apparently when he learned that Western sympathizers with movements like Hizbullah were promoting the term Islamist. "I object to the word 'fundamentalism,'" he told the same English-language periodical six months later, "a term which has overtones of exclusivism. I prefer the term 'Islamist movement,' which indicates a willingness to interact and live harmoniously with other trends of opinion, rather than to exclude them. In the Western perspective, 'fundamentalism' has implications of violence, and the Islamists have never chosen violence. Rather, violence has been forced upon them."

Fadlallah had taken his cue from foreign friends. But like other so-called Islamists, he was ambivalent about being called one—and with good reason. If Islamism came to be presented by its critics as a deviation from Islam itself, it too could appear pejorative.

New Permutations

To all intents and purposes, Islamic fundamentalism and Islamism have become synonyms in contemporary American usage. An author's choice can no longer be regarded automatically as a substantive statement about the subject itself. The choice of one term or another has been reduced to a matter of style. Yet the Muslims whom these terms purport to describe are in constant motion, and their actions are sure to have an impact upon Western perceptions and the categories created in the West to explain them. The pressures will come from two directions.

The first will be the theory mills of France, which twice invented Islamism, in the eighteenth and twentieth centuries. The wheels are turning again. The same French scholars who defined *islamisme* twenty years ago have now determined that it is *passé*, since it never succeeded in seizing power. Where there was once *islamisme*, there is now only *postislamisme*, also sometimes labeled *néofondamentalisme*. Its adherents are supposedly more interested in Islamizing society than pursuing power.

This purported discovery has prompted a debate in France over whether Islamism ever existed in the first place. Alain Roussillon, an authority on Egypt, claims that it didn't. The concepts of *islamisme* and *postislamisme*, he argues, are impositions of ethnocentric Western sociology. Orientalist in effect, they make Muslims into exceptions and postulate one "truth of Islam" that supposedly defines Muslims from one end of the Islamic world to the other. And the inevitable confusion between Islam and *islamisme* "reduces the analysis of contemporary Muslim societies to the discourse and practices of their most radical and marginal components."

Not so, responds Oliver Roy, one of the chief interpreters of the new movements (and father of the term *postislamisme*). *Islamisme* may be a construct, he admits, but Muslims themselves constructed it. If it appears to be Western in origin, this is because thinkers like Ayatollah Khomeini were deeply influenced by radical Western thought. Arcane as this debate may sound, it touches on the question of whether Western scholars have a license to represent "the other" in categories they themselves label and define. At some point, the debate is sure to cross the

Atlantic, and it is not impossible that scholars who once embraced the term Islamism as non-prejudicial may yet repudiate it.

The second source of pressure will come from the ascent of other terms that have gained in popularity since September 11. "It was called 'Muslim Fundamentalism' in the beginning. Now the term 'Jihadism' is in vogue." So wrote a columnist in Pakistan's leading English-language daily in 2000. At that time, the use of jihadism was largely confined to the Indian and Pakistani media. But the terror attacks in the United States, the war in Afghanistan, and the battle against al-Qa'ida, have facilitated the term's migration to the West. At present, jihadism is used to refer to the most violent persons and movements in contemporary Islam, including al-Qa'ida. But the widespread Muslim reaffirmation of the duty of jihad, coupled with expressions of Muslim sympathy for al-Qa'ida and suicide bombings, could transform jihadism into a household word in the West. Since September 11, it has figured in the titles of several university-press bestsellers dealing with Islamism or Islamic fundamentalism as a whole, such that the transformation may already be underway.

Some media outlets have adopted the phrases militant Islam and militant Muslims. The dictionary definition of a militant is someone prepared to do battle; in American English, its clearest association is with the violent fringes of the antiwar and civil rights movements of the 1960s. The implication of militant Islam is that the new Muslim movements have a propensity toward violence. In contrast, sympathizers of these movements have shown some preference for the phrase political Islam. This choice suggests that the defining characteristic of the new movements is not their inclination to do battle, but their willingness to engage in the give-and-take of politics. Political Islam may well be an oxymoron, since nowhere in the Muslim world have politics been separated from religion. But political Islam, like militant Islam, is immediately intelligible to the English reader, and one or both phrases might overtake Islamism in the future.

Western Desires

The actions of Muslims will affect the Western choice of terms. But Western perceptions, hopes, and prejudices will play an equal or greater role. Debate over terminology has always surrounded the West's relations with Islam, and its outcome has been as much a barometer of the West's needs as a description of the actual state of Islam. At the turn of the seventeenth century, the traveler Sir Thomas Shirley complained about fellow Englishmen who called the "Great Turke" (the Ottoman sultan) the "king of the Muslims" (*Musselmanni*). Why? "Musselman" meant believer, and any Christian who acknowledged "a Maho-metan to be a faithful believer doth confess himself to be an infidel."

At various times, Westerners have needed Muslims to be infidels or believers, threatening or peaceable, foreign or familiar. It is impossible to predict which terms will prevail in the West's own struggle to come to terms with change in contemporary Islam. It will depend on what Muslims do—and on what the West desires.

Responses to Western Society

Whereas the fundamentalist battle against Western thought, which is reflective of the whole of modernity, is largely an intellectual struggle against the non-Muslim world, the battle over the status of the family is a street-level campaign to resist Western influence by conforming Muslims to the strict commands and demands of *sharia* law. Within the modern Islamic world, much of the ongoing debate between fundamentalist Muslims and secular Muslims has focused on the status of women, marriage, and family law.

The Quran and *hadith* are explicit in addressing such issues; fundamentalists believe the demands of Islamic law are strict, divine, unchanging, and central to the vitality of Islamic society. Islamic faith itself is the key to Muslim social order; the term *Islam* literally means "obedience." A just and holy society can be achieved only when Muslims live in obedience to God's divine revelation mandating human relationships to God and to one another. Fundamentalist Muslims, in seeking to enforce the sovereignty of God upon the entire universe, begin with the individual and the family in obedience to God and His plan for the sexes.

Only when families in a community are living according to Islamic law can the community be in harmony with God; only when all communities in a nation are living according to Islamic law can the nation be in harmony with God; and only when all nations are living according to Islamic law can the universe be in harmony with God. In the context of attempts to interject strict *sharia* law upon Muslim society and government, women have been, and remain, the primary focus of attention. Even as western influences led many Islamic states to reform the legal and political status of women in the mid-twentieth century, Islamic fundamentalists came to view the strict suppression of women's "rights" as vital to the revitalization and purification of Islamic society.

Islamic fundamentalists see basic morality at stake in the fight over women's rights. Wives are morally bound to be obedient to their husbands; social justice cannot be achieved if women are in violation of their proper sphere of existence. In Pakistan in the 1960s, for example, Mawdudi and the Jama'at-i Islami struggled unsuccessfully to reverse the trend towards the liberalization of marriage and divorce laws in the form of legal codes which gave more rights to women. In the 1980s, Muslims in India successfully influenced the government to retain Muslim

Family Laws, despite the fact that such laws were opposed to the Uniform Civil Code. In many countries throughout the Muslim world, fundamentalists continue in their efforts to keep women out of the job market, to force women to remain fully veiled in pubic, and to keep wives in strict submission, if not virtual bondage, to their husbands.

Such efforts take the form of seeking to enforce strict implementation of Islamic law in terms of marriage, divorce, inheritance, and succession. Fundamentalists have achieved varying degrees of success in these matters. Among the most notable instances are Afghanistan's Taliban (now removed from power) and Saudi Arabia's Wahhabi-driven suppression of women. Although repulsive to modern Western societies, the strict suppression of women is pivotal to Islamic fundamentalists. Disorderly women signify a society apart from the will of God. Doubtlessly the coming years will bring repeated clashes between Islamic fundamentalists and the Westernized world concerning the role of women in society.

Islamic fundamentalists also see modern economic systems as a threat to faith. Although there are differences of opinion in terms of the specifics of market processes, Islamic fundamentalists are united in their belief that modern economic systems are at fault for inflicting "severe injustices, inefficiencies and moral failures." For fundamentalists, the solution is to base economic activity on the Quranic verses which touch upon the subject. Reclaiming the ancient, pure social order is imperative; the economic changes that have taken place in the world since the seventh century are of no concern.

Finally, in the larger context of perceived threats from Western society, the concept of freedom is resisted by Islamic fundamentalists. In the first place, the concept of obedience leaves no room for individual freedoms. Furthermore, Western ideals of self-individualism are anathema in the sense that they glorify the individual and his or her abilities and achievements apart from God. On the other hand, as already noted, Islamic fundamentalists have co-opted self-individualism, placing the concept within the framework of each individual having a responsibility to work for the ultimate securing of God's sovereignty over the entire universe. Freedom is contained because it is opposed to social order predicated upon strict hierarchical structures of unbending obedience.

Responses to the Secular State

The larger goal of Islamic political fundamentalism is to overthrow secular states and impose theocratic political law. Only under theocratic law can the dangers of Western science and society effectively be eliminated. Only under theocratic law can the sovereignty of God be extended into that realm of existence which is now controlled by the "ignorant." The Iranian Islamic revolution of 1979 provided a model of how Islamic fundamentalists could achieve national political dominance. Against the backdrop of rapid modernization on the one hand and a repressive state on the other, the masses in Iran, incited to action by Ayatollah Ruhollah Khomeini, a fundamentalist Islamic cleric, revolted against Prime Minster Bakhtiar.

When the military declared neutrality, Khomeini assumed leadership of the nation, installing a theocratic government based on his interpretation of Shi'ite jurisprudence. The manner in which Shi'ite law was imposed into state governance provides insight into the ongoing struggles between advocates of strict Islamic political law and advocates of secular rule. In theory, Iran has been ruled by a constitutional monarchy for most of the twentieth century. Constitutionalism, however, was a political product of Western Europe. Thus when constitutionalism arrived in the Muslim world in the late nineteenth century, the concept underwent modifications which made it compatible with the Islamic faith. In Iran, the result was a constitutional monarchy more in name than in practice.

By the late twentieth century, however, Islamic fundamentalists throughout the Muslim world, including Khomeini, were convinced that state constitutions were too accommodating of other faiths and were thus diluting the purity and power of the Islamic faith. Iran's new constitution as crafted by Khomeini dealt with this problem by radically breaking with all other modern constitutions. Entitled "The Fundamental Law," it is an ideological and thoroughly Islamic document based on the "Mandate of the Jurist," Khomeini's belief that a religious jurist has the right to establish the governance of a nation-state and demand allegiance of other religious jurists.

The constitution defines the purpose of the nation-state in terms of imposing the worldview of Islam, restricts the civil liberties of individuals, assigns sovereignty and legislative powers to the One God as interpreted by clerical jurists, and establishes social order based on a strict understanding of Shi'ite basic articles of faith. Islamic fundamentalist have met with varying political successes in other nations. As previously mentioned, Saudi Arabia with its Wahhabi revivalist heritage has long been ruled by a version of *sharia* law, while at the same time welcoming Western influence and the material benefits thus afforded to the ruling royal family.

In addition, Afghanistan, under Taliban rule from 1996 to 2001, was governed by a mixture of *sharia* law and local tribal customs which sought to eradicate all Western influence and enforced strict Islamic law upon Afghan society in an effort to tightly control social behaviour. Within many other countries, fundamentalist pressure on government structures has increased significantly in the decades following the 1967 Arab-Israeli War. In Pakistan in 1977 General Zia, a devout Sunni, seized control of the country and immediately invoked an Islamization program to establish Islam as the official ideology and identity of Pakistan. His larger purposes were to legitimize his military dictatorship and quell calls for democracy. In so doing, he made alliances with Sunni clerics and fundamentalist groups, including the Jama'at-i-Islami.

Although Zia sought to establish an Islamic constitution in Pakistan, he was ultimately unable to do so without destabilizing his regime, and thus settled for an informal common law system based upon Islamic law. In the 1980s, Pakistan's government encouraged the military training of seminarians ("taliban"), who in turn created an Islamic state in neighboring Afghanistan following the Soviet withdrawal from that nation. Today, Pakistan is still a harbor for Islamic fundamentalists, although the aftermath of the September 11, 2001 attacks on America's World Trade Center has led President Musharraf to increasingly crack down on Islamic fundamentalists involved in terrorism.

In Sudan, the Muslim Brotherhood has championed the imposition of *sharia* law since the country's independence in 1956. Despite independence, civil war between Muslims in the North and non-Muslims in the South raged on into the seventies. Accordingly, political upheavals and attempted coups kept the issue of *sharia* law on the back burner. By the 1970s, Hassan al-Turabi, a local Muslim Brotherhood leader and high-profile spokesperson for the fundamentalist cause, had secured a prominent role in Sudanese politics. At the same time, the long running civil war came to an end, marked by the implementation, under President Jafar al-Numayri, of the 1973 Sudanese Constitution which recognized the rights of Islam, Christianity, and traditional religions, and forbad the usage of religion as a constitutional means of limiting citizens' rights. However, ten years later Numayri did an about-face and began pursuing a policy of Islamization in an effort to co-opt the growing influence of fundamentalists.

The tactic split fundamentalists in Sudan, with many

supporting Numayri, who one year later, in 1984, proclaimed him to be the nation's *Imam* (supreme religious leader and authority). Numayri's hastily implemented Islamization program had his own version of *sharia* penal law as its centerpiece. The hybrid *sharia* law code soon became unpopular and led to his downfall in 1985. Since that time, fundamentalists have continued to play a powerful role in the government. The Sudanese legal system is a combination of English common law and Islamic law, with the later being imposed on all residents of the northern states since 1991.

In other countries, Islamic fundamentalism has been historically active, but as of yet unable to achieve significant political gain. Egypt epitomizes the difficulties that fundamentalists face in their campaign to implement their radical agenda into government structures. Despite the fact that the Muslim Brotherhood originated in Egypt over seventy years ago, only in the past decade has Egyptian fundamentalists gained enough influence in parliament to raise the issue of *sharia* law on the national level.

6

Ideology of Islamic Fundamentalist

The Western public sees religious fundamentalism chiefly through the lens of news coverage related to acts of terrorism and other sensational events. Western perceptions of fundamentalism, preoccupied with the equating of it with extremism, are thus misperceptions. True, most of the published views of fundamentalists reflect rather more a new variety of totalitarianism than an effort to "Islamize democracy." But it is deplorable to see some observers taking at face value the window dressing of eloquent Islamic fundamentalists living and acting in exile in the West. After all, no deeper understanding of Islamic fundamentalism is to be reached simply by pinpointing the anti-democratic direction of the movement. Being preoccupied with democracy is a characteristically Western way of looking at things, but in the ideology of Islamic fundamentalism—or, for that matter, in the minds of the Islamic peoples—democracy is not an important issue.

To understand the currents that *should* concern us, we need to study the ideology and major themes of Islamic fundamentalism, as it is propounded by operatives within Islam. The pivotal concept of its ideology is what the fundamentalists call *nizam*/order. Their goal is an Islamization of the political order, which is tantamount to toppling existing regimes, with the implication of de-Westernization. Thus each theme in their ideology is related to a set of dichotomies, divine order versus secular order, *nizam* Islami/Islamic system versus the secular nation-state, *shura*/consultation versus secular democracy, *shari'a*/Islamic law versus positive law or human legislation, and, above all, *hakimiyyat Allah*/God's rule versus government of the people by the people.

My focus is on the Arabic sources. This approach is justified by the fact that the Arab part of Islamic civilization is the religiopolitical center of Sunni Islam. In the West there have been great exaggerations of the impact of the Islamic Revolution in Iran on the rest of the World of Islam. These exaggerations overlook the fact that Sunni Muslims have a concept of order different from that of the Shi'i Muslims in Iran. Ideologies do not fall from heaven, and they do not stand in isolation. They are always articulations of specific historical conditions. But in arguing thus, I do not mean to suggest that ideologies are simply reflections of an objective situation. Ideologies that are based on religions as cultural systems are shaped by the realities, and they in turn contribute to shaping the reality by giving it symbolic meaning.

This was the Geertzian approach I employed in my earlier book, *Islam and the Cultural Accommodation of Social Change,* and I have kept true to it here. In studying the social context of Islamic fundamentalism I do not reduce its ideology to existing social and political structures. I am inclined rather to discover the interplay between the ideological and structural components of this context. Islam is a religious belief, not an ideology. As a Muslim I believe in Islam as a faith and honor its precepts as a source of ethics for humans and of orientation in their conduct. But this is not the way fundamentalists see Islam. Fundamentalisms, of whatever stripe, are not expressions of a renaissance of religion, but rather reflect political ideologies ostensibly drawn from religions in an effort to remake the world, thus clearly for political ends.

The true fundamentalist is basically a political man with a political outlook, and in some cases a political activist with little or no interest in religious ethics and divinities. It becomes obvious, then, that my concern here is to study Islamic fundamentalism as a political ideology, not to inquire into the religion of Islam itself. The distinction between Islam as a faith and the political ideology of Islamism as a variety of religious fundamentalism is most important to denying Islamists their claim that they are the true representatives of Islam. They are not!

The Repoliticization of Islam in Pursuit

The repoliticization of the Islamic cultural system occurring today in the shape of a political revival has been the most salient feature of public life in countries belonging to Islamic civilization. In the age of Arab liberal thought and secular nationalism, Islam was maintained as a belief and a cultural identity but was, however, depoliticized in the decoupling of concepts of political order from religious faith. Traditional Islamic political thought is based on the religious universalism of Islamic revelation, and a political interpretation of this universalism runs, of course, counter to the modern institution of the nation-state. But although the current revival of political Islam is an expression of an Islamic revolt against the prevailing international order of nation-states and its local configurations, it is *not* a revival of traditional Islamic political thought.

Islamic fundamentalists do not speak about the restoration of the traditional Islamic order of the caliphate, but rather of the *nizam Islami*/Islamic order, with clearly modern implications. Western academic literature on the phenomenon of the repoliticization of Islam can be classified in three categories:

1. Writing that deals with the phenomenon in terms of day-to-day events, its authors relying on the news coverage by the media and on other published

secondary materials in Western languages, mainly English. (There are also some books and articles in French and German.) This category can be further subdivided into (a) survey, articles and books, consisting largely of narratives of events, and (b) conceptually oriented works informed by social science theories. All of the literature in this category is hampered by its apparent failure to use primary sources. Most of these authors do not watch the phenomenon at first hand, do not read Arabic or other Middle Eastern languages, and thus fail to encounter fundamentalism on the ground.

2. Scholarly writing that deals with various movements related to political Islam, as well as writing that extends this scope to deal with the phenomenon empirically, within the framework of field work on a national level (case studies). These studies, though at times suggestive, lack the conceptual overview that would have produced a better grasp of the phenomenon. Some of the authors who have encountered political Islam on the spot, such as the French writer Olivier Roy in Afghanistan, tend to generalize from their one-country experience while lacking an appropriate conceptual framework, Any generalization from one case must be flawed, aside from the fact that the lack of an overarching concept leads to a sweeping impressionism.
3. Scholarly writing that requires the ability to read materials in Arabic and other Middle Eastern languages and to find ways of gaining access to them, requirements that are often neglected. An analysis of the writings of the current revival promises major insights, and studying political literature in its native languages is an excellent way to seek an understanding of its ideology. Aside from a handful of scholarly works on political Islam, such as those of Emmanuel Sivan, Nazih Ayubi, and Youssef M. Choueiri, we find not much of this category. Few of the authors of the large

and continually growing body of writings on political Islam published in the West over the last two decades seem to make use of primary sources.

In the following I shall be focusing on Sunni Islam and thus dealing with the literature produced by the Sunni Arab fundamentalists published in Arabic. Shi'i material is published mostly in Farsi, the dominant language of Iran. The major topic of the literature of resurgent political Islam is the Islamic system of government, *al-nizam al-Islami.* In the view of the authors of these works, all existing political systems in the Middle East, except those of Iran and Sudan, and in some cases Saudi Arabia, are un-Islamic. It is time, they infer, to return to true Islam, to the divine order established in Medina by the Prophet Muhammad himself. In so doing, they are pursuing for their prospects a decidedly backward orientation. But the choice of the neo-Arabic term *nizam* to denote the old order of the seventh century that so enthralls these authors reveals a typical confusion between the old and the new. It is therefore hardly surprising to discover in their effusions a great many projections of the present into the past.

Understandably, most of the concerns of Islamic fundamentalists are related to the current crisis situation, but they articulate them in the traditional language of Islam. Still, a closer look at their belief in the authority of scripture discloses its embedding in the modern context. Moreover, even the language used (for example, the term *nizam*) often consists of modern additions to the classical Islamic lexicon.The fundamentalists are thus not so much reviving classical Islamic concepts as they are introducing new ones that have grown out of the modern context. For fundamentalists, whatever they may claim, are not traditionalists, the much touted *nizam Islami* is something new that resembles more a religiously legitimated dictatorship or an otherwise totalitarian rule than it does the traditional caliphate.

Islamic political groups in the Arab states of the Middle East resort to Islam as a frame of reference (and a source of legitimacy and respectability) in their opposition to the nondemocratic orders of these states. They invoke the concept of *shura*/consultation, integrate it into their concept of an Islamic political system, and present it as an Islamic alternative to Western democracy. Again, we are confronted with the old religiopolitical symbols rilled with new meaning, in the Geertzian sense. As we shall see, there are just two very brief sentences in the Qur'an encouraging the Prophet Muhammad to have consultation (*shura*) with his companions, and the content of these two lines can scarcely be considered a "concept" unless radically reinterpreted—which is, in fact, what the advocates of the new political Islam do. Despite being anti-democratic by nature, the new concept of *nizam Islami* is adorned with the trappings of democracy through reference to the notion (lacking in the Qur'an) that counsel is *incumbent* on Muslim rulers. Thus our reading of the contemporary political writings of Islamic fundamentalists must focus on the related notions of the *nizam Islami* and *shura,* which fundamentalists consider central.

All Muslim fundamentalists set the implementation of the *shari'a*/Islamic law *(tatbiq al-shari'a)* as the primary condition for the realization of an Islamic system of government. Our examination of the *nizam Islami* must therefore be cognizant of the call for the implementation of *shari'a.* With its reappraisal of political Islam in the guise of current Islamic *usuliyyal* fundamentalism, contemporary Arab political thought has undergone a major change, a shift from secular to religiopolitical commitments. Even once-leading Arab Marxist authors such as the celebrated Anwar 'Abd al-Malek have suddenly discovered that the Qur'an had enjoined political practice long before Marx did, "Twelve centuries ahead of the praise of *praxis* in the Marxian 'Theses on Feuerbach' the Qur'an had urged the believers to commit themselves ... to the practice [of politics]." The ex-Marxist 'Abd al-Malek thus speaks with contempt of the authors of various secular writings, including 'Ali 'Abd al-Raziq and Sadiq Jalal al-'Azm. This shift to a religiopolitical commitment is compelling to the extent that a discussion of the major themes of the currently prevailing political writings published in Arabic will remain incomplete if the discussion fails to deal with this issue.

The publication dates of the politically salient contributions to the fundamentalist ideology in question lead us to conclude that the rise of political Islam clearly began in the Arab part of Islamic civilization; it did not take hold, as commonly believed, through the Iranian Revolution. The prominent contemporary ideologue of Islamic fundamentalism, Yusuf al-Qaradawi, published his call for *al-hall al-Islami/the* Islamic solution in the early 1970s, at a time when Khomeini's name and the ideology of Khomeinismwere completely unknown in the Arab areas of the Middle East. The first printing of the major contemporary treatise on the alleged political system of Islam, written by Muhammad Salim al-'Awwa, was published in 1975 in Cairo, without reference to Khomeini or to Iran. Only in the later editions do we find such references. For this reason, it seems justifiable to exclude the Shi'i Iranian Revolution from the arguments of this chapter and to focus on Sunni Arab Islam, without denying (or exaggerating) the later interplay between the two.

In their writings, the Islamic fundamentalists present themselves as true scripturalists, though they invoke the scriptures (wittingly or unwittingly) in a highly selective manner. In any event, I shall not restrict myself to a scriptural approach in studying the relevant writings. Instead I will offer a contextual understanding of their content, concentrating on the political structures within which Islamic fundamentalism operates. There exists no geographically isolated Islamic world, but rather a religioculturalry diverse Islamic part of our current world, addressed here as an Islamic civilization.

Ideologically, political Islam is based on the rejection of the global system of nation-states. Thus the spirit of rejection that we see set forth in the political writings of Islamic fundamentalists, even though political Islam claims a new alternative to the prevailing order, it is based rather on reviving old dreams and, hence, is primarily millenarian in character. Still, Islamic fundamentalists are not traditionalists; their ideal is the selectively perceived and arbitrarily purified state of seventh-century Islam. This primeval golden age is presented as a referent for solving the problems of the present crisis on a global basis, that is, as an alternative world order. The selectively scriptural recourse to the past is assumed to set the norms for the future of Islamic civilization. But this millenarian notion helps us little in understanding the real issues. In fact, Islamic fundamentalism addresses current issues with a new ideology. I shall spell out this contention.

7

The Context of the Fundamentalist Writings

Our context here is a global one, our time is world time, and the history involved, as affected by modernity, is global history. As earlier outlined, the Peace of Westphalia in 1648 marked the decay of the divine order and the emergence of the modern international system of secular states. In the three hundred years following the Peace of Westphalia, Europeans imposed this system of states, each enjoying internal and external sovereignty, on the rest of the world. In much of the World of Islam this sovereignty exists in only nominal form, and I have therefore coined the term "nominal nation-state." The decline of the Ottoman Empire was not the result of a "Western conspiracy against Islam," but a part of unfolding global history; it marked the end of the long historical epoch of divine orders that had reigned virtually throughout the world.

After the abolition of the caliphate in 1924 the Arabs adopted the idea of the nation as a concept for political action, but chose not to restrict it to any one of the Arab nation-states that had come to exist in reality. The Arab dream of a pan-Arab state embracing all individual Arab states remains technically feasible, and is not incompatible with the framework of international order as a system of nation-states. This was the dream that gripped the thinking of Arab nationalists and thus superseded and deferred the dream of an Islamic universalism. As we have seen, the political option of an Arab nation is consonant with a real structure, the modern, globally prevailing, international system of nation-states.

Arab nationalism, though irredentist in nature, has been imprisoned in the idea of the nation-state for the simple reason that it has aspired to the larger goal of an overarching Arab nation-state. Pan-Arab nationalism was at odds with the notion of Islamic *umma* because, on the one hand, it excluded all non-Arab Muslims (for example, those in Indonesia, the largest Islamic nation) from this entity and, on the other, because it included Arab Christians (for example, those in Lebanon and Egypt) as citizens and no longer as *dhimmi*/protected people, that is, minorities. The writings of Sati' al-Husri are a literary manifestation of this period, which began in the early 19205 and lasted until the late 1960s.

The Arab defeat in the Six-Day War of 1967 was a turning point, because the war's outcome contributed to the de-legitimization of the secular Arab regimes involved in this crushing defeat. In an authoritative book published in French, Arabic, and English, the preeminent Moroccan historian Abdallah Laroui views the historical period triggered by the Six-Day War as a period of crisis, and the crisis has not receded since, but rather has intensified. The Gulf War only complicated matters, by adding its own bitter legacy to the post-1967 Arab predicament. In an article in Arabic published in Beirut in the literary/critical journal *Mawaqif,* edited by the preeminent Arab poet Adonis, I called the process of self-chastisement in the years 1967-70 "From Self-Glorification to Self-Criticism."

Secular pan-Arab nationalism, as once reflected in the many writings of Sati' al-Husri, had to step aside to make way for political Islam. The new political pamphleteering has superseded the voluminous, hitherto prevailing writings of pan-Arabism, and reflects more recent attitudes. In one of the politically pioneering works of this new genre, the previously mentioned Egyptian Muslim Brother Yusuf al-Qaradawi declared *al-Hall al-lslami faridha wa darurah*/ The Islamic Solution as an obligation. This option provides the *"ma'alim fi/ial-tarq*/signposts" (Sayyid Qutb) on the road to the future of Islamic civilization.

In the Arab part of the Middle East, the repoliticization of Islam began as a response to the repercussions of the Six-Day War. Spillover effects soon spread far beyond the Arab core of the "abode of Islam" to its periphery. In the process, political Islam has become a global issue related, in varying degrees, to all of Islamic civilization. Again, one could question this statement by observing that Islam has always been political, even after the abolition of the caliphate in 1924. The birth of the Muslim Brotherhood movement in Egypt in 1928, as well as the emergence of Wahhabi-inspired Saudi Arabia, could be advanced as further evidence against the argument of a retreat of political Islam since the 1920s. Furthermore, one could cite the involvement of Islamic symbols in the struggle against French colonial rule in Algeria, as well as in Morocco.

In fact, secular ideologies, primarily pan-Arab nationalism, emerged in the post-World War I period as the dominant political discourse, while Islam as a political ideology, but not as a religious belief, seems to have receded ever since, at least until the early 19705. This assessment is not meant to so exaggerate the dynamics of the period that one might conclude that the political understanding of Islam had vanished altogether. Students of the contemporary history of the Middle East know that even Sherif Hussain of Mecca, the "leader" of the Arab Revolt of 1916 against the Islamic (essentially Turkish) order of the Ottoman Empire, coveted the thought of becoming the caliph of all Muslims himself. In fact, he made just such an attempt, in his abortive caliphate of 1924, shortly after the abolition of the Ottoman caliphate. Nevertheless, and notwithstanding the fact that Hassan al-Banna, the founder of the Muslim Brotherhood movement, considered the *i'adat al-khilafa al-mafqudahl* restoration of the lost caliphate to be the chief political goal of his party,political Islam had by then receded and was no longer the driving political force in the Arab part of the Middle East.

In the global context of world time those political ideologies based on the idea of a secular nation uniting the Arabs replaced the then seemingly abandoned understanding of a universal *umma* that included all Muslims. Even a leading Syrian *shari'a* scholar, Muhammad al-Mubarak, at times dean of the faculty of *shari'a* at the University of Damascus, drew a clear distinction between *al-umma al-'Arabiyya,* the uniting of both Muslim and Christian Arabs as one nation, and *al-umma al-Islamiyya,* a very loose understanding of solidarity *(al-ukhuwwa/* brotherhood) among Muslims, lacking decisive political consequences. In Arabic there exists no particular term for the secular meaning of *la nation,* as defined in the historical context of the French Revolution.

In classical Arabic and in the formative years of Islam there was a clear distinction between a *qawm,* that is, the particular tribe to which an Arab belonged, and the *umma/* community, which is the supreme frame of reference of identity for all Muslims. In modern times *la nation* has been translated into Arabic as the very term *umma,* thus confusing the religious meaning of the political community established by the Prophet Muhammad in the seventh century with the secular meaning that had unfolded in Europe in the course of the eighteenth century. "Nationalism" has been translated into Arabic as the neo-Arabic term *al-qawmiyya,* which is based on the classical Arabic term *qawm* meaning tribe, people. This translation opened the way for the polemical cry of Islamic fundamentalists that secular Arab nationalists are reverting to the pre-Islamic *jahiliyya*/age of heedlessness of tribes. Truly, the Islamic *umma* historically aimed at replacing the *qawm*/tribe in uniting all Arab tribes in one community.

In the secular literature of pan-Arab nationalism we confront chiefly projections of modern European meaning, such as that of *la nation,* into the classical Arab history and lexicon. Most of the authors of this literature trace the Arab nation back even into pre-Islamic times. The ethnic conflict between Arabs and the *mawali* (non-Arab Muslims) is being translated into a national conflict between those who want to maintain the Arab purity of Islam and those who want to welcome non-Arab elements into it. Enmity and confusion—between tribes, ethnosectarian communities, and the modern nation—have been at work among Islamists and secularists alike.

Political thought always reflects a worldview. In interpreting Islam as a cultural system along the lines of the anthropology of Clifford Geertz, I want to advance the hypothesis that Islam has always been the underlying cultural basis of the particular worldview of Muslims, and even of pan-Arab secularists. In the Middle East there has never been a process of structural and cultural changes underlying an orderly shift of the world-view from a religious to a secular one, as happened in the historical process that once unfolded in Europe. In this sense, there has never been a real societal process of secularization underpinning secular ideologies in the Middle East, not even in secular Turkey. In Turkey the state claims to be secular, but the society is not; and it cannot be described as secular in the sociological meaning of the term.

We can argue, in fact, that the continuity of the Islamic worldview, persisting even in the midst of social change, has facilitated the recent shift from secular ideologies to those of political Islam and to the worldview it reflects. In examining Islam's function as a cultural system underlying a worldview, one cannot escape the fact that secular ideologies were never able to put down strong structural roots in Islam, or to affect the prevailing worldview. Thus, secularization as a separation of religion and politics has remained a surface function. Long before the rise of Islamic fundamentalism a former sheikh of al-Azhar who received his academic education as well as his doctorate from a German university defined the worldview of Muslims as one based on a separation of the world into "the West" and the "abode of Islam." To him, the West has intruded upon the World of Islam, and in the process has provoked a deviation from Islam.

The concern of Muslims should ultimately be to return their people and their ideas and institutions to Islam. It follows, then, that the desire "to rebuild Islamic social life on the very principles of Islam" has always been a salient feature of Muslim thinking. Preoccupation with the glorious Islamic past characterizes the views of both the secularists and the fundamentalists in the Middle East. This preoccupation is a major obstacle to the unfolding of a worldview adjusted to the structure of the real, existing world of today. Muslim fundamentalists for the most part continue to be preoccupied with dichotomizing the world into an Islamic East and a Christian West, but our world can no longer be reduced to such a simplifying dualism.

Although the war in Bosnia enforced this dualistic worldview, the realities of our modern world are characterized by far more complex structures, and the preoccupation with West/Islam dualities hampers the development of insights into these structures. If one agrees with Edward Said that the "East" is a creation of the "West," then one can hardly exclude modern Arab and Islamic writers from culpability for creating a "West" that is the enemy. The alleged holistic "West" does not exist; it is a creation of Islamic thought. It seems to me fruitless to continue such a debate. Still, we do need to understand how Islamic fundamentalists deal with the issues of government, democracy, and the disruptive effects of rapid social change, for these are the dominant issues informing the present ambiance of crisis, and it is dismaying to see them debated within the framework of the "Orient/ Occident" dichotomy. I have no inclination to engage in the polemics of the debate on orientalism, but it is nonetheless appropriate and fair to concede that orientalism is not an invention of Edward Said.

The label describes a real attitude of some ethnocentric Western authors writing about the "Orient," not to mention the trappings of decades of Western cinematic melodramas. Said, however, stretches the argument too far. Those who, in his footsteps, adopt the concept simplify the issue and even reverse the idea of orientalism. A Damascene critic of Said, Sadiq Jalal al-'Azm, in a piece no less polemical than Said's *Orientalism* itself, has argued that Muslim authors *orientalize themselves* when they claim for themselves a frame of reference different from those of the rest of humanity. In al-'Azm's view, this is orientalism in reverse. While giving Said his due, I cannot overlook the trap of romanticizing manichaeism he unwittingly falls into while dealing with the Orient/Occident dualism.

Many Muslim writers argue that Islamic thought is distinct, altogether different from the analytical tools of social science. Implicitly, then, they subscribe to the idea of *homo islamicus* originally put forward by Western orientalists themselves. The program of "Islamization of knowledge" is one of the discouraging aspects of current political Islam. I argue that we Muslims, like peoples of any other civilization and their traditions, can engage in dispassionate reasoning. It is true that ostensibly neutral tools of analysis can have sensitive cultural connotations, since by necessity they originate in a specific cultural context. It is; however, wrong to infer from this acknowledgment of an existing cultural diversity the disputable generalization that there can *be* no general knowledge in these terms, owing to the lack of a universal civilization. Islamic fundamentalists insist that there is an Islamic knowledge that by its nature divorces them from the West, but surely political Islam can be understood and analyzed by thoughtful interpretation of its texts in the light of the concomitant historical context.

The literary production of Muslim authors, like that of any group embedded in a given civilization, is generated from encounters with real issues and is based on human knowledge and experience. Studying and understanding these issues in their historical context is possible even for non-Muslims. To concede the distinctive character of a culture is not tantamount to contending that these specifics can be properly understood only by members of the culture itself. All political thought reflects continuity. Topical issues relate to recent events, but their articulation often reveals far older concerns and, hence, a conspicuous historical continuity. Fundamentalist writers—like writers elsewhere—seldom embark upon truly new grounds. For the most part, they revive the discussion that arose in the aftermath of the abolition of the caliphate in 1924, though in a new language and with new concerns.

Most of the new writers find time to refer to the aforementioned book by 'Ah' 'Abd al-Raziq, *al-Islam wa usul al-hukm*/Islam and the Basis of Government, either to continue refuting and demonizing him or to set new precedents. In discussing Islam and government only a few of the adherents of political Islam insist on the restoration of the caliphate. The larger debate is on "the Islamic system of government". Most fundamentalist writers stress the political character of Islam, but no longer insist on maintaining the term "caliphate," as we shall see later. Fundamentalist thought is clearly embedded in a new context, one that differs markedly from that of classical Islam. In short, the issue of whether Islam is basically a religious belief or is, rather, a system of government manifested as an expression of a divine order—whether domestic or global in purview—situates the fault lines between secularists, liberal Muslims, and fundamentalists in the Islamic world.

The Distortion of History and Scripture

The ongoing debate on Islamic government may raise expectations that the fundamentalist approach is in fact dealing with the real problems emanating from the crisis of the nation-state. There is a need for finding an appropriate political system for the people of Islamic civilization, but in the course of reviewing the literature of Islamic fundamentalism, we find that the political thought expressed seldom goes beyond the self-congratulatory assertion that divine order in general is preferable to any secular one. In keeping with the classical tradition of Islamic thought, in which politics was inseparably linked with the *shari'a,* the political writings of Islamic fundamentalism are convictional in attitude and scriptural in method. One's first glimpse of this literature reveals that in addressing the current state of affairs it neither offers a political analysis nor shows a way out. The notion of *al-nizam al-Islami* is set forth as a conviction lying beyond evidence and the need for firm grounds.

Those who share it are viewed to be true Muslims; those who question it, whatever their sympathies are scorned as deviants of the Islamic *umma,* or even "infidels." Since the symbol of Islamic order so easily projects different patterns of meaning, it is not surprising that it is an issue in contention even among its own adherents. Islamic fundamentalists of various currents insist on the righteousness of their own views, and deny righteousness to their fellow Muslims, other fundamentalists included. Scriptural argumentations provide the logic of the debates, for only the scripture is conceded to uphold or to reject any given interpretation of the notion of an Islamic system of government.

The lessons of history, the actuality of existing political structures, and the efficacy or inefficacy of institutions do not matter as a source or defense of argument, for if their reality does not accord with the precepts invoked, then they are merely refutable deviations from true Islam. A liberal Muslim thinker, Mohammad Arkoun, recently denounced this sort of anti-intellectualism and made the point that every religion, Islam not excluded, is subject to rethinking, that is, to the lessons and forces of history. Needless to say, the response by the representatives of political Islam has been mostly hostile. Again, there is considerable historical continuity in Islamic thought, as there is in the thought of cultures elsewhere.

Most of the Arab-Islamic contributions to the debate on the *shari'a* draw upon two Islamic writings of the early twentieth century, works that are already acclaimed as classics. One is Rashid Rida's *al-Khilafah wa al-imamah al-'uzma/The Caliphate and the Great Imamate*; the second is 'Ali 'Abd al-Raziq's *al-Islam wa usul al-hukm*/Islam and the Basis of Government. In the first we encounter the idea that Islam is *din wa dawla*/unity of religion and state; in the second we learn the opposite, that although such a unity has been imputed to Islam, the notion lacks any justification in the primary sources, that is, in the Qur'an and the *Hadith.* The Muslims who stand besides Rida against 'Abd al-Raziq cannot insist that the caliphate is the only the legitimate Islamic system of government.

True, there was a protracted silence concerning the issue of Islamic government in the years preceding the reappraisal of political Islam. Anyone who follows the intellectual currents of Arabic publications is familiar with such books as Muhammad Yusuf Musa's *Nizam al-hukm fi al-Islam/ The Political System of Islam,* Muhammad Dia'ud- din al-Rayes's *al-Nazariyyat al-siyasiyya al-Islamiyya/Political Theories of Islam,* and 'Abdulhamid Mutawalli's *Mabadi' nizam al-hukm fi al-Islam/Principles of the System of Government in Islam,* none of them less than 30 years old.

This category of Islamic political writings was rare, however, before the 1970s or, at the least, was not the dominant genre in the political literature. Moreover, these writings were not generally as appealing upon publication as they have become since. But one cannot infer from their newfound following that Muslims had earlier done away with Islam, as most of the current fundamentalist writings suggest. Islam never ceased to be the major source of the Islamic world-view. It did recede, however, as a framework for the legitimation of a political order. Prior to the rise of political Islam, the dominant understanding of Islam was to be found in the authoritative textbook on Islam, *al-Islam, 'aqidah wa shari'a*/*Islam, Doctrine and Law,* by the late sheikh of al-Azhar, Mahmud Shalrut.

Shalrut argues that Islam does not restrict the meaning of *umma*/community to a specific *dawla*state, because this would lead to a "delimitation and narrowing, contradicting the universalism of Islam." Shaltut stresses the *ukhuwwa al-Islamiyya*/Islamic brotherhood. The fraternity of Muslims, which is the ethical value and the content of solidarity among Muslims, is the salient meaning of the Islamic *umma.* Fundamentalists refute this view by invoking the Islamic principle of *shura,* as a principle of Islamic government. Shaltut states unequivocally that "neither the Qur'an nor the Prophet set a specific system of *shura.*"

In other words, no less an authority than Mahmud Shaltut indirectly depoliticizes Islam while putting greater emphasis on the ethical content of *umma,* in the sense of moral fraternity, than on *dawla*/state, as an expression of a political system. In denying that the primary sources of Islam provide a "specific system of *shura,*" Shaltut clearly intends to reduce this Islamic precept to an ethical norm and virtually dismisses the notion *of hukumah Islamiyya*/ Islamic government. This term, which has been used extensively by Khomeini, conveys the same meaning as the term *hakimiyyat Allah*/God's rule preferably used by Sunni

Arab fundamentalists. To be sure, all fundamentalists subscribe to this concept of divine order. Shaltut's understanding of modern international relations, to which he adheres in this work, is also striking.

In his view, Islam is primarily a mission of peace: "If non-Muslims maintain peace, so they must be in this case, from the point of view of Islam, considered brothers to the Muslims, comprising with them humanity. Each has his own religion...." In so stating, Shaltut formulates an Islamic alternative to fundamentalism. Although his book, along with the more recent two-volume handbook by al-Azhar, *Bayan li al-nas/Declaration to Humanity*, is not a particularly enlightened contribution to an Islam quite capable of embracing the cultural accommodation of social change, it is nevertheless a significant effort to adjust the Islamic worldview to the changed conditions of our age. In reviewing the political writings of Islamic fundamentalism, we no longer encounter this notion of plurality in humanity ("each has his own religion").

Political Islam is of a completely different caliber. Those Muslims who regard their religion more as and ethical than a political context, as a source of conduct and not a system of government, are considered by fundamentalists to be "misguided Muslims," or even apostates. Thus the fundamentalists draw the conclusion that they are justified in slaying these Muslims they arbitrarily declare apostates. In a widely read popular book by two exponents of political Islam, *Asalib al-ghazu al-fikri li al-'alam al-Islami/Methods of the Intellectual Invasion of the Muslim World,* we encounter some of the new fundamentalist attitudes. The authors of this book, Jarisha and Zaibaq (professors teaching in Medina), do not exclude even 'Abduh, the foremost intellectual father of Islamic modernism, from their polemic. Muhammad 'Abduh (1849-1905) lived in Cairo and after the years of exile in Paris became Grand Mufti of Egypt in 1888. 'Abduh made an effort at a synthesis between Islam and cultural modernity.

In the view of fundamentalists 'Abduh and all Islamic reformers are themselves products of the "intellectual invasion" by the West and are therefore indicted. The edge of the polemic becomes even sharper when the authors turn to Rifa'a R. al-Tahtawi, who, in his well-known diary of his experiences as *imam*/religious and political leader to the contingent of Egyptian students in France in the 1820s, gives an enthusiastic account of Parisian life. Tahtawi viewed Europe as a model for Muslims. The fundamentalists Jarisha and Zaibaq condemn Tahtawi. For them the only adequate understanding of "true Islam" is the one that first acknowledges that "the major task of the Qur'an is to govern *[an yahkuma]*... [and] the unity of state and religion is the crucial part of this understanding, not such that religion is a partial dimension of the state, but on the contrary, such that religion is the major element of the state [*qism lahu la qasim*/a part of it, not a partner to it]".

As Jarisha and Zaibaq put it, there has been a colonial *mu'amarah*/conspiracy directed against Islam, a conspiracy that resulted in the destruction of the caliphate. The authors apparently do not consider the fact that the concept of a caliphate cannot be found in the Qur'an. True, the verb *khalafa*/to succeed does occur in several of the Qur'anic *suras* (the Qur'an is subdivided into 114 suras) but in meanings quite different from "to succeed in office." A role in this alleged conspiracy is assigned to Arab nationalism, which is seen by Jarisha and Zaibaq as a product of "missionizing crusaders." Moreover, "Arab nationalism was disseminated by the British spy Lawrence". Arab nationalists are mostly secularists, in the sense that they distinguish between a divine order and the secular nation-state. But in the view of Jarisha and Zaibaq, Arab nationalists are victims of the Jews, who are held to be the precursors in the conspiracy to separate religion from state in order "to destroy religion.... Islam, however, does not permit such a separation.

The state is in the *fiqh*/ Islamic jurisprudence of Islam

an indivisible part of the religion, so that there can be no religion without the state and vice versa." The fact that the political culture of our age is based on the nation-state denotes, for Jarisha and Zaibaq, a "return to the *jahiliyya,*" that is, to the pre-Islamic age of heedlessness. The "return to Islam" promoted by the *sahwa al-Jslamiyya/* Islamic awakening expresses an Islamic determination to overcome the setbacks suffered by Islam. The call for *al-nizam al-lslami/the* Islamic system of government is considered the major feature of this awakening, which in the view of these authors, as a return to the divine, focuses on three issues:

1. Islamic legitimacy *(al-shar'iyya al-Islamiyya);*
2. The Islamic *umma,* which supports the *shar'iyya;* and
3. The political power necessary for upholding this concern, that is, the implementation of the *shari'a.*

Quite apart from their obsession with conspiracy it is striking to see Jarisha and Zaibaq drawing on a neo-Arabic term simply translated from modern Western languages, *al-shar'iyya.* Students of Islam are familiar with the traditional Islamic concept of *al-siyasa al-shar'iyya,* in which the adjective *shar'iyya* is derived from the noun *shari'a.* The traditional concept of the classical jurist Ibn Taimiyya gives *siyasa* the meaning "the running of a state." This concept renders the state authority valid only if standing in conformity with the *shari'a.* In the language used by Jarisha and *Zaibaq* the adjective *shar'iyya* becomes a *noun* that in modern Arabic means "legitimacy." In this equation the term *shar'iyya* covers the meanings both of "legitimacy" and "s/iari'fl-based policy."

This acrobatic wordplay results in the formula *"la shar'iyya bighair shari'a"* there can be no legitimacy without implementing the *shari'a,"* which epitomizes the view that every political system of government is devoid of legitimacy if the commitment to the practice of Islamic *shari'a* is missing. This striking example reveals the fundamentalists' play of language in mixing old and new concepts, as well as introducing new meanings and simultaneously claiming both originality and authenticity. The question arises now whether the caliphate is indeed the political system our authors acclaim in their formula of *al-shar'iyya al-lslantiyya,* supported by the Muslim *umma* and upheld by the true Muslim rulers.

Jarisha and Zaibaq do not evade the question; they present their position as follows:

If political rule, first, is based on the *shari'a* of God and, second, is accepted by the Muslims, then the form matters little. We may name it *caliphate, imamate,* or we may refer to whatever names so long as the aforementioned requirements are fulfilled. If, however, these requirements are missing, then no political authority can claim to have legitimacy.... This is the true understanding of the protection of religion and of... how to refer to it as guidance for worldly affairs. In fact, this is the definition of the *caliphate,* and properly the definition of any legitimate order.

As this passage shows, the authors no longer insist in their *fetwa* on the restoration of the caliphate. Their goal is a political system based on the *shari'a* or, more properly, on their understanding of it, because, as outlined above, the *shari'a* is a post-Qur'anic construction. As most of the Islamic fundamentalists do, Jarisha and Zaibaq resort to the neo-Islamic and neo-Arabic term *al-nizam al-lslami.* They plead, too, for the absolute imposition of the Islamic *shari'a* as the incontestable framework or orientation for resolving all issues, to be applied in all times, in all places, and for all peoples. "If the *shari'a* is established in this sense and if the Islamic law is practiced under the aforementioned conditions [that is, unlimited, absolute validity], then it follows that there is an Islamic system *(nizam Islami)"*. Any other option, and especially options based on secular views, is considered contrary to the tenets of Islam. For Jarisha and Zaibaq, "Secularization is an assault *('udwari)* on Islam".

The suspension *(ta'til)* of the *shari'a* is equated with the suspension of God's will and therefore considered to be the source of all evils. As a liberal Muslim with a Middle Eastern background I agree wholeheartedly with Mark Juergensmeyer's plea that the West ought to overcome its arrogance and be more tolerant toward non-Western cultures. This must not amount, however, to consent to religious fundamentalism (or, as Juergensmeyer names it, religious nationalism). Indeed, I would not care to live in a divine order overseen by Islamic fundamentalists. When one learns of the *fetwa*/religious decree by the late Egyptian fundamentalist sheikh Muhammad al-Ghazali (died in 1996), the renowned authority on the Islamic concept of human rights, the limits of tolerance are reached. In his *fetwa* of June 1993 he declares that "every Muslim who pleads for the suspension of the *shari'a* is an apostate and can be killed.

The killing of those apostates cannot be prosecuted under Islamic law because this killing is justified." There is no justification in the Qur'an for such an entree to the slaying of fellow Muslims. There is not one revelation in the Qur'an that sanctions the killing of *murtad*/apostates. The command to slay reasoning Muslims is un-Islamic, an invention of Islamic fundamentalists. The *shari'a,* after all, is a post-Qur'anic construction. The right to view religious belief as an ethics and to refuse to permit its politicization to be part and parcel of intellectual freedom ought not to be questioned. Freedom of belief is a basic human right, and the Qur'an rigorously forbids the killing of Muslims (Qur'an-Surat *al-Nisa,* 4/92).

It is thus frightening to realize that on the authority of this *fetwa* the killing of the Egyptian essayist Faraj Fuda (in June 1992) was justified. Algerian fundamentalists, who in 1993 alone slew twelve leading Algerian intellectuals, also resort to this *fetwa* and legitimize their killing of Muslims as *shari'a*-decreed executions. Islam as a religious belief is thereby distorted, and the fundamentalists defile Islam not only by legitimizing the totalitarian rule they seek but also by silencing reasoning liberal Muslims. In the terms of scriptural fundamentalism, simply coining the formula "Rethinking Islam" puts the enlightened Algerian Muslim Mohammed Arkoun at grave risk, for fundamentalists view "rethinking" of this sort as heresy. Rethinking Islam can lead to one's being listed among those apostates to be executed. Arkoun is careful, but courageous enough to use this formula as the title of one of his important books. "Rethinking Islam" may suggest to some that *shari'a* and human rights are at odds.

An unbiased reading of the political writings of current fundamentalists leads one to conclude that we are dealing with a brand of political propaganda. The style, language, and method of argumentation of these works all reveal propagandistic tactics, not a theology or an intellectual discourse. Reasoning is for these zealots a heresy. The importance of books produced by Islamic fundamentalists' lies, of course, in their great political impact. I have encountered the cited Jarisha and Zaibaq volume throughout the Islamic world. Other, more serious works are being published to meet the increasing demand among Muslims to learn more about the caliphate as the historical form of political rule in Islam.

Among these current writings is a fairly scholarly work, based on historical sources, titled *al-Islam wa al-khilafah/Islam and the Caliphate,* by 'Ah' Husni al-Khartabuli. Although he defends the Islamic caliphate, al-Khartabuli indicates clearly that there exists no single scripture, either in the Qur'an or in the *hadith,* supporting the idea that this is the true Islamic system of government. He nevertheless insists that "despite the fact that the caliphate was abolished in Turkey, it is still divine and respected by all Muslims. Ever since its abolition Muslims have never stopped asking for its restoration." This is the only judgment related to the present that is included in this most comprehensive book, which covers the history of the caliphate from its inception after the death of the Prophet Muhammad until its abolition in 1924.

Without so much as a blush, al-Khartabuli refers to events of the tenth century, during which Muslims had simultaneously *three* caliphs, one in Baghdad, the second in Cairo, and the third in Cordoba (now Spain), *each one* claiming to be the true Islamic successor of the Prophet. Al-Khartabuli merely describes this bizarre state of affairs and restricts himself to reporting that the rule of the caliph over the two holy shrines (in Mecca and Medina) was no longer a requirement for establishing the caliphate. More outspoken is the liberal Muslim and jurist Muhammad Said al-Ashmawi in his courageous book on the Islamic caliphate, published in Cairo. Ashmawi bluntly states that neither in the Qur'an, as the Islamic revelation, nor in the sayings of the Prophet *(hadith)* does there exist a religious justification for the political order of the caliphate. "The caliphate has no Islamic grounds ... it did disservice to Islam in confusing religious belief and politics." Ashmawi is among the Muslim intellectuals in Cairo hunted for his rational arguments by fundamentalists.

Aside from these references to the debate on the caliphate we can conclude from the study of Islamic fundamentalist literature that the caliphate and its restoration are no longer pivotal issues in contemporary political Islam. The focus now is on another concept, the *nizam* Islami—the formula of the search for a divine Islamic order in the age of fundamentalism. Within Islam there is considerable dissent on the authenticity of the concept *of nizam* in Islamic sources. There are neo-Islamic advocates of an Islamic system of government based on implementing the *shari'a.* These are the fundamentalists. Then there are Muslims who believe that in Islam there exists no clear precept that might determine how a government should be assembled if it is to have an Islamic legitimacy.

And there are also Muslims to whom Islam—in the tradition of Sufism/Islamic mysticism—is a source of ethics and a way of life, not a formal system of government. Islamic Sufi-mystics believe that religious faith is spiritual and based on "love of God," not on a rigorous implementation of *shari'a*/Islamic law. In the Middle East and North Africa, the warriors of political Islam have seized the lead from these tolerant Muslims. Some bright liberal Muslim thinkers do not contest the political character of Islam.

They do, however, refuse any dogmatic solution to the crisis of the nation-state in Islamic civilization, be it purely secular *or* fundamentalist. It is unfortunate that these Islamic thinkers are such a small minority and that they are already exposed to the threat of being slain as *murtad*/apostates. It is not only Westerners who denounce this distressing intolerance in contemporary Islam. Muslim liberals do also. Must we who condemn intolerance then feel "guilty of intolerance of our own," as Juer-gensmeyer himself does for not having been perceptive enough to anticipate the anti-secular views of those who plead for a divine order?

8

Religious Fundamentalism and Terrorism

Although fundamentalism is neither new nor limited to one culture, globalized communications and recent political events have highlighted Christian and Muslim forms. Since links are often perceived between fundamentalism, extremism and terrorism, most commonly with respect to Islamic fundamentalism, it is desirable to delineate a model of fundamentalism which permits some degree of prediction as to its possible extension into political action. The term 'religious fundamentalism', it is argued here, can denote a type of worldview that can in fact be found in various religions of the world of today. Specifically, it may denote a shift in mentality from the relative harmlessness of an otherwise quaint, ultra-religious belief system to the readiness to pursue aggressively impositional, and in some cases terrorist activity. The article seeks to work out the details of these potential connections paradigmatically.

The term 'fundamentalism', broadly speaking, names today a religio-political perspective found in many if not all major religions in the contemporary world. Most disturbingly, it is associated with variant forms of religious extremism and thus religiously-oriented terrorism, in particular – though by no means exclusively – that of an Islamic ilk. Movements of a fundamentalist type are evident in Islam, certainly, but they may be found also in Christianity, in Hinduism, in Judaism and other religious communities. Contemporary fundamentalism is not the sole province of any one religion. And an upsurge in the totalising claims of fundamentalist ideologues, of whatever religion, together with the utilisation of globalized communication, transportation and related modern technologies, means that the issue of religious fundamentalism itself requires, once again, some careful attention. Although both Christianity and Islam are susceptible to imperialist impositions of one sort or another, as history only too clearly has demonstrated, it is nonetheless the case that Islamic modalities of terrorism have presently taken centre-stage in current world affairs. However, the religious fundamentalism with which Islamist extremism is associated arguably follows an identifiable paradigm that has a wider purview.

Given the pressing need to be able to identify, predict, locate and so counter any potential terrorising extremism born of certain expressions of religion, then the task of analysing the phenomenon of religious fundamentalism so as to construct a heuristic paradigm capable of providing a measure of predictability would seem both obvious and urgent. In this paper I shall explore the nature of fundamentalism as such, examine fundamentalism and also terrorism in respect to Islam, then outline a paradigm of fundamentalism that, I contend, could enable the development of a predictive capability in respect to identifying genuine possibilities for religious extremism and terrorism.

I suggest that 'religious fundamentalism' denotes a worldview-type that can be found across different religions in the world of today. Specifically, the term denotes, as I will seek to demonstrate, a paradigm that paves the way for a shift in mentality from the relative harmlessness of an otherwise quaint, ultra-conservative – or in some *apropos* sense idiosyncratic relative to an orthodox 'norm' – religious belief system; to a religiously motivated and fanatically followed engagement in aggressively impositional, even terrorising, activity. Understanding the structure, logic, and implementation of this paradigm is, I suggest, of vital importance in the endeavour to create any meaningful counter terrorist capability able to address religiously motivated and sourced terrorism.

Fundamentalism

The term 'fundamentalism' and its usage arose in a uniquely Christian context, whence it has migrated into other arenas of discourse. A series of booklets, simply titled *The Fundamentals,* was published in America early in the twentieth-century to promote the view that there is a fundamental defining and non-negotiable set of traditional Christian doctrines. As a distinctive term, 'fundamentalism' arose to refer to the generic idea proposed by the publication of the booklets. In an age where theological liberalism had been in the ascendancy, a fresh term enabled a new countering viewpoint to be identified and promoted. There was abroad the sense of needing to do battle royal for the fundamentals of the faith, and in this context the badge of fundamentalism was proudly worn. However, subsequent and wider application of the term has not been without problems and difficulties. It does not transfer well into religious contexts other than Christian, and it is imprecise enough even within the Christian camp. Nevertheless, it has gained wide coinage.

In a nutshell, 'fundamentalism' may be understood in terms of whatever it is 'against'. Often it is used as "a pejorative description for anyone who is regarded as having a closed mind with regard to a particular issue." As a subject of critical academic scrutiny, fundamentalism, in its Christian context, has been the focus of a number of notable books and studies in the closing decades of the twentieth century. This has broadened out into studies on a wide-ranging front, inclusive of both religious and political variants of fundamentalism. The five-year 'Fundamentalism Project' sponsored by the American Academy of Arts and Sciences has made a major contribution. This project commenced in 1987 and led, during the 90s, to the publication of several substantial volumes of research output. More recently there have been a number of studies where the focus has been on Islamic fundamentalism.

The result of such academic development has been, among other things, to identify a number of generic elements or dimensions of fundamentalism *per se*. For example, Martin E. Marty observed that "fundamentalisms look backward and set out to 'freeze' some moment, some event, some text or texts from the past as the perfect place in time or space from which to measure" life in the present. An imagined 'golden-age', believed to have pertained at the religion's foundation, is held up as the model and reference point for contemporary reality. In response to the critique that religion, and in particular fundamentalist religion, is but an epiphenomenon riding on what are really political ideas and actions, or that fundamentalism is really just a passing fad, such studies have only served to highlight what subsequent history and recent events underscore, that religious fundamentalism is a deeply rooted phenomenon that can give rise to, rather than itself relies upon, political acts.

One significant conclusion that arose from the Fundamentalism project was the recognition that fundamentalists "fear loss and change through whatever serves to relativize the world and their worlds. There is constant fear of pluralism, or the stranger who brings other ways which may be alluring or threatening. ... Pluralism confuses; it presents not only the threatening but also the attractive neighbour at hand, and that could lead to loss of identity in a group." Furthermore, far from being archaic and fossilized, fundamentalist movements are instead "lively, intense, creative", setting out to make a difference, indeed to change the world.

Religious fundamentalism can imply a narrow, strict and limited metaphysics and set of doctrines, which to a greater or lesser degree hardly impinge on the wider life of a society; it can mean a worldview perspective that engenders, if not demands, the advocacy of a socio-political ordering and action to achieve an intended outcome. There is nothing startlingly new about that, of course. But the key difference between religiously-driven political actions today, in contrast with any previous point in history, is the pervasive context of globalisation. Instead of localised and regional levels of action, the technology and mentality of a globalized world now allow for a degree of internationalisation of the ideologies and activities of fundamentalist movements as never before.

Fundamentalism and Islam

Bassam Tibi, an outspoken critic of much of contemporary Islam, was one of the researchers involved in the American Fundamentalism Project. Islamic fundamentalism, he says, "strongly rejects (the) spirit of religious pluralism, dismissing it as a heresy threatening the neo-absolutist claim for the dominance of political Islam throughout the world. The intellectual father of Islamic fundamentalism, Sayyid Qutb who inspired Bin Laden, was also the one who claimed an Islamic world order to replace the present one. Fundamentalism is not only an intellectual challenge; it is a challenge to security inasmuch as it proposes to topple the existing order. ... The challenge (is) a very concrete one posed and practiced by ... *jihad*-fighters willing to sacrifice their lives."

Tibi further asserts: "There is a real challenge of fundamentalism as a threat that results in creating disorder. This challenge is not only posed to the West and to its civilization, but also to decent Muslims – men and women – who suffer the intolerance and totalitarian views and practices of the Islamists". However, he views fundamentalism *per se* as primarily, if not solely, a political phenomenon that is first and foremost "an aggressive politicization of religion undertaken in the pursuit of nonreligious ends". Thus, in his view, fundamentalism is only secondly and "superficially a form of terrorism or extremism". Nevertheless he issues a salutary warning:

"In the long run the Islamic fundamentalists are far more dangerous as ideologues of power than as extremists who kill ... Fundamentalism is a *Weltanschauung*, or worldview, that seeks to establish its own order, and thus to separate the peoples of Islamic civilization from the rest of humanity while claiming for their worldview a universal standing. ... Islamic fundamentalists challenge and undermine the secular order of the body politic and aim to replace it with a divine order ... Certainly Islamic fundamentalists will not be able to impose their "order" on the world, but they *can* create *disorder*, on a vast scale."

Tibi views religious fundamentalism as a generic politicization of religion. Thus, in effect, he views fundamentalism as but one variety of a relatively new global phenomenon in international politics. He states:

"I identify religious fundamentalism not as a spiritual faith, but as a political ideology based on the politicizing of religion for sociopolitical and economic goals in the pursuit of establishing a divine order. ... this ideology is exclusive, in the sense that it attacks opposing options, primarily those secular outlooks that resist the linking of religion to politics."

For him it is a political ideology, not the religion linked with the ideology, which is the point at issue. But it is the advocated assumption of a deep dichotomy between religion and politics which is problematic for much religious fundamentalism generally, and certainly for Islamic fundamentalism. Islam, broadly speaking, has ever championed an inherent linking of religion and politics, the necessary symbiosis of Islam as religion and Islam as civilization is the default position which Tibi seems to be overlooking. Certainly, as himself a devout Muslim, Tibi is deeply concerned about the identification of Islam, *per se*, with fundamentalism, "Islam as a religion is definitely not a threat, but Islamic fundamentalism is". He is thus most concerned about the blurring of the distinction between Islam and Islamic fundamentalism in the media, "it is important to not only distinguish clearly between the two but also to make clear that the phenomenon [that is, religious fundamentalism as such] is not restricted to the Islamic world".

Tibi sees current Islamic fundamentalism as an outgrowth of tensions that hold between the secular worldview of western cultural modernity and the monotheistic worldview of Islam. It is these tensions which can become a source of international socio-political conflict. Nevertheless it is an interpretation and application of religious sources that predominate in the forming of Islamist ideologies, and Tibi acknowledges that. As he notes, "In their writings ... Islamic fundamentalists present themselves as true scripturalists, though they invoke the scriptures in a highly selective manner". Furthermore, such Muslim fundamentalists, he argues, "are not traditionalists; their ideal is the selectively perceived and arbitrarily purified state of seventh-century Islam".

That Islamic fundamentalists go beyond the Qur'an is given credence by an Egyptian example of a fundamentalist sheikh, or legal scholar, a "renowned authority on the Islamic concept of human rights" who declared in a *fatwah* of June 1993 – published in a London-based Arabic newspaper – that "every Muslim who pleads for the suspension of the *shari'a* is an apostate and can be killed. The killing of those apostates cannot be prosecuted under

Islamic law because this killing is justified". However, nowhere in the Qur'an is there support for such a *fatwah*. "The command to slay reasoning Muslims is un-Islamic, an invention of Islamic fundamentalists". Tibi's critique is trenchant and far-ranging, although he does tend to gloss the religious basis and component of Islamic fundamentalist ideology. In the end I think he provides an example of the critical scholar who yet underplays the religious dimension. I suggest it is the ideology of *religious* fundamentalism as such that needs to be addressed if there is to be any sustained successful counter to the contemporary threat of Islamist terrorism, or indeed of any terrorism that arises out of, or in conjunction with, a particular religious milieu.

Islamist Terrorism

What 9/11, the subsequent bombings in Madrid, and more recently London 7/7, have revealed is that suicide-bombing Muslims, enacting out their warped jihad, are by no means the poor, oppressed, and dispossessed of this world. Whatever their lot in life they have been well educated for the most part; they have had sufficient affluence to travel with impunity; they have had access to sophisticated technology. Indeed, in the aftermath of the London bombings there is increasing evidence of the recruitment of affluent middle class Muslims in British universities to the radical Islamist cause.

A joint Home Office and Foreign Office dossier on Young Muslims and Extremism places likely recruits in two categories, those well educated, especially in the engineering and IT (Information Technology) fields, together with those who may not be unintelligent, but who have emerged in their youth as underachievers, often having already come to the attention of authorities in relation to criminal activities.

Furthermore, the report claims that young professionals from privileged backgrounds, as well as students, "have become involved in extremist politics and even terrorism". Such young Muslim men have enjoyed all the benefits and opportunities of the contemporary globalized industrialised world. These are not the warrior peasants of old, intent on sweeping out the corrupt and decayed administrations in order to inaugurate a renewal of their society. There may have been an echo of that ancient Islamic paradigm motivating Pashtun tribesman of the Taliban. It is most certainly not the agenda of an al Qaeda terrorist cell.

Extreme actions are not being called for in the name of a societal reformation and the overthrow of evil. Rather evil is being employed for no more reason, practically speaking, than a cruelly quixotic tilting at the windmill of Western society *per se*. As Johann Hari remarked of the July 2005 London bombers, they "were not poor, they were not persecuted, they were not personally humiliated". For Hari, any explanation of their actions can only lie in "the extraordinary power of political ideas". But the political dimension is clearly embedded in the religious, as Hari implies, "With one leap of faith ... they were soldiers in the International Jihad, doing the work of Allah himself to liberate Muslim peoples across the world."

A template for this can be found in the three-way relationship between Britain, Pakistan and globalized Islamism. Muslims from England have been active in various Pakistan-based militant groups, engaged in a jihad in Kashmir, since the early 90s; the Kashmiri-focussed groups – whose jihad is against Indian occupation of Kashmir – later in the 90s established links with the Taliban in Afghanistan. Significantly, the clue to this linking is found in the shared Deobandi ideology of an "ultra-conservative strand" of Sunni Islam that in turn has links to the hard-line Wahhabi ideology emanating from Saudi Arabia. From this it is evident that some of these initially quite locally-focussed groups, in terms of the outworking of jihad, have now been linked to international terrorism jihad is thus globalized, by virtue of the logic of extending jihad beyond a local context together with applying the logic of an ultra-conservative and militant form of Islam.

Further, as the *Observer* report that discusses this development notes, modern globalized militancy works by way of "a long chain of personal and organisational associations". Thus the difficulty in identifying and locating – let alone rooting out – potential terrorist groups before they act, there are few overt institutional or structural elements whereby such potential terrorists can be identified. The implication, of course, is that the first component in any countering strategy has to be in respect to identifying, and addressing, ideological rhetoric and elements within communities from which potential terrorists are likely to come, and by which they are likely to be nourished.

The war on terror is a war of ideology; in particular, it is a war against the dominance of certain religious fundamentalisms. Of course, by virtue of being "extremists", the individuals who carry out terrorist atrocities are properly disowned by the community of faith with which they are otherwise identified. Their actions are condemned as un-Islamic, as contrary to Quranic dictate, and inimical to normative Islam. Alongside this rejection of aberrant behaviour there is also a direct and outright denial by some – possibly many – from within the Muslim community of any Islamic link to the situation in the first place. Attempts to redirect responsibility elsewhere, including claiming the attacks were the work of America or Israel, are not unknown.

Such paradoxical and absolute denial of Islamically-driven terrorism, by Muslims, is based on an ideological stance which goes, in effect, "Given that such terrorism harms Muslims and besmirches Islam, any true Muslim could not possibly commit it." This line of thought surfaced after the 9/11 attacks when a Muslim mentality of denial led to rumours of Jewish conspiracy theories as the root cause and not Islamic disaffection, let alone an Islamic ideology as such. Straws of denial and deflection are being desperately clutched at by some. As Waleed Aly remarks:

"An emotive confusion drives denial and this is demonstrated by the inconsistency of the reasoning that accompanies it. Too often, those who deny that Muslims are in any way responsible for terrorism also blame a belligerent Western foreign policy towards Muslim nations for the terrorist backlash. Such Orwellian doublethink destroys the necessary credibility to inspire honest engagement."

On the one hand there is a refusal, on ideological grounds, to believe fellow-Muslims could even commit such acts of terrorism; on the other hand Islamic extremists will target Muslim and non-Muslim alike on equally ideological grounds. One result is that the many moderate and peace-loving Muslims in western secularised communities "are just angry and tired of being held hostage by the acts of other Muslims". So what is driving contemporary globalized Islamic extremism and terrorism? Is it just a contemporary socio-political aberration in a religious guise? Are these little more than the anarchists of our age?

The joint report, referred to above, noted that among likely candidates for anarchic terrorist cells of the present-day Muslim variety are "loners" who gravitate to ethnic or religious university clubs, or the like, and who also clearly register "disillusionment with their current existence". The issue at this level is not with the clubs as such, but with the possible psychological profile of certain of their members. Neither of these variables, even taken together, would help to identify a potential suicide-bomber. However, the report goes on to identify the rhetoric of communal disillusionment as a third factor, noting in particular the oft-repeated disapproving response to the double standard attributed to "the foreign policy of western governments, in particular Britain and the US".

This may provide the prospect of a more obvious measure of discontent, except that there are many mainstream Christian Churches and their congregations which express similar critiques, cater for ethnic identities, are by definition 'religious clubs', and very often encourage 'loners' into their midst. Identifying a religious extremism inclining to criminal activity is not going to be easy. Arguably, when the matter of attending to public discourse is pressed, a potential measure of the propensity to terrorism can be identified in terms of a scrutiny of certain forms of Muslim rhetoric, namely when there is unequivocal advocacy of the view that, vis-à-vis an Islamic context, 'passive oppression' – as evidenced within the UK, for example, by a foreign policy of non-action in Kashmir or Chechnya – has been eclipsed by an intentional 'active oppression' against Muslims and Islam.

That is to say, in regards to the advocating rhetoric, military interventions in Afghanistan and Iraq, the so-called 'war on terror', or whatever else may be deemed to express 'active oppression', may be taken by Muslims as, indeed, acts perpetrated against Islam *per se*. Acts against Muslims in a specific context are interpreted as acts conducted against Islam generally and universally, thereby calling forth and legitimating, *qua* the logic and rhetoric of jihad, an aggressive Islamic response. Where such rhetoric of advocacy and argumentation is fomented there may well be a case for pre-emptive countering action on the part of the authorities concerned. The problem, of course, is that such action only reinforces the rhetoric.

It is certainly the case that Muslim tendencies to reform and modernise that emerged in the late 19th and early 20th centuries have been eclipsed, in recent decades, by the rise of Islamism, and more latterly by globalized and internationalized Islamic extremism. Islamists assert Islam as a revolutionary idea and programme with the aim of utterly destroying the social structure of the world in order to build it anew. Jihad is thus revolutionary combat in a transcendent cause. In the view of such an extremist perspective, Islam is not a matter of optional belief but is inherently a total and totalising socio-ideological system. Thus, the message of Islam is believed to have been addressed to all humankind.

For the Islamist, this means every person who believes in the message becomes, *ipso facto*, a member of the 'Islamic party' or the 'party of God', which is engaged in an inherent struggle to put in place a new civilisation explicitly based on the 'word of God'. This is the essence of the paradigm that has motivated the pattern, found throughout Islamic history, of popular overthrow of Muslim governments deemed corrupt and un-Islamic, jihad is taken up as a tool of social salvation; deep disaffection finds resolution in assertive jihadic action. Jihad is viewed as a Muslim liberation struggle to be engaged in on multiple fronts, and terrorism becomes a legitimate tool of jihad. Or so the logic, born of the rhetoric, can go and so religious terrorism derives from an ideology of religious fundamentalism.

One political correspondent, writing in the aftermath of the 2005 London bombings, seemed to get the point when he noting that, rather than taking up arms in the so-called "war against terrorism", the real issue has to do with the "battle to discredit an ideology ... it is an idea that caused the attack, and it is the idea that must be undermined". And another *Observer* report noted that authorities are intent on "examining literature for clues to the precise ideology" that may have inspired the bombers. Investigations are said to have revealed that as far back as January 2005 there was mounting concern within the young men's own Muslim communities that their hardening fundamentalist and extremist attitudes and opinions were taking them far beyond the pale of normative Islam. Indeed, they had been ostracised and told they were not welcome in certain mosques because of their advocacy of "inappropriate teachings".

Their "increasing fundamentalism" had estranged them from their own. Yet, local Muslim acquaintances could not foresee the possibility of terrorist action, suggesting that there is as yet a very real difficulty for religious people to understand the range of ideological options, and the significance of the shifts that occur in an individual's ideological stance, from within a given religion. This appears acutely the case for Muslim communities right now, but should in no way be deemed a uniquely Muslim issue.

Paradigm for terrorism

Fundamentalism is both a specifically focussed mindset and a certain kind of narrow worldview, a *modus operandi*, which can apply to just about any sphere of human activity, but especially so to religion and politics, for both are concerned with the context and aims of human existence. Fundamentalism, as a framework phenomenon that applies across more than just one religion, and which can be applied also to other non-religious spheres of human commitment and worldview, is marked, I suggest, by at least twelve key factors. Others may be adduced, but these twelve, and the way they are interconnected, need to be carefully understood. For it is these features, collectively and cumulatively that, I contend, move a fundamentalist mindset from the quirky to the critical, from atavism to aggression, from benign eccentricity to socially endangering activity. The factors comprise six sets of paired features, and it is the particular sequential combination which is important, not just the factors themselves.

Set 1 – Principal Presuppositions:

i. Perspectival Absolutism and
ii. Immediate Inerrancy

A fundamentalist perspective is inherently absolutist, all other relevant phenomena are explained on its terms or viewed in a relativising way with reference to it. Fundamentalism, as a mindset, is first and foremost a mentality that expresses the modernist project writ large, only one truth; one authority; one authentic narrative that accounts for all; one right way to be. And, of course, that way is my way, declares the fundamentalist. Further, a fundamentalist perspective deems itself privileged in respect to this absolutism, for it implies superiority of knowledge and truth. Indeed, this is inherent to holding an absolutist perspective as such. Absolutism of outlook or worldview is a mark of fundamentalism, but not of itself a signal of potential terror.

Allied to absolutism is the view that the grounding text – be it political manifesto or holy writ – is to be read as conveying an immediate truth or value, without error; that is, it is inherently or effectively inerrant. However, the assertion of the immediate inerrancy of the text – namely reading the text as being immediately applicable and providing a non-mediated access to ultimate or divine truth – in fact involves an implicit assertion that there is only one normative interpretive reading allowed, that which is undertaken through the fundamentalist's lens. Now a fundamentalist's presumption of textual immediacy and inerrancy is, of course, but one interpretive option. Nevertheless, from the fundamentalist perspective, alternative and variant interpretations are deemed inherently false or heretical, and so are rejected, there can only ever be one truth, one verity, one valid interpretation.

So far as religion is concerned, these two interconnected factors – perspectival absolutism and immediate inerrancy – comprise the foundational or principal presuppositions of a religious fundamentalism that, on their own, might simply indicate little more than one among many options for the expression of religious belief. Most often a secularist, an agnostic, or a religious liberal in the West would view these factors to be the essence of fundamentalism, an atavistic expression of religious thought, a quirky mindset, a rather odd out-of-step religious mentality; easily ignored, best avoided, of no consequence or significance in the greater scheme of things. But, I contend, this is not all there is to fundamentalism.

Set 2 – Authority Derivation:

iii. Apodicity Assumption and
iv. Narrow Narrative Indwelling

Building directly upon the preceding set, the third and fourth factors together constitute the basis of authority claimed by fundamentalism as such, namely, in the first instance, the assumption that the authority source, most usually textual (though not necessarily scriptural, together with the relevant scripture there are many other possibilities of textual sources upon which a fundamentalist might rely), is unambiguous, thus requiring no interposing hermeneutic. This is sometimes understood in terms of 'literalism', but for a fundamentalist the key issue is that the authority of the text is such that no intermediary interpretive framework is required – the text itself provides pellucid expression of truth, whether in terms of an abstract universal, or in respect to a pragmatic or programmatic articulation of the values and views espoused by the fundamentalist *as* the truth. This provides the authorisation underlying the preceding presupposition of immediate inerrancy.

Paradoxically, of course, any so-called 'literalist' reading, or regarding a text as not requiring intentional hermeneutical application, is itself a modality of interpretation, namely a fundamentalist one. It is often assumed, by a fundamentalist, that a 'direct' reading of the text can be made so as to avoid the murky waters of interpretation. That is to say, there is no need to apply any sort of intellectual critique or scrutiny of the text, meaning can be immediately read off; the text at hand is clear in its composition; the message conveyed by the text is apodictic. Not so. The fundamentalist makes the assumption that meaning and truth can be directly read without recourse to a frame of meaning that supplies a key to understanding.

Again, not so, every fundamentalist reading of the *Bible*, the *Qur'an*, or whatever, necessarily requires a prior-held framework of understanding about the nature of the text and the meanings of the key terms and concepts employed. Nevertheless, allied to the assumption of apodicity is the factor of narrow narrative indwelling. Arguably all religious people 'indwell', to a greater or lesser degree, their respective religious narrative. The life references, points of meaning, and various frameworks of understanding which inform a religious individual's existence are more often than not traceable to the paradigms, models, values etc that are given within the religious narrative – both the scriptural record as well as ancillary histories/stories and so forth – than derived from the intellectual ratiocination of doctrine and dogma.

Where the narrative base is broad, the religious life that indwells therein likewise reflects breadth. But where the base is narrow, the resultant indwelt religious life is correspondingly confined. So, I suggest, in the case of fundamentalism a distinguishing factor has to do with the narrowness of narrative indwelling that is manifest. It is, indeed, this very narrowness which often marks a fundamentalist out from the wider religious tradition and community that might otherwise be regarded as conservative, for example.

Set 3 – Contextual Scope:

v. Ideological Exclusivism and

vi. Polity Inclusivism

Fundamentalism's third set includes two factors which, in their apparent paradoxical juxtaposition, yield the scope of the context of fundamentalism. The first is ideological exclusivism wherein, because there is only one reading, only one interpretation, of the grounding text allowed, the ideological view expressed therein, or built thereon, is inevitably an exclusive one. No competing or variant ideological view is granted credibility. A fundamentalist perspective will exclude, virtually automatically, anything that relative to it appears 'liberal', that is, that admits of, for example, any limitation, provisionality, otherness, openness or change. Religious fundamentalism excludes religious liberalism. Similarly, secular fundamentalism often excludes religion *per se* on the same sorts of grounds. Ideological exclusivism works in multiple directions.

But alongside this exclusivity there may be discerned, somewhat paradoxically, as a sixth factor to fundamentalism, a form of inclusion, namely polity inclusion. This refers to the propensity to include, in respect to considerations of the policies and praxis of social organisation, all others that fall within the fundamentalist's frame of reference or worldview understanding. This may still appear innocuous, especially if the fundamentalists concerned are a minor or marginalised group in terms of the wider society in which they exist, or where such an inclusivist stance finds a more benign setting within a normative or orthodox religious tradition.

Nevertheless, in terms of the paradigm analysis I am here pursuing, the fundamentalist for whom polity inclusiveness is a primary element is now poised to become activist – to act on this inclusivism in terms of polity, whether covertly (as in the Church of Jesus Christ of Latter Day Saints vicariously baptising the dead) or overtly (as in the Taliban's insistence that everyone in Afghanistan live according to their application Islam, and variations on this theme found currently in parts of Pakistan and Nigeria). So, the apparent paradox of fundamentalism evincing both exclusivism and inclusivism as two of its core features is resolved.

Excluding all other ideological variants and perspectives necessarily implies the wholesale inclusion of a society in terms of the outworking of polity considerations. Thus, for example, the fundamentalism of a resurgent Islamist perspective naturally insists not just that all Muslims should live according to Islamic Law, but that all members of the society in question, irrespective of religion, should likewise submit to this Law Code – understood, of course, to transcend human values and codes by virtue of being "God's law". The imperative force of this element of fundamentalism means that all are expected automatically to submit – or be made so to do. We hear of this call being made by activists from time to time in different parts of the Islamic world; we may find some variant expressions of it closer to home, if only albeit wistfully, or merely in principle, entertained.

Set 4 – Implicit Verification:

vii. Narrative Correlation and

viii. Rhetorical Corroboration

Principal presuppositions granted, the derivation of authority established, and the contextual scope adumbrated, the evolving fundamentalist perspective begins now to move from a variant conservative expression of a religious worldview to a more intentional advocacy of religious outlook as being, *par excellence,* the expression of authenticity and truth applicable for all. This comes about, initially, with the deepening of the correlation between the religious narrative espoused and the reality, or *sitz-im-leben,* of the religious community concerned. Any phenomenology of religion will be able to articulate some such measure of narrative correlation as an otherwise quite normal feature of religion as such. That is to say, normatively speaking a religion will proffer some degree of correlation between its narrative and the 'real world' in which the followers of the religion live – otherwise religion would reduce to a simple and obvious fairy-tale superimposed upon the 'real' world, or set aside from it.

However, a distinction can be made between the broader traditions of a religion whose narrative correlation will be relatively loose, flexible or at least provisional, and the fundamentalist whose degree of correlation will be that much greater and intense. Indeed this factor sharpens – and is prefaced by – the elements of absolutism and inerrancy as adumbrated above. For a fundamentalist the correlation will be such as to yield an unambiguous outcome – America *is* the Great Satan, ontologically, for example – whereas, for a non-fundamentalist critical of the West, America may be deemed or judged satanic in a more general way. The difference is one of the supposed degrees of correlation between the religious narrative and the external realities of the world in which the fundamentalist lives.

Allied, clearly, to the factor of narrative correlation is that of rhetorical corroboration. Here the discourse of fundamentalism can be readily tested. For in the articulation of narrative correlation there is likely to found a corresponding intensification of a corroborating rhetoric that situates, endorses, and justifies the fundamentalist perspective vis-à-vis the judgements and assessments made about the external world in terms of narrative correlation. Rhetoric will be sharp and self-affirming; judgements will be clear and reflective of both the correlation factor as well as the corroboration factor. Thus the perspective of the fundamentalist derives implicit verification and the scene is set for the next step, namely the application of the values espoused from out of the fundamentalist's narrative.

Set 5 – Value Application:

ix. *Otherness Negated*

x. *Self-Superiority Asserted*

At this stage in the development of a fundamentalist's outlook the sense of self-affirmation and confidence is such that the values of fundamentalism are actively and intentionally applied. And these values are primarily two, the negation of otherness or alterity *per se,* and the corresponding assertion of self-superiority over all opponents, real and putative. The negation of otherness is perhaps critical at this juncture for the scene set by the third set of factors – contextualising exclusivism and inclusivism – now emerge into a devaluing and dismissal of the 'other', whether in terms of rival community or competing alterities, ideological or otherwise. Indeed, such alterities may be – and in fact often are – demonised. The religiously 'other' on this view is often cast as 'satanic', or at least seriously and significantly labelled as a hostile opponent, and so hostilely regarded.

In the process of negating the other, the self is asserted as inherently superior. My God is greater than your god. My Truth reigns over your ignorance. The authenticity of my faith contrasts with the feeble delusion you entertain. My laws express the divine reality directly which is infinitely superior to the laws which derive merely from human ideas. The salvation offered by my faith is the real thing by contrast to the lost way that you proclaim. And so we might go on. However it is expressed or referenced, it will be clear enough that the fundamentalist is applying the key value set of negativity to 'otherness' and a corresponding assertion of self-superiority. The scene is now well set for the sixth and final set of factors I have analysed as the components of the paradigm of fundamentalism – the rendering of an explicit justification not just for a viewpoint but also for actions premised on that viewpoint.

Set 6 – Explicit Justification:

xi. Sanctioned Imposition

xii. Legitimated Extremism

It should be clear that, once the preceding sets of factors are in operation, it is but a short step to the final two, which denote the expression of fundamentalism in some form of direct socio-political action. For the eleventh factor sees the very imposition of the fundamentalist's views and polity as, in fact, sanctioned by a higher or greater authority – whether that authority is conceived in terms of deity or the dynamics of historical necessity, or whatever. This reference transcends the local, particular, ordinary taken-for-granted freedoms of everyday life with the requirement to be, live and act, in accord with the fundamentalist's ideological dictates.

The sanctioning of the imposition of the fundamentalist's programme leads naturally to the twelfth and final factor of this analysis, extremist action is now legitimated. Once there is in place a sense of transcendent sanction for programmatic action, the way to the legitimising of extreme behaviours in order to achieve the requisite outcomes, is eased. Japanese *kamikaze* pilots and Palestinian suicide bombers are two examples – now 'classical' in terms of recent history – of the outworking of the features of fundamentalism that culminate in extreme actions. More complexly, as we have recently seen in Afghanistan, not only was it the case that all good Muslims ought to submit naturally to the *Shari'a,* according to the fundamentalist ideals of the Taliban, but indeed all of society should be made to submit, like it or not, for impositional submission is an inherent element of Islamic extremism.

Submission to the dictates of the fundamentalist is at this juncture a matter of necessary imposition, as Afghani women found to their cost, for example. And the alternative to even an involuntary submission is outright destruction, hence, from the Taliban's fundamentalist perspective, the Buddha 'idols' had to be destroyed. How else does the fundamentalist ensure that the imposition that has been sanctioned can actually be effected? Sanctioned imposition and legitimated extremism are the two sides of the one coin in the currency of terror. Fundamentalism is not simply a religious or political option in terms of belief perspective. It is a package-deal phenomenon marked by a sequence of factors whose cumulative impact can be devastating.

The Taliban, to return to this example of extreme

Islamist fundamentalism, took an absolutist, inerrant and exclusivist line with respect to religious identity and behaviour, which was extended to include all who were within their purview – namely, the inhabitants of Afghanistan. Actions taken to effect their aims were deemed sanctioned by the highest authority – *Allah* – and their extreme measures were in consequence deemed legitimated. Thus no opposition was brooked; all had to submit and obey, or face the consequences. Whether political or religious, of local or global scope, fundamentalism is a phenomenon to be seriously reckoned with. Religious fundamentalism, in the form of contemporary Islamism, is the seedbed of Islamic extremism and terrorism.

To the extent my analysis of the paradigm of religious fundamentalism *per se* is in any way apposite and accurate, and to the extent that empirical evidence – for example from speeches, pamphlets etc. – can be adduced, from any given situation, such that there is a clear correlation with the above paradigmatic factors, then I suggest that the analysis provides a basis, at least, for an empirical measure for the detection, and so hopefully countering, extremist religious fundamentalism – Islamic as well as any other – likely to lead to terrorist activity. Furthermore, and perhaps more significantly in the long run, such a paradigm analysis may assist in the task of tackling the ideology of Islamist extremism head-on. A war on terror is inherently unwinable as a military exercise. It requires a change in mindset, in worldview, brought about by a shift in religious ideology, if the likelihood of terrorism emerging from within any religious community is to be successfully countered. Unmasking the underlying ideological framework of an extreme religious fundamentalism is the first step in formulating a countering ideology; developing it is a demanding challenge of interreligious and intercultural dialogical engagement.

9

Faces of Political Islam Today

Islamic Fundamentalism, diverse political and social movements in Muslim countries of North Africa, the Middle East, and South Asia that have as their goal the creation of more Islamically oriented states and societies based on the principles and values of Islam. For many people in the West, the term "Islamic fundamentalism" evokes images of hostage crises, embassies under siege, hijackings, and suicide bombers. But these images hardly present a comprehensive picture. While some Islamic militants try to reach their goals through violence, the majority of Islamic activists work within mainstream society, participating in the electoral process.

The ranks of Islamic fundamentalists include members of non-governmental Muslim organizations that provide much-needed services to the poor through Islamic schools, medical clinics, social welfare agencies, and other institutions. At the fringes are extremist groups like the al-Qaeda network of Saudi-born millionaire Osama bin Laden that engage in a global war of terrorism. The reassertion of Islam and Islamic values in Muslim politics and society over the past 30 years is often referred to in the West as the rise of Islamic fundamentalism.

However, the word *fundamentalism*, which originated in Christianity, can be misleading when it is used to describe

Islam or Muslim countries. The conservative monarchy of Saudi Arabia, the radical socialist state of Libya, and clerically governed Iran have all been described as "fundamentalist," but this description fails to take into account vast differences in their governments and policies. Political analysts prefer to use the expressions "political Islam" or "Islamism" when discussing Islam's many-faceted roles in current social and political movements.

Islam and Politics

Like Judaism and Christianity, Islam originated in the Middle East. Adherents of all three religions are considered to be the children of Abraham. Muslims believe that God (Allah in Arabic) sent his revelation first to Moses (through the Hebrew Scriptures, the Torah), then to Jesus (through the Gospels of the Christian Bible), and finally to Muhammad (through the Islamic scriptures, the Qur'an). Islam is based on the Qur'an and the example of the prophet Muhammad, who Muslims believe is the last of God's prophets.

Islam's involvement with politics dates back to its beginnings with the founding of a community-state in Medina by Muhammad in the 7th century AD. Under the political leadership of Muhammad and his successors known as the caliphs. Islam today claims more than 1.3 billion followers, more than any religion except Christianity. Islam has exercised considerable political and social influence throughout its history. Early rulers in the Middle East and elsewhere claimed legitimacy for their authority in the name of Islam, and Islamic teachings gave structure to almost every facet of society. But these early Muslim states and empires were not theocracies—that is, governments ruled by religious leaders or clergy—until the creation of the Islamic Republic of Iran in 1979.

The Resurgence of Political Islam

The causes of Islam's resurgence vary by country and

region, but there are several common threads. Among these is a widespread feeling of failure and loss of self-esteem in many Muslim societies. Most Middle Eastern and North African countries achieved independence from colonial rule by the mid-20th century, but the expectations that accompanied independence were shattered by failed political systems and economies and the negative effects of modernization. Characterizing many of the newly independent Muslim nations were autocratic leaders, repressive governments, overcrowded cities with insufficient social support systems, high unemployment rates, government corruption, and a growing gap between rich and poor.

Many Muslims blamed Western models of political and economic development for these failures. Once enthusiastically pursued as symbols of modernity, these models increasingly came under criticism. Modernization, a process of Westernization and secularization of society, was seen as responsible for an excessive dependence on the West; for a weakening of traditional family, religious, and social values; and for a loss of identity that contributed to the breakdown of Muslim society. Consequently, many countries became disillusioned with the West, and in particular with the United States. United States support for authoritarian Muslim rulers such as Iran's Mohammad Reza Shah Pahlavi, as well as what was seen as America's uncritical support for Israel, strengthened anti-Western feelings.

Israel's crushing victory over its Muslim neighbors in the 1967 Six-Day War became a symbol of this sense of failure. After defeating the combined forces of several Arab nations, Israel seized conquered territory from Egypt, Syria, and Jordan. The loss of Jerusalem, the third holiest city of Islam, was particularly devastating to Muslims around the world. The Islamic revival has affected both the private and public lives of Muslims. Many Muslims have become more religiously observant, attending mosque, fasting, wearing Islamic dress, emphasizing family values, and abstaining from alcohol and gambling. Publicly, the revival has manifested itself in the form of Islamic banks, religious programming in the media, a proliferation of religious literature, and the emergence of new Islamic associations dedicated to political and social reform.

As Islamic symbols, slogans, ideology, and organizations became prominent fixtures in Muslim politics in the 1970s and 1980s, Egypt's Anwar al-Sadat, Libya's Muammar Qaddafi, Pakistan's General Muhammad Zia ulHaq, and other government leaders appealed to Islam in order to enhance their legitimacy and authority and to mobilize popular support. Movements in opposition to the government in Afghanistan, Egypt, Iran, Saudi Arabia, and other countries did the same. The most successful Islamic opposition movement culminated in the establishment of the Islamic Republic of Iran in 1979. Throughout the 1980s, Iran inspired antigovernment protests in Kuwait and Bahrain, and helped create Islamic militias, such as Lebanon's Hezbollah (Party of God) and Islamic Jihad, both of which were involved in hijackings and hostage-takings.

These acts, combined with the 1981 assassination of Egypt's president Sadat by religious extremists, contributed to the image of a monolithic radical Islamic "fundamentalist" threat to governments in the Muslim world and the West. Distinguishing between moderate Islamic groups that participate within society and violent revolutionaries is critical to understanding the resurgence of Islam. Many opponents of political Islam have charged that all Islamic movements are extremist groups that seek to "hijack democracy" and manipulate the political system in order to gain power and impose their will. Some experts argue that this type of reaction contributes to the radicalization of moderate Islamists.

Beliefs behind Political Islam

A number of beliefs and assumptions lie at the heart of the Islamic political revival. The first of these is that the

Muslim world is in a state of decline, and the cause of this decline is departure from the straight path of Islam. The cure, therefore, is a return to Islam in personal and public life, which will ensure the restoration of Islamic identity, values, and power. Moreover, Islam is a total or comprehensive way of life as stipulated in the Qur'an, mirrored in the example of Muhammad and the first Muslim community-state organized by Muhammad at Medina, and embodied in the comprehensive nature of the Sharia (Islamic law). Thus, the renewal and revitalization of Muslim governments and societies require the restoration or reimplementation of Islamic law, which provides the blueprint for an Islamically guided and socially just state and society.

Although political Islam condemns the Westernization and secularization of society, it does not condemn modernization as such. Science and technology are accepted, but the pace, direction, and extents of change are to be subordinated to Islamic belief and values in order to guard against the penetration of and excessive dependence on Western values.

Beliefs of the Radical Minority

While the majority of Islamic activists seek to work within the system and bring about change from within society, a relatively small but significant radical extremist minority believe they have a mandate from God to carry out God's will. This extremist minority further believes that because the rulers in the Muslim world are authoritarian and anti-Islamic, violent change is necessary. They seek to topple governments, seize power, and impose their vision or interpretation of Islam upon society. Radical Islamic movements often operate on the assumption that Islam and the West are locked in an ongoing battle that reaches back to the early days of Islam; a battle that has been heavily influenced by the legacy of the Crusades and European colonialism, and that today is the product of a Judeo-Christian conspiracy.

This conspiracy, they believe, is the result of superpower neocolonialism and the power of Zionism (support for a Jewish nation, now the state of Israel). These radical movements blame the West (Britain, France, and especially the United States) for its support of un-Islamic or unjust regimes and biased support for Israel in the face of the displacement of the Palestinian people. Thus, violence against such governments and their representatives as well as Western multinationals is regarded as legitimate self-defense. Islamic radicals also believe that Islam is not simply an ideological alternative for Muslim societies but a theological and political imperative. Because it is God's command, implementation must be immediate, not gradual, and the obligation to implement is incumbent on all true Muslims. Therefore, those who hesitate, remain apolitical, or resist—individuals and governments—are no longer to be regarded as Muslims. They are atheists or unbelievers, enemies of God, against whom all true Muslims must wage holy war in the form of *jihad*.

Faces of Political Islam Today

In the early 21st century, Islam remains a major presence and political force throughout the Muslim world. The question is not whether Islam has a place and role in society, but how best for it to assume that role. While some Muslims wish to pursue a more secular path, others call for a more visible role of Islam in public life. The majority of Islamic activists and movements function and participate within society. A distinct minority are radical extremists who attempt to destabilize or overthrow governments and commit acts of violence and terrorism within their countries.

During the late 1980s and the 1990s Islamic political organizations began to participate in elections, when allowed, and to provide much-needed educational and social services in a number of countries. Headed by educated laity rather than the clergy, these Islamic organizations attracted a broad spectrum of members, from professionals and technocrats to the uneducated and poor. Candidates with an Islamic orientation were elected to high office in several countries. In Turkey, the leader of the Islamist Welfare Party held the office of prime minister from 1996 to 1997. In Malaysia, Anwar Ibrahim, a founder of the Malaysian Islamic Youth Movement (ABIM), served as deputy prime minister from 1993 until his dismissal in a power struggle in 1998.

In the first democratic elections in Indonesia, Abdurrahman Wahid, leader of perhaps the largest Islamic movement, the Nahdlatul Ulama, was elected president in 1999. But popular support for him eroded as Indonesia's economic problems worsened. Wahid was removed from office in 2001 after the national legislature unanimously voted to impeach him and replace him with the vice president, Megawati Sukarnoputri. Although the primary catalysts and concerns of most Islamic movements have been domestic or national, international issues also have shaped Muslim politics. Among the more influential issues have been Palestinian-Israeli conflict and Israel's occupation of East Jerusalem; the Soviet occupation of Afghanistan during the 1980s; the devastating impact of United Nations (UN) sanctions against Iraq on hundreds of thousands of Iraqi civilians, especially children, following the Persian Gulf War (1991); forceful efforts to suppress Muslims in Bosnia, Chechnya, and Kashmîr; and the U.S.-British invasion and occupation of Iraq, beginning in 2003.

In addition, countries such as Iran, Libya, and Saudi Arabia have sought to extend their influence internationally by supporting government Islamization programs as well as Islamist movements elsewhere. A review of the current situation in key areas of North Africa, the Middle East, and Southwestern Asia indicates the directions and diverse forms that Muslim politics has taken during recent decades.

Tunisia

Until the late 1980s analysts believed that North Africa, like Turkey, was beyond the reach of any serious challenge from Islamic activism. Tunisia had had one-man rule after gaining independence from France in 1957; Habib Bourguiba served as the country's president from 1957 to 1987. In 1987 Tunisia's prime minister Zine al-Abidine Ben Ali seized power from Bourguiba, who had been declared senile. Ben Ali, like Bourguiba, insisted on taking a tough stance against Islamists.

Ben Ali promised democratization and held parliamentary elections in 1989. Islamic candidates won 14.5 percent of the vote nationwide and a stunning 30 percent in several cities. The Tunisian government responded by suppressing the most effective Islamic opposition movement, Ennahda, through widespread arrests and trials held before specially created military courts. International human rights organizations strongly criticized these repressive actions. The government's brief flirtation with democratization came to an end as President Ben Ali in 1994 and 1999 won reelection by 99 percent of the vote. Tunisia's constitution was amended in 2002 to enable Ben Ali to seek a fourth term in 2004 and a fifth term in 2009. Ben Ali was reelected in 2004 with more than 90 percent of the vote, after the opposition withdrew from the elections so as not to legitimize "a one-party state with a facade of democracy."

Algeria

Whereas the Tunisian government decapitated the Islamic movement, driving its leaders into exile or underground, in Algeria the military set in motion an escalating spiral of indiscriminate violence and counterviolence. Under its constitution Algeria had single-party rule by the National Liberation Front (Front de Libération Nationale, FLN), the group that won Algeria's independence from France in 1962. A revised constitution in 1989 permitted other political parties to challenge the FLN. That year the Islamic Salvation Front (FIS) became North Africa's first legal Islamic political party.

Led by a university professor, Shaykh Ali Abbasi al-Madani, the FIS flourished as the FLN-led government failed to resolve Algeria's social and economic problems. Through mosques and an effective social welfare network, the FIS built a national organization and emerged as the strongest opposition party. Substantial support for FIS came from the unemployed, at a time when Algeria's unemployment rate had surpassed 30 percent, and from socially marginalized youths. But FIS supporters also included small-business owners and prosperous merchants, civil servants, university professors, physicians, lawyers, and other professionals

In 1990 Algeria held local elections, its first multiparty election since independence. The FIS captured 55 percent of the vote, and it scored an even more surprising victory in 1992 in the first round of parliamentary elections, winning 188 seats, and appeared to be on its way to winning an absolute majority in the second round. As Islamists celebrated the first round of elections, the Algerian military intervened, canceled elections, and forced the resignation of Algeria's president. The military arrested more FIS leaders, outlawed the FIS, seized FIS assets, and imprisoned more than 10,000 Algerians in desert camps.

These actions led to a protracted civil war in which the majority of Algerians found themselves caught between extremist factions. On one side were hardline military and security forces whose only strategy was the eradication of Islamism; on the other, the equally uncompromising radical Armed Islamic Group. Brutality and bloodshed, which claimed the lives of some 150,000 Algerians, continued into the late 1990s and early 2000s. The FIS was excluded from the 1997 elections for the National Assembly (lower house of the Algerian legislature), but two other Islamically oriented parties together won 107 of the 380 seats. Presidential elections in 1999 were flawed by the last-minute withdrawal of all six opposition candidates, who charged that the military had rigged the elections.

Abdelaziz Bouteflika, elected president in 1999 and reelected in 2004, brought relative stability to Algeria by releasing imprisoned opposition leaders and granting amnesty to Islamist rebels. In 2005 Algerians approved by referendum the president's Charter on Peace and National Reconciliation, which closed the chapter on a decade of violence. It pardoned Islamist militants on the run or in prison as long as they renounce violence, but it also protected Algeria's army and security forces from bearing responsibility for the thousands of people who "disappeared" after being arrested. A series of terrorist bombings in late 2006 and early 2007 dispelled Algerians' hopes that the violence had finally ended. A new group claiming to represent al-Qaeda in northern Africa took responsibility for the bombings and hinted that it would attack again.

Morocco

A constitutional monarchy, Morocco has been ruled by the same family since its independence in 1956. Mohammed VI succeeded his father, Hassan II, as king in 1999. Mohammed VI was hailed as a reformer and pushed through reforms in family law, economic liberalization, and politics. Morocco's parliamentary elections in 2002 were billed as Morocco's first freely contested elections since the country's independence. The Islamist Justice and Development Party (PJD) tripled its representation in parliament from 14 seats to 42 seats after securing 13 percent of the vote.

In 2003 a series of suicide bomb attacks in Casablanca killed 41 people and left more than 100 others injured. The

PJD kept a low profile afterward, fearing the government would use the attacks as a pretext to crack down on the party. Although the PJD claimed not to be a religious party, it was the only legal Islamic party in Morocco. The Islamist movement in Morocco also comprises unauthorized Islamic associations and numerous underground groups, including the Salafia Jihadia, which was blamed for the Casablanca bombings.

Egypt

Political Islam in Egyptian society includes a spectrum of organizations, from radical and violent to mainstream and nonviolent. The Muslim Brotherhood gained strength during the 1970s under Egypt's president Anwar Sadat and began participating in the political process during the 1980s under his successor, Hosni Mubarak. By the 1980s the Islamist movement had split into those who advocated the violent overthrow of the government in order to create an Islamic state and those who believed in peaceful, grassroots organizing as the most effective way to establish an Islamic society. The Muslim Brotherhood joined the latter, renouncing violence and focusing their efforts on organizing among the poor.

Radical Islamic organizations, such as Islamic Jihad and the Islamic Group (al-Gama'a al-Islamiyya), turned to violence in the 1990s, attacking government officials, institutions, fellow Muslims, Christians, and foreign tourists. Their goal was to destabilize and overthrow the Egyptian government. The Mubarak government launched a counteroffensive against the radical groups, imprisoning more than 20,000 Islamists, many of them without charge. Military courts not subject to law were created, and laws were enacted to restrict freedom of the press, take control of mosques, and prevent elected Islamists from heading professional associations.

The slaughter of 58 foreign tourists at the historic town of Luxor in 1997 seemed to indicate the powerlessness of the government. By 2000, however, the Mubarak government had gained the upper hand and weakened the radical movements. Despite the government's apparent success in containing Islamic radicalism, Egyptian society has become more Islamized by moderate Islamists at the grassroots level. Young, university-educated professionals preach to middle- and upper-class audiences. Physicians, journalists, lawyers, and political scientists—male and female—speak out and write on issues of Islamic reform, such as *pluralism* (different beliefs) within Islam, women's rights, and social justice for the poor. Islamic schools, clinics, hospitals, and social services, as well as Islamic banks and publishing houses, offer an alternative set of institutions and an indirect indictment of the government's inability to meet peoples' needs.

Elections in 2000 were the first to be supervised by Egypt's independent judiciary and thus free of the ballot tampering that characterized previous elections. Although the Muslim Brotherhood was banned from participating as a legal party, its members, running independently or with other parties, won 17 of the 444 contested seats in the legislature. Egypt held its first-ever presidential election with multiple candidates in 2005, a sign of short-lived optimism that the country might be heading toward full democratic reform. Mubarak won a fifth six-year term as Egypt's president. He had promised sweeping reforms if he won, including repeal of emergency laws that allow for arbitrary arrest and have been in place since Mubarak came to power in 1981.

Instead, the government extended Egypt's emergency laws for two more years. Furthermore, Mubarak's closest challenger in the elections, Ayman Nour, the leader of the liberal Al-Ghad party, was thrown into jail, despite doctors' pleas that he was dangerously ill. In subsequent parliamentary elections in 2005, the Muslim Brotherhood—outlawed since 1954—won an unprecedented 88 seats in parliament (one-fifth of the seats), its largest gain since participating in the political process. However, the Brotherhood's candidates had to run as independents because of the party's illegal status. In recent years, its members have been targeted by the state security services, arrested, and sometimes tortured. Islamist leaders claim that the arrests were motivated by the government's desire to curb opposition in parliamentary elections in 2007. Many of those arrested were likely contenders in the elections, according to the Brotherhood's leader.

Iran

In 1979 Ayatollah Ruhollah Khomeini, an aging, white-bearded Muslim cleric, came to power in Iran, having toppled Mohammad Reza Shah Pahlavi, a modern ruler and close ally of the United States. The Iranian revolution was the product of a long, slow buildup of opposition to the shah, who came to power in 1941. In 1953 the shah was forced to flee the country after a failed coup by supporters of Iran's Prime Minister, Mohammad Mosaddeq, whose efforts to nationalize Iran's oil industry angered Great Britain. Fearing that Iran might develop close ties with the Soviet Union as the Cold War got under way, the U.S. Central Intelligence Agency (CIA) spearheaded another coup after the original failed and the shah was reinstated within a week. The shah maintained a close relationship with the United States and Europe afterward.

During the 1960s and 1970s, the shah used his country's enormous oil revenues to finance a modernization program. But the reforms tended to benefit urban areas and the educated elite rather than Iran's thousands of rural villages. Opponents warned that the shah's uncritical economic, military, and cultural dependence on the West, referred to as "Westoxification," threatened Iranian identity, autonomy, and culture. The Iranian revolution (1978-1979) was supported by a broad-based alliance of religious and political opponents, mobilized under the umbrella of Shia Islam, the dominant form of Islam in Iran.

An existing network of clergy, mosques, and seminaries in every city, town, and village provided necessary organization and a means for communication and mobilization of the people. Although the government had banned political meetings, it could not close the mosques, where Iranians heard sermons denouncing injustice and oppression. Khomeini, exiled in 1964 for criticizing the shah, became a symbol of the opposition. As the shah's military and security forces responded with increased ferocity against opponents, the shah's unyielding stance transformed his opponents into revolutionaries. As a stunned world looked on, the shah's government fell. Khomeini returned from exile, and the Islamic Republic of Iran was born.

Although many Iranians expected the clergy would return to their mosques and seminaries soon after the revolution, Iran became a clergy-governed state within a year. Khomeini sat at the apex of power and served as the final authority on all domestic and international matters. He silenced all effective opposition, secular and religious, and many Iranians fled the country. After Khomeini's death in 1989, Iran witnessed an expansion of political participation and dissent. Public discussion and debate became more open, and the number of independent newspapers, magazines, and journals grew significantly. But perhaps the most stunning example of increased moderation and pluralism in Iran was the victory of Muslim cleric Mohammed Khatami in Iran's 1997 presidential election.

Widely seen as moderate and progressive, Khatami pursued two major policies, creating a more open and tolerant society at home and promoting dialogue with the West abroad. In 1998 Khatami proposed cultural exchanges with the United States as a means of breaking down the "wall of mistrust" between the two countries. As a result, Iran and the United States embarked on more open communication and exchange.

In its third decade, the Islamic Republic of Iran was locked in a struggle to redefine its political and economic future at home and abroad. The 2004 legislative elections marked a defeat for Khatami's reformist movement. Since then, the Majlis (legislative assembly) has been dominated by a conservative coalition, chiefly the Developers of Islamic Iran. That alliance was made up of the "second generation" of the Islamic revolution—men and women who had been in their 20s and 30s when Khomeini came to power and who defended the values of Ayatollah Seyed Ali Khamenei, Iran's supreme spiritual leader.

In the 2005 presidential elections, Mahmoud Ahmadinejad, a Khamenei loyalist, was elected with the backing of the Developers of Islamic Iran, his main political base. Domestic supporters and critics alike soon became weary of Ahmadinejad's fiery rhetoric, which placed Iran under the threat of a military attack by the United States. Some Iranians blamed Ahmadinejad's provocative statements for the UN's passage of economic sanctions against Iran late in 2006. Iran also rejected UN demands to halt its program to develop nuclear fuel. Further criticism of Ahmadinejad, at home and abroad, followed his hosting of a Holocaust-denial conference in Iran in 2006.

Iraq

The United States-British invasion of Iraq in 2003 overthrew the authoritarian and secular regime of Saddam Hussein. The ouster of Hussein, who had long repressed Shia Muslims in Iraq, gave breathing space for the Islamist parties known as the Da'Wa Party and the Supreme Council of the Islamic Revolution in Iraq (SCIRI). These two parties joined with other mainly fundamentalist Shia parties to form the United Iraqi Alliance (UIA). The UIA established warm relations with the clerical regime in Iran. In Iraqi legislative elections held in December 2006, the UIA gained the single largest bloc of seats, with 128 out of 275.

The Kurdish Alliance, which was allied with the UIA, won 53 seats, leaving the Shia and the Kurds only three seats shy of the two-thirds majority needed to elect a president and push through constitutional reforms. Among Sunni Muslims in Iraq, the fundamentalist religious coalition, the Iraqi Accord Front, did best, winning 44 seats. The deputy leader of the Shia Da'Wa Party, Nouri al-Maliki, became Iraq's prime minister in May 2006. Kurdish leader Jalal Talabani was elected to the largely ceremonial post of president, becoming the first non-Arab to lead an Arab country. From early 2007 al-Maliki's government met with increased confrontation from the Medhi Army, the strongest Shia militia in Iraq. Led by young, radical cleric Moqtada Sadr, the Medhi Army was accused of inciting sectarian violence against Sunni targets and against U.S.-led forces. However, al-Maliki was reluctant to take action against the militias because he relied on Sadr's influence and political support to maintain power. Unlike Sunni insurgents, Sadr was involved in the political process and controlled 30 seats in the Shia bloc that dominates the Iraqi parliament.

Pakistan

Pakistan moved toward greater Islamization of state and society under General Zia ul-Haq, the country's president from 1978 to 1988. A side effect of Pakistan's Islamization was increased conflict between different religious communities and organizations, especially between the Sunni Muslim majority and the Shia Muslim minority. Although anti-Shia sentiment had existed in Pakistan, the 1990s saw a dramatic upsurge of religious radicalism and violence. Armed with automatic weapons and explosives, militant Sunni organizations fought equally militant Shia organizations. During this period of religious violence, Pakistan, long regarded as a stable ally of the United States, became a training ground for guerrilla warriors and Islamic terrorists.

The Soviet Union had invaded Afghanistan in 1979, and a ten-year Soviet-Afghan War followed. Afghan rebels set up camp in Pakistan, where Muslims from other countries joined them to train as guerrillas. Known as *mujahideen,* the guerrillas were regarded as freedom fighters in their campaign against Soviet forces, and they received substantial financial and military assistance from the United States, Saudi Arabia, and other countries throughout the 1980s. After the war ended and Soviet withdrawal from Afghanistan in 1989, many of the mujahideen returned home to such countries as Algeria, Egypt, and Pakistan. There they contributed to the spread of radical Islam. Others remained in Afghanistan and Pakistan.

Pakistan's military, Islamized under Zia, supported the mujahideen. The military developed close ties with the Taliban (the movement that controlled most of Afghanistan from 1996 until November 2001) and with militant Pakistani groups. So did many of Pakistan's *madrasas* (religious seminaries). Pakistan and Afghanistan together supported the mujahideen in their struggle against India in Kashmir, disputed territory claimed by both Pakistan and India.

In a bloodless coup in 1999, Pervez Musharraf seized power as president of Pakistan and chief of its army staff. During parliamentary elections in 2002 Musharraf formed an alliance with a coalition of six hardline Islamic parties known as the Muthida Majlis-e-Amal (MMA; United Council of Action). Until the 2002 election, the religious parties had never won more than 5 percent of the total vote in the country, but their alliance with Musharraf in 2002 brought them 11 percent of the vote. With 50 seats, the MMA became the second-largest opposition party in Pakistan.

The MMA parted ways with Musharraf in 2005 after he ordered the army to attack tribal lands along Pakistan's border with Afghanistan. Some of the Islamist political parties in the borderlands, which receive support from the tribes, were supposedly "hosting" members of Al-Qaeda. After a U.S. invasion toppled the Taliban in Afghanistan in 2001, Musharraf provided critical support to the U.S. war on terrorism and aid in the effort to capture Osama bin Laden. As a result, however, Musharraf became labeled an "American puppet" in Pakistan, where anti-Americanism has steadily increased on account of the war in neighboring Afghanistan. In October 2006 Pakistanis erupted in outrage after Pakistan's military bombed a *madrasa* (Islamic school) near the Afghan border, killing at least 80 people. Musharraf also came under criticism from the United States and Afghanistan for allegedly providing refuge for the Taliban.

Palestine

The political views of Palestinians in the Israeli-occupied territories of the West Bank and the Gaza Strip have long been regarded as primarily secular and nationalist. But Islamist groups, such as Islamic Jihad and Hamas, have won popular support. Hamas was influenced by the Muslim Brotherhood, and like the Muslim Brotherhood, it provided social services. Hamas rejected the Oslo accords that established the Palestinian National Authority (PNA) and gave hope for a two-state solution to resolve the Israeli-Palestinian conflict. For a long time it continued to wage terrorist attacks against Israel while the Fatah leadership of the PNA sought to enforce a cease-fire with Israel and continue negotiations for a Palestinian state.

In elections for the Palestinian Legislative Council in 2006, Hamas won a surprising victory, claiming 76 of the 132 seats and emerging as the dominant political force. Many political observers, however, believed that Hamas's showing was largely a rejection of Fatah's corruption and inefficient administration rather than an embrace of militant Islam. Fatah, which had dominated Palestinian politics since the 1960s, won only 43 seats in the legislative elections. Signs of Palestinians' dissatisfaction with Fatah had been visible for years, and its alleged misappropriation of funds only intensified the discontent of Palestinians.

After Hamas's election to government in 2006, sanctions by Western countries crippled the Palestinian economy. The United States froze its aid package, and the European Union (EU) followed suit. Israel refused to release taxes and custom duties collected from Palestinians on behalf of the PNA. The Palestinian government's bankruptcy created a volatile situation that soon led to clashes between Hamas and Fatah supporters. Fighting in late 2006 and early 2007 left 90 Palestinians dead and the government in complete chaos. Saudi Arabia's king Abdullah brokered a peace agreement between Hamas and Fatah in Mecca in February 2007.

The agreement called for Hamas to abide by previous PNA agreements with Israel, including Israel's rights to its pre-1967 borders, which Hamas agreed to respect. The United States and the EU withheld judgment on the peace accord. Fighting between Hamas and Fatah militias in June 2007 left Gaza under the control of Hamas and the West Bank under Fatah control. Palestinian Authority president and Fatah leader Mahmoud Abbas dissolved the power-sharing government with his rivals in Hamas and set up a Fatah-led administration to govern the West Bank. The United States, EU, and Israel moved quickly to recognize the new government and offer aid to the West Bank while continuing to withhold recognition and aid from the democratically elected Hamas government in Gaza.

Lebanon

Hezbollah is the most powerful political and military organization of Shia Muslims in Lebanon. It was formed in response to Israel's invasion of Lebanon in 1982 and the subsequent 18-year Israeli occupation of southern Lebanon. As a political party with a popular base, it holds seats in parliament and in the Lebanese cabinet. It also provides a wide range of social services. At the same time, it is a resistance movement that the United States has labeled as a terrorist organization. Hezbollah's military wing, the Islamic Resistance, has highly trained and motivated fighters. Hezbollah earned broad-based support among Lebanese after Israel withdrew from southern Lebanon in 2000, as Hezbollah's attacks on the Israeli Defense Forces (IDF) were widely perceived as responsible for the pullout.

The Israeli withdrawal also vindicated, in the minds of Hezbollah's supporters, the tactical use of violence and suicide bombing. Further vindication came during a 34-day war with Israel in 2006. Israel launched a military offensive against Lebanon in July 2006 in retaliation for a Hezbollah raid on the IDF. Hezbollah responded to Israeli air strikes on Lebanon with rocket attacks targeting cities in northern Israel. After 34 days of intense warfare, the U.N. Security Council called for a cease-fire. Hezbollah's leader, Hassan Nasrallah, declared a strategic victory over Israel and emerged as the most popular figure in the Middle East. Lebanon found itself under the threat of a civil war early in 2007. In January, Hezbollah and its allies in parliament, including several Christian factions, called a general strike against the government, demanding early elections and a greater share of power. Clashes between Sunnis and Shias on the streets of Beirut, Lebanon's capital, led Hezbollah and its allies to call off the strike, fearing it might unleash an unstoppable sectarian war. Sunni-Shia tensions escalated sharply in the polarizing Lebanese political crisis.

Turkey

A secular republic, Turkey has a strategic location as the bridge between Europe and Asia that makes the country a significant player in global politics. With a fast-growing economy and a rising population, Turkey has emerged as an important trade and investment partner in the global market. It also is significant militarily, with the second-largest army in NATO. Above all, Turkey stands out as an example of a predominantly Muslim country that is a thriving democracy and a secular republic—a model that political analysts say the West should encourage.

Turkey experimented with Islamic political parties during the 1970s and 1980s but eventually outlawed all of them. Necmettin Erbakan founded several Islamist parties that were banned but in 1996 and 1997 served as Turkey's first Islamist prime minister. Erbakan's policies alienated Turkey's secular political elites and he was forced to step down by the military in 1997 after his coalition government fell apart. Reformists who were disenchanted by Erbakan's anti-Western policies broke off from his latest Islamist party in 2001 and formed an independent party, the Justice and Development Party (AKP).

The landslide victory of the AKP in 2002 parliamentary elections reflected a drastic shift in Turkey's political landscape. The AKP, a party with strong religious roots, albeit not an Islamist party, won a huge overall majority in parliament, replacing three parties and nearly all the former political heavyweights. The AKP won 363 seats, just four short of the plurality needed to rewrite the constitution drawn up by generals after an army coup in 1980. The election of an overwhelmingly pro-Islamic parliament and prime minister in the Muslim world's only strongly secular state seemed astonishing.

Turkey's new government pushed through some significant reforms, dramatically weakening the political power of the military, the proclaimed guardians of the country's secular constitution, and granting limited amnesty to Kurdish militants. The parliament stripped the National Security Council of executive powers and put it under civilian control in 2004. By bolstering democratic government, that reform advanced Turkey's chances of joining the European Union. The government walked a fine line in seeking to appease Turkey's secular elites as well as its increasingly popular Islamic groups.

Afghanistan

Although Afghanistan's mujahideen succeeded in driving out Soviet occupation forces in 1988 and 1989, their victory did not bring peace to Afghanistan. The rebels ousted Afghanistan's central government in 1992, but civil war then broke out among factions within the mujahideen. The shared Islamic identity that had served to inspire, mobilize, and unify the mujahideen in their jihad against the Soviet Union was eclipsed by Afghanistan's age-old tribal, ethnic, and religious (Sunni-Shia) differences and rivalries.

Rise of the Taliban

A new militia, Taliban, first appeared in late 1994 and subsequently swept across Afghanistan, uniting 90 percent of the country under its rule and declaring the Islamic State of Afghanistan in 1996. Taliban, which means "group of madrasa students," included many veterans of the Soviet-Afghan War (1979-1989) who had returned to the madrasas after the departure of the Soviet troops. Although portrayed as seminary students with no military background, they were in fact a highly trained force.

The Taliban were initially hailed as liberators who secured towns, made the streets safe for ordinary citizens, and cleaned up corruption and graft. But they also imposed puritanical doctrines. The Taliban barred women from school and the workplace, required that men wear beards and women the full-length all-enveloping chador, banned music and television, and imposed strict physical punishments on those who deviated from these policies. The Pashtun, Afghanistan's dominant ethnic group, dominated the Taliban. Using religion for legitimacy, the Pashtun Taliban fought "holy" wars to subdue other ethnic and Muslim groups in Afghanistan.

The Taliban's intolerance led to the slaughter of many of Afghanistan's Shia minority, whom the Taliban disdained as heretics. Many Muslim religious leaders denounced the Taliban's policies as too extreme and a deviation from Islam. Muslim governments as diverse as Iran's and Egypt's condemned the Taliban's violations of human rights, as did Western governments and international human rights organizations. The Taliban brand of Islam produced a "jihad culture" of Islamic radicalism and revolution. In classical Islam it is believed that jihad is a defense of Islam and the Muslim community against aggression was transformed into a militant worldview that targeted Muslims and non-Muslims alike.

This worldview fed off political fragmentation and economic failures, as well as religious and ethnic differences and conflicts. Many groups that embraced the jihad culture received support from Saudi Arabia. With the funding came the influence of Saudi Arabia's ultraconservative Wahhabi reform movement, which promotes a narrow, militant worldview? Afghanistan under the Taliban provided a sanctuary and training ground for young Islamic rebels in Southeast and Central Asia. The effects were felt from Chechnya, an autonomous republic in Russia, to Xinjiang Uygur Autonomous Region in China. Afghanistan also provided a haven for Osama bin Laden, the Saudi-born veteran of the Soviet-Afghan War, and his export of global terrorism.

Osama bin Laden and Global Terrorism

Attacks on the World Trade Center in New York City and the Pentagon in Arlington, Virginia, on September 11, 2001, provided a grim reminder of Osama bin Laden's reputation as the godfather of global terrorism. The Afghanistan-based millionaire and his umbrella organization of international terrorist groups, al-Qaeda, were soon identified as the prime suspects in the attacks. Intelligence analysts have linked bin Laden and al-Qaeda to a series of attacks, many of them in his self-declared jihad against the United States. American intelligence experts regard Osama bin Laden as a major funder of terrorist groups involved in the following attacks, firefight in Somalia in 1993 that left 18 Americans dead; bombing of a military training center run by the United States in Riyadh, Saudi Arabia, in 1995; bombing of the Khobar Towers, an apartment complex that housed U.S. servicemen in Dhahran, Saudi Arabia, in 1996; the killing of 58 tourists at Luxor, Egypt, in 1997; bombings of U.S. embassies in Tanzania and Kenya in 1998; and an attack against the USS *Cole* while it refueled in Yemen in 2000.

He has admitted his complicity in the attacks in Somalia; expressed his admiration for the "heroes" responsible for the Riyadh and Dhahran bombings, while denying his involvement; threatened attacks against Americans who remain on Saudi soil; and promised retaliation internationally for cruise missile attacks. In 1998 he announced the creation of a transnational coalition of extremist groups known as The Islamic Front for Jihad against Jews and Crusaders. After the September 11 attacks, the United States declared a war on terrorism to capture bin Laden, destroy al-Qaeda training bases in Afghanistan, and replace the Taliban with a government less friendly to terrorists. Aerial bombing attacks destroyed al-Qaeda bases and helped a coalition of anti-Taliban forces called the Northern Alliance gain control of Afghanistan. The whereabouts of bin Laden, however, remained unknown.

Osama bin Laden's message resonates with the feelings of many in the Arab and Muslim world. A sharp critic of

U.S. policy toward the Muslim world, bin Laden has denounced U.S. support for Israel, which he blames for the failure of the Middle East peace process. He has condemned U.S. refusal to censure Israel's 1996 shelling of civilians in Qana, Lebanon, and U.S. insistence on continued economic sanctions against Iraq, which resulted in hundreds of thousands of deaths, especially among children. He has been equally critical of what he dismisses as "new crusades" in the Persian Gulf, in particular the substantial U.S. military and economic presence and involvement in Saudi Arabia. He has embraced populist causes such as the "liberation" of Muslims in Bosnia, Chechnya, Kashmir, Kosovo, and other areas.

Bin Laden and other Islamic extremists justify their use of violence with the claim that most Muslim and Western governments are corrupt oppressors that resort to violence and terrorism. These extremists use Islam to motivate their followers and rationalize their actions. However, they misinterpret and misapply Islamic beliefs. Claiming that Islam and the Muslim world are under siege, they call for a jihad. Although jihad refers to the right and duty of Muslims to defend themselves, their community, and their religion from unjust attack, extremists use the concept to legitimate acts of violence and terrorism.

Post-9/11 Terrorism

In the wake of the September 11, 2001, attacks, terrorist bombings took place in Morocco, the Philippines, Indonesia, Saudi Arabia, Jordan, and Turkey. The groups responsible for the attacks had loose ties or no ties to al-Qaeda. Madrid, Spain, and London, England, were the targets of the deadliest terrorist attacks against Western countries following September 11. On March 11, 2004, a chain of suicide bombs exploded on commuter trains in Madrid at the height of the morning rush hour, killing 191 people and wounding more than 1,500. The militant Moroccan group blamed for the bombings in Casablanca in May 2003 was charged with responsibility for the Madrid terrorist attacks. Although there is uncertainty regarding the group's origin, it is widely believed to be linked to al-Qaeda and operating in Belgium, Denmark, Egypt, France, Morocco, Spain, Turkey, and the United Kingdom.

On July 7, 2005, a series of bombings on three London subway trains and a double-decker bus during the morning rush hour killed 56 people and wounded more than 700 others. Four young Britons, who led seemingly ordinary lives, carried out the attacks. Their relationship with al-Qaeda remained unclear. However, one year after the bombings, the al-Jazeera television network showed a videotaped message from one of the suicide bombers, Mohammad Sidique Khan, on the same tape as al-Qaeda's Ayman al-Zawahri, who praised the London bombings. Khan said that he was "a soldier" who had given up his life for his beliefs and was inspired by Osama bin Laden.

Jordan became a prime target for al-Qaeda because it is used as a base for Westerners who fly in and out of Iraq for work. Four al-Qaeda suicide bombers from western Iraq attacked two wedding parties in Amman, Jordan, in November 2005, killing 57 people and wounding nearly 100. Al-Qaeda's leader in Iraq, Abu Musab al-Zarqawi, who was of Jordanian origin (he was killed near Baghdad in 2006), claimed responsibility for the terrorist attacks. Saudi Arabia also became the target of terrorist attacks after 9/11. In May 2003 al-Qaeda operatives in Saudi Arabia attacked a housing compound, killing 34 people, including 8 Americans.

In 2004 al-Qaeda struck Saudi Arabia again, launching suicide attacks in downtown Riyadh in April and on the U.S. consulate in Jiddah in November. Osama bin Laden has listed the presence of U.S. troops in Saudi Arabia as one of the motives for his jihad against the United States and Saudi Arabia. However, the threat of terrorism has led to greater cooperation between the two countries. Al-Qaeda took responsibility for attacks in Istanbul, Turkey, in November 2003. Car bombs exploded near two synagogues, the British consulate, and a British bank. Casablanca, Morocco, became the scene of a deadly terrorist attack in May 2003 that was blamed on a radical group, Salafia Jihadia, which is allegedly linked to al-Qaeda.

Abu Sayyaf, a militant group in the Philippines, has carried out terrorist attacks since the early 1990s with the aim of establishing an independent Islamic state on the island of Jolo. These attacks include kidnappings, murders, robberies, and bombings. The United States believes that Abu Sayyaf has links to al-Qaeda. Indonesia experienced its deadliest act of terrorism in recent history in 2002, when terrorists attacked nightclubs, killing more than 200 people, most of them tourists. Since then terrorists have struck Indonesia a number of times.

10

Necessity in Islamic Thought

Metaphysical Issues

The understanding of causality that prevailed among the classical Islamic philosophers was decidedly Neoplatonic in character. Intellectual coherence was assured by a scheme of emanation itself modelled on the necessity inherent in a logical system. Thus the connections between events shared in the connections between propositions that followed logically from one another. In this fashion, al-Farabi's emanation scheme offered a cosmic pattern for all causality as well as a master metaphor for causal interaction. All that is and all that happens was conceived as depending, for its being and its intelligibility, ultimately on the first cause (or 'the One') by way of intermediary influences which are cosmic in character yet linked together by an intellectual inherence assuring necessary linkage between cause and effect.

Aristotle's ideal of 'scientific explanation' in the *Posterior Analytics* could only have been projected, after all, if the world itself was so constructed that things and events were properly connected with one another so as to form a coherent whole. That is the sense to be made of Ibn Sina's division of 'being' into 'necessary being' and 'possible being', with 'necessary being' restricted to the one from which all the rest emanates while the remainder is characterized as 'possible in itself yet necessary by virtue of another'. In this way the order of the natural world is assured, since it derives from the one principle of being in a way that is modelled on logical derivation. In this way also, the necessity of causal interaction becomes virtually identical with that of logical entailment, thereby linking the entire universe in a necessary order with the first cause.

Furthermore, the pattern of logical entailment extends to the action of that first cause as well, the universe comes forth from it necessarily, as premises from a principle. Such a model for causal activity cannot be easily imported into a world believed to be freely created by one God. The order described by the emanation scheme threatened the hegemony of the God revealed in the Qur'an, by removing the freedom of that God to reveal as well as to create. Accommodation with Neoplatonic thought required too much by way of concession from believers in the Qur'an, and it was only a matter of time before this effort to harmonize creation with emanation was challenged.

That challenge came notably from al-Ghazali, whose frontal attack, entitled Tahafut al-falasifa (The Incoherence of the Philosophers) was in turn countered by Ibn Rushd in his Tahafut al-tahafut (Incoherence of the Incoherence). But while Ibn Rushd's defence of a repristinated Aristotle would continue to influence Western thought, al-Ghazali's spirited attack succeeded in virtually marginalizing such philosophical reflection on metaphysical matters in the Islamic world to the activities of an elite who would come to be known as 'the philosophers', and whose adherence to Qur'anic faith would often be suspect.

Human Action and Divine Action

If such quasi-logical necessity attributed to causality in the universe ran counter to the freedom of the divine agent, it also threatened by implication the freedom of human beings to respond to divine revelation; and such freedom is clearly presupposed by the very structure of the Qur'an, which calls constantly for a response to its warnings and means to elicit wholehearted response to the guidance it offers. Yet the controversy here was not carried out on the terrain staked out by the philosophers but rather among expressly religious thinkers (called *mutakallimun* because of their desire to articulate the faith by way of argument). The earliest among these, the Mu'tazilites, could only see their way to securing human freedom by considering free human actions as utterly autonomous, and so as the creations of human agents, not of God.

These early Islamic thinkers fashioned their position on such matters without benefit of the later philosophical reflections noted above, and appear to have conflated notions of origination, causation and creation in an effort to assure that humans bear complete responsibility for the actions for which they will be rewarded or punished. Their concern was for justice, as it can be applied to human beings and to the God of the Qur'an. Again, however, to withdraw a sector of creation from the purview of the creator of heaven and earth, and to insist that human actions be our creation and not God's, could hardly be sustained in Islam. The challenge this time came from one of the theologians' own number, al-Ash'ari, who shared their conceptual conflations; he developed a purportedly intermediate position, whereby human actions are *created* by God yet *performed* by us.

The key notion introduced was *kasb* (or *iktisab*), which attempts to distinguish responsibility for one's actions from their sheer origination. Originating in the marketplace to describe transactions, it alludes to the fact that actions which God creates are 'acquired', or perhaps better, 'performed' by human beings as created agents. While this position obviates the removal of human actions from the domain of God's creation, it seems to complicate unduly the issue of human agency and responsibility. The conceptual question turns on the extent to which the notion of 'agent' can be used of both creator and creature. Can there be an authentic agent other than the creator?

This is a question, of course, which touches every religious tradition which avers the free creation of the universe by one God, how does the first cause relate to other causes? Indeed, can there even be other causes in the face of a sovereign 'First'? The response of *kalam* thinkers to this question was complicated by their commitment to an atomistic metaphysics, which seemed designed to remove all causality other than the divine from the realm of nature, this is the celebrated 'Islamic occasionalism'. Later, however, the question was debated by al-Ghazali without reference to any such metaphysical theses. Rather, the terms were those introduced by 'the philosophers', turning on the necessity of the connections between events in nature, specifically between those which we recognize as causes and their effects.

Clearly these connections could not be akin to logical necessity, or there would be no room whatsoever for miracles like the 'descent' of the Qur'an; yet if the universe is the result of God's free action and not of necessity, the creator will continue to be free to act within creation. Thus the account given of causal agency in general and of personal agency in particular, will have to allow for just that, a kind of agency proper to creatures, yet always subordinate to the influence of a free creator. al-Ghazali responds to this challenge by comprehending created causes under a patterned regularity of the *Sunna Allah*, action willed by God, creatures do indeed contain such powers, yet always subject to the will of the One who so created them. In this way, a key Islamic religious thinker such as al-Ghazali can simultaneously insist that God alone is the only agent and yet, by God's power, others are agents as well. Thus causality can be attributed to creatures, but not causal connections of the quasi-logical sort demanded by the emanation scheme.

Natural Philosophy

Early *kalam* thinkers, as noted above, presumed an atomistic conception of nature by which the universe was divinely sustained by being freely created at 'each moment' by God. This conception is clearly an attempt to affirm the omnipresence of divine causal action in the universe God creates, and just as clearly evacuates created causal efficacy. It also runs foul of Aristotle's refutations of atomism in terms of the irreducibility of the continuum of time, space and matter to discrete moments. It is these arguments which persuaded al-Ghazali that the Ash'arite presumption of the atomistic constitution of nature was gratuitous and unnecessary as a ploy to assure the omnipresence of the creator's action in nature. Thus Islamic thought has not been caught between the two extremes of 'occasionalism' (whereby all action is effectively God's) and the pervasive necessity associated with the Neoplatonic emanation scheme of its notable philosophers; there is a middle course, intimated by al-Ghazali and explicitly developed in the early twentieth century in Egypt in the celebrated Qur'an commentary *al-Manar*, whereby the *sunna Allah* is evoked to explain the consistency of a created world of nature.

In summary, Islamic thought must always reconcile the assertion that the entire universe is the free creation of God, who neither requires anything in order to create it nor stands to gain anything by creating it, with the fact that this created world has a consistency associated with causes and effects as we observe them and as we use them to explain natural phenomena. If that causal consistency is articulated in terms which presume a necessity inimical to the free action of a creator, either in the beginning or at any moment of the universe's duration, then Islamic thinkers will feel constrained, as some indeed have, to deny created causality in favour of divine sovereignty.

However, as might be expected, developments internal to Islamic thought on this matter have found a way of affirming the free creation of the universe together with its causal consistency, and in doing so have suggested a pattern for causal connections in nature which distances them from the quasi-logical while respecting their reality, specifically by invoking an analogy with the patterns which the God who reveals the Qur'an sets up between human actions and their recompense, the *sunna Allah*. In this way the world of nature can be seen to have a consistency proper to it, yet at the same time is affirmed to be the result of an intentional agent whose order it reflects in the operations proper to it. The pattern to be found by scientific investigation will be a reflection of that with which the natural world has been endowed by its creator, the celebrated *ayat*, or 'signs' of divine wisdom and ordering available to human reason.

Aristotelianism in Islamic Philosophy

Early Influence

Among the major differences between the Islamic philosophers and Aristotle are the questions of the eternity or creation of the world, the nature of Being and a real-world distinction between essence and existence. The ninth-century philosopher al-Kindi used Aristotle, in Arabic translations, as a base for his own philosophical works. Among other works, al-Kindi wrote one treatise specifically dealing with Aristotle, Fi kammiya kutub Aristutalis wa ma yahtaj ilahi fi tahsil al-falsafa (The Quantity of the Books of Aristotle and What is Required for the Acquisition of Philosophy).

The early part of this treatise gives an accurate summary of various logical works by Aristotle, such as *Categories* and *De Interpretatione*, before diverging into a decidedly non-Aristotelian précis on questions found in the physical treatises. Though he owed a large debt to Aristotelian thought, al-Kindi parted company with Aristotle in espousing the idea of creation from nothing by a Creator. Furthermore, in writing about creation al-Kindi does not ascribe the idea to Aristotle in the text of his treatises. Debate still continues over whether al-Kindi should be considered more 'Platonic' or 'Aristotelian'.

An inventory of those works attributed to Aristotle which were available to early Islamic philosophers appears in the Fihrist of the tenth-century bibliographer Ibn al-Nadim. The work known as the *Theology of Aristotle* appears in the Fihrist, although it is mentioned only in passing. Greater attention is paid to other correctly attributed works of philosophy and logic by Aristotle, including such detailed information as the translator, the number of sections and the work's Arabic commentators, suggesting the relative importance of these works to Ibn al-Nadim and his audience.

Judging from the list available in the Fihrist, the Islamic philosophers would have been able to appreciate Aristotle's logic, physics and metaphysics. However, since the *Theology of Aristotle* was really a Neoplatonic work, based on the *Enneads* of Plotinus, accepting this attribution would have obscured understanding of Aristotle. Whatever the influence of Aristotle on Islamic philosophy, the Muslims were nonetheless obliged to work out for themselves certain underlying issues, such as conceptualizing ideas in their own language. In particular, they had to implement a philosophical terminology, as there was a lack of abstract nouns in Arabic.

Ibn Sina and al-Farabi

The Islamic philosophers picked and chose from Aristotle's texts, using him as an authority when it suited their purposes, and knowing that philosophy was a 'foreign science' in need of an external authority as it lacked an indigenous authority. While aspects of Avicennan philosophy continue the Aristotelian tradition in broad terms, Ibn Sina's ideas about the Necessary Existent and the Possible Existent do not have their antecedents in Aristotle's philosophy.

However, as Ibn Sina himself hailed from Khurasan, one cannot dismiss the possible influences of Buddhism, Zoroastrianism and Hinduism on his philosophy. The differences with Aristotle go back to the fact that the philosophers are writing in an Islamic milieu, and certain changes had to take place to correlate with the religious ideology. Seen in some lights, these changes may be considered peripheral; the philosophers continued to hold a solidly Aristotelian view of such basic ideas as the relationship of form and matter. Among the scholars of the Middle Period - the fourth and fifth centuries ah (tenth and eleventh centuries ad) - al-Farabi is considered the foremost Aristotelian, and was indeed known as the Second Teacher.

Some scholars have divided his works into those which admit Aristotelian influence, such as Kitab al-huruf (The Book of Letters), and more popular works, such as *Kitab fi mabadi' ara' ahl al-madina al-fadila (The Book of the Principles of the Opinions of the People of the Virtuous City),* usually known simply as *al-Madina al-fadila (The Virtuous City),* a utopian treatise which espouses Neoplatonic theories such as emanation, in which everything is said to flow from the One. His internalization of Aristotle is apparent in his treatment of the four causes in Tahsil al-sa'ada (The Attainment of Happiness), echoing those found in *al-Tabi'a (The Physics)*. Here he shows a complete familiarity with the Aristotelian idea of the four causes, but is equally willing to propound his own interpretation, preferring the word *mabadi'* (literally, principles) rather than *asbab* (causes), which was the translator Ibn Ishaq's choice.

On another important point, however, al-Farabi is not conceptually Aristotelian. In *al-Madina al-fadila,* we do not find the long discourses on the inherent weakness of women, children and slaves, which are found in Aristotle;

rather, he distinguishes the inhabitants of the virtuous city from those of the ignorant cities by their moral character. Al-Farabi considered his Kitab al-huruf, which takes its title from the Greek letters which entitle Aristotle's chapters, to be a commentary on Aristotle's *Metaphysics*. While *al-Huruf* is inspired by Aristotle's concerns, and deals with many of the same subjects, it does not slavishly imitate or even follow the order of the *Metaphysics*. Al-Farabi also believed in the ultimate harmony of the opinions of Plato and Aristotle, a difficult notion for many philosophers today to accept.

One might ask why Ibn Sina (Avicenna) would be taken in by a false treatise, the *Theology of Aristotle*, when he had such a good command of Aristotelian concepts that he could quote accurately from memory. In his *'Letter to Kiya'*, Ibn Sina expresses doubt about the authorship of the *Theology of Aristotle*, remarking that the text is 'somewhat suspect'. The tone of his discussion indicates that while he included this work with other Aristotelian treatises, he has by no means concluded it is genuinely an Aristotelian text. On the other hand, in the Danashnama-i 'ala'i (The Book of Knowledge for 'Ala'), his account of metaphysics, Ibn Sina derives a quotation from Aristotle where he claims that Aristotle describes the First Being as having complete happiness in itself. It is uncertain to which part of the *Metaphysics* Ibn Sina is referring; as such a passage does not appear to exist.

Elsewhere, Ibn Sina claims to quote Aristotle from memory when discussing the theory of definition for his treatise on Definitions, when he suggests that in the *Topics*, Aristotle defines definition as 'a statement indicating the quiddity of a thing'. This is an exact quotation. It is remarkable that Ibn Sina appears to remember Aristotle's important ideas word for word after having, he says, read the books only once and thereafter being unable to refer to them. Given his life as a wanderer, this statement is credible.

The Legacy of Aristotelianism

Unlike the Islamic east, where a Hellenistic tradition of philosophy flourished from the ninth century, philosophy reached al-Andalus later. Ibn Bajja, known as Avempace in Latin, was one of its first practitioners, active in the early part of the twelfth century. His heavily Aristotelian commentaries on the logical works of al-Farabi still survive. The socio-historian Ibn Khaldun ranked him with Ibn Rushd, and Ibn Bajja no doubt influenced this, the most famous, philosopher of Muslim Spain. Ibn Rushd, better known in the West as Averroes, is considered not nearly as influential in the Islamic world as he was in medieval Europe.

Here, either because he lived on the Western periphery of the Islamic world or because he wrote such extensive commentaries on Aristotle, he became renowned. Latin translations of Ibn Rushd's texts were available in Europe within a century of his death. Coming from a family of eminent jurists, Ibn Rushd had legal as well as philosophical training. He wrote commentaries on a wide range of Aristotle's works, including his *Physics, Metaphysics, Book of the Soul, On the Heavens* and *Posterior Analytics,* the last dating from 1170. In both long and intermediate commentaries as well as short paraphrases, Ibn Rushd tried to analyse the extent of his Islamic predecessors' deviation from Aristotle. He also exerted himself in reconciling religion and philosophy in his Fasl al-maqal (Decisive Treatise On the Harmony of Religion and Philosophy). He discovers a duty to reflect with the intellect on existing beings and to seek knowledge in the Qur'anic injunction found at Surah 49: 2, 'Consider, you who have vision.'

There is good reason to consider another of Ibn Rushd's works, the Tahafut al-tahafut (The Incoherence of the Incoherence) to be an attack on Neoplatonism and a defence of true Aristotelianism. On the question of the origin of the world, Ibn Rushd promulgated eternal creation but did not accept emanation. While he wrote the *Tahafut* primarily as a rebuttal of al-Ghazali's attack on the philosophers, he also disagreed with Ibn Sina's ideas about necessity. Ibn Rushd was also to be the last in the line of Islamic Aristotelians. Throughout the classical period of Islamic thought, there were always some thinkers who distrusted rationalism and logic, certain that the study of philosophy results in a loss of faith.

Al-Ghazali and Ibn Taymiyya are the two best known examples. Al-Ghazali studied philosophy to be able to rebut it; he suggested that knowledge is inferior to faith, as knowledge could not overcome doubts. His Tahafut al-falasifa (The Incoherence of the Philosophers) had a lasting influence. Here al-Ghazali attacked Aristotle and his followers, al-Farabi and Ibn Sina, particularly objecting to the Aristotelian notion of the eternity of the world, which he found irreconcilable with the Qur'anic description of God's creation of the world from nothing. Al-Ghazali also saw this as an idea which limited God in a totally unacceptable manner. Two centuries later, Ibn Taymiyya wrote al-Radd 'ala al-mantiqiyyin (Against the Logicians) as an attack on the method of definition and demonstration used by the philosophers who were influenced by Aristotle. He argued that logic is based on the faculty of human reason, which is necessarily inferior to divine revelation.

Despite the efforts of Ibn Rushd to rehabilitate philosophy, many scholars believe that Islamic philosophy never completely recovered from al-Ghazali's massive and brutal assault on it. In the Latin West, Islamic Aristotelianism was reincarnated as Averroism, that is, Aristotle's works as taught by Ibn Rushd and translated into Latin. His works also came to have great influence in Jewish philosophy, and for many years led to a strong strain of Aristotelianism among Jewish philosophers. Aristotelianism continued to have an effect on Islamic philosophy through opposition to it from Illuminationist philosophy, and in particular thinkers such as al-Suhrawardi, al-Shahrazuri, Ibn Kammuna and others, often based in Persia. The latter sought to attack what they took to be the principles of Aristotelianism, especially its logical and ontological axioms, and produced critiques of Aristotelian essentialism which are sometimes quite similar to that of William of Ockham. It is accurate to say, however, that Aristotelianism as a school of philosophy in the Islamic world found no Muslim successors after the death of Ibn Rushd.

Aristotle Commentators

The commentary movement followed and is commonly thought to have been inspired by the work of Andronicus of Rhodes, who, perhaps around 60 BC, began a massive study of Aristotle's writings. Of the extant commentaries, the earliest come from Peripatetics of the first half of the second century AD, Adrastus and Aspasius. The early commentaries culminate in the work of the greatest Peripatetic elabourator of Aristotle, Alexander of Aphrodisias. But the later commentaries by Themistius (fourth century), though presented as mere paraphrases, and though informed by certain Neoplatonist developments, are similar in content to those of Alexander.

Outside the Peripatetic school, the chief interest in the first century BC and the first two centuries ad focused on Aristotle's *Categories*. Under the influence of the Neoplatonist Porphyry (third century), who rejected the complaint of his teacher Plotinus Aristotle's *Categories* ignores the Platonic Forms, Aristotle's logic and a wide selection of his other texts became a standard prerequisite for studying Plato in the Neoplatonist schools, Neoplatonism being by then the dominant philosophy.

Porphyry's insistence on the harmony of Plato and Aristotle inaugurated a Neoplatonist tradition. His pupil Iamblichus (third to fourth century) and Iamblichus' pupil Dexippus further defended the compatibility of Aristotle's *Categories* with Plato's theory of Forms, and Iamblichus is even said to have denied that Aristotle contradicted the theory of Forms at all. In fifth-century Alexandria, first Hierocles and then Ammonius, son of Hermeas represented Plato and Aristotle as agreeing that god was the artificer of a beginningless universe. This harmonization, though historically untenable, proved philosophically fruitful, producing a new amalgamation of the ideas of Plato and Aristotle.

After Iamblichus, the study of Aristotle as a propaedeutic to Plato acquired a new significance, because the study of Plato himself was seen as leading to the Neoplatonist ideal of ascent to god. In Iamblichus' Platonic curriculum, Plato's *Timaeus* and *Parmenides* were put last, and seen as theological treatises describing the supreme divinities. From Ammonius onwards formalized introductions were prefixed to commentaries on Aristotle's *Categories*, the first Aristotelian work in the curriculum. The introductions covered ten points which, we are told, had been made standard by Ammonius' teacher Proclus (fifth century), one of them being that the eventual aim of studying Aristotle is ascent to god through the theological works of Plato. Even before the *Categories*, the curriculum included Porphyry's introduction to the *Categories*, known as the *Isagog* or *Quinque Voces*. Commentaries on that work were prefaced by a description of the nature of philosophy.

The commentaries of the Alexandrian Neoplatonist School after Ammonius are sometimes divided into portions which would have taken an hour to deliver as lectures. Often there is a double discussion, a *protheoria* or treatment of Aristotle's doctrine in a passage, followed by an exegesis of the exact wording of the text.

In Alexandria, the Christian Platonist Philoponus (490-570s) worked out a complete alternative to the Aristotelian physics which the Neoplatonists had accepted, and thus went on to influence the development of Islamic and Western physics. Many of his unorthodox ideas were included in his attack *Against Proclus*, published in 529, but he also began to introduce them into his commentaries on Aristotle. Meanwhile Simplicius, a pious devotee of Neoplatonist religion, had left Athens for Persia as one of the seven displaced Athenian philosophers after the Christian emperor Justinian closed the Athenian Neoplatonist School in 529. He wrote bitterly about Philoponus' Christianity and about the unorthodox interpolations in his commentaries. He emphasizes the harmony of virtually all Greek thought, partly in order to rebut Christian charges of contradictions. It was from Harrn that Thbit ibn Qurra later went, to found the Platonizing School in Baghdad. This school became the driving force behind the translation into Arabic of Aristotle and his commentators in the ninth century, which was to inspire new philosophizing in the Islamic world.

Meanwhile commentaries were made available in Latin by Boethius (died *c*.525), but only on two logical works of Aristotle and on Porphyry's introduction to that logic. The Alexandrian School may have survived until the Arab capture of the city in 642, and a tradition continued in Constantinople. There in the twelfth century the princess Anna Comnena organized a circle that included the commentators Eustratius and Michael of Ephesus, whose commentaries were completed in 1138 or later. It may have been from Michael's workshops that James of Venice was able, around 1130, to collect Greek commentaries for translation into Latin. In the same century, Gerard of Cremona was translating Aristotelian commentaries into Latin from the Arabic versions.

During the next century, the process of transmission from both languages to the Latin-speaking world turned from a trickle into a flood, and Thomas Aquinas was a beneficiary of this development. He was thus responding not just to Aristotle, but to Aristotle transformed by the ancient commentators. The commentaries embed fragments from all 1,150 years of ancient philosophy from 550 BC to ad 600, notably those of the Presocratics. And many ideas which were previously thought to date from later times can actually be traced back to the commentators. In dynamics, the idea of an impetus, which in its medieval context has been hailed as a scientific revolution, can be seen to have travelled by an Arabic route from the sixth-century commentator Philoponus. Galileo in his early works mentions Philoponus more often than he mentions Plato. And Brentano in the nineteenth century got from the commentary tradition, and not from Aristotle himself, his idea that all activity of the mind is directed towards intentional objects.

Greek Philosophy

The Rise of Neoplatonism

Neoplatonism has been described as the final summation or synthesis of the major currents in Greek philosophy, Pythagoreanism, Stoicism, Platonism and Aristotelianism, into which an oriental religious and mystical spirit was infused. Its founder, Plotinus, was born in Lycopolis in Egypt, studied at Alexandria and lectured in Rome. He studied with Ammonius Saccas and was a classmate of Origen, who became a Christian. Plotinus was so profoundly interested in oriental religions that he joined the abortive expedition of the Roman Emperor Gordian to Persia, as we are told by Porphyry, Plotinus' disciple and biographer, in search for 'the ways and beliefs of the Persians and Indians'. When the Emperor died on the way and the expedition came to grief, Plotinus sailed to Rome in ad 244, where he achieved great success as a teacher.

The other great representative of Neoplatonism was Diadochus Proclus, whose metaphysical outlook, like that of Plotinus, marks the final phase in the struggle of Greek paganism against Christianity at Athens, where he taught, and Alexandria, where he studied under Olympiodorus. It also marked that version of Greek philosophy which exerted a particular fascination upon Muslim minds. Other representatives of Neoplatonism during the Byzantine period include Syrianus, the teacher of Proclus, Damascius, Proclus' pupil, Simplicius and Philoponus. All those philosophers or commentators were known to the Arabs and some of their writings, sometimes lost in Greek, were translated into Arabic.

In ad 529 the Byzantine Emperor Justinian ordered the school of Athens, the last bastion of Greek paganism, to be closed. Seven of its teachers, including Syrianus and Damascius, immigrated to Persia and were well received by the Emperor Chosroes I, who was an admirer of Greek learning and the founder, in AD 555, of the School of Jundishapur which was destined to become a major centre of Greek medical and scientific studies.

Subsequently, due to its proximity to Baghdad and the close political links between the Abbasids and the Persians, Jundishapur served as a staging station in the process of transmitting Greek medical and scientific learning into the Islamic world. However, the first phase in the process of transmitting Greek learning into the Near East was the translation of theological treatises, such as Eusebius' *Ecclesiastical History* and Clement's *Recognitiones*, into Syriac. As a prelude, a series of logical texts were also translated into Syriac, including the *Isagog* of Porphyry, Aristotle's *Categories, De interpretatione* and *Prior Analytics*. Beyond these, for theological reasons, the Syriac translators were not allowed to proceed.

Arabic Translations

The Arab conquest of Syria and Iraq in the seventh century did not, on the whole, interfere with the academic pursuits of Syriac scholars at Edessa, Nisibis, Qinnesrin and other centres of Syriac-Greek learning. To these Christian centres should also be added Harran in Northern Syria, home of a sect of star-worshippers known in the Arabic sources as the Sabaeans and alleged to have been founded by Alexander the Great. Throughout the eighth and ninth centuries (second and third centuries AH), a new impetus was given to the translation movement thanks to the enlightened patronage of three of the early Abbasid caliphs at Baghdad, al-Mansur, Harun and his son al-Ma'mun, who founded the House of Wisdom in Baghdad to serve as a library and institute of translation.

It was during the reign of al-Ma'mun that the translation of medical, scientific and philosophical texts, chiefly from Greek or Syriac, was placed on an official footing. The major translators who flourished during al-Ma'mun's reign include Yahya ibn al-Bitriq, credited with translating into Arabic Plato's *Timaeus*, Aristotle's *On the Soul, On the Heavens* and *Prior Analytics* as well as the *Secret of Secrets*, an apocryphal political treatise of unknown authorship attributed to Aristotle. However, the shining star of al-Ma'mun's reign was the Nestorian Hunayn ibn Ishaq, who hailed from al-Hirah in Iraq and, jointly with his son Ishaq, his nephew Hubaysh and other associates, placed the translation of Greek medieval and philosophical texts on a sound scientific footing.

The chief interests of Hunayn himself were medical, and we owe to him the translation of the complete medical corpus of Hippocrates and Galen, but Hunayn and his associates were also responsible for translating Galen's treatises on logic, his *Ethics* (the Greek original of which is lost) and his epitomes of Plato's *Sophist, Parmenides, Cratylus, Euthydemus, Timaeus, Statesman, Republic* and *Laws*. (Only the epitomes of the *Timaeus* and the *Laws* have survived in Arabic.)

The interest of Hunayn and his school in Galen, the outstanding Alexandrian physician and Platonist, is noteworthy and this philosopher-physician is a major figure in the history of the transmission of Greek learning into Arabic. Not only his sixteen books on medicine but a series of his logical and ethical writings were translated and played an important role in the development of Arabic thought. Apart from the epitomes of Plato's *Dialogues* already mentioned, his *Pinax* (list of his own writings), *That the Virtuous can Profit from Knowing Their Enemies, That One Should Know His Own Faults* and especially his *Ethics* have influenced moral philosophers from Abu Bakr al-Razi to Ibn Miskawayh and beyond.

Of the works of Aristotle, Hunayn's son Ishaq is responsible for translating the *Categories, De interpretatione, On Generation and Corruption,* the *Physics, On the Soul,* the *Nicomachean Ethics* and the spurious *De Plantis,* written by the Peripatetic philosopher Nicolaus of Damascus (first century BC). By far the most important Aristotelian treatise to be translated into Arabic during this period is the *Metaphysics,* known in the Arabic sources as the *Book of Letters* or the *Theologica* (*al-Ilahiyat*). According to reliable authorities, a little-known translator named Astat (Eustathius) translated the twelve books (excluding M and N) for al-Kindi, as did Yahya ibn 'Adi a century later. However, Ishaq, Abu Bishr Matta and others are also credited with translating some parts of the *Metaphysics.*

Equally important is the translation by Ibn Na'imah al-Himsi (d. AH 220/AD 835) of a treatise allegedly written by Aristotle and referred to in the Arabic sources at *Uthulugia* or *Theologia Aristotelis.* This treatise, which consists of a paraphrase of Plotinus' *Enneads* IV-VI, made by an anonymous Greek author (who could very well be Porphyry of Tyre), together with Proclus' *Elements of Theology* (known as the *Pure Good* or *Liber de causis*), thoroughly conditioned the whole development of Arab-Islamic Neoplatonism.

Al-Kindi is said to have commented on the *Theologia Aristotelis* as did Ibn Sina and others, and al-Farabi refers to it as an undoubted work of Aristotle. A series of other pseudo-Aristotelian works also found their way into Arabic, including the already mentioned *Secret of Secrets, De Plantis, Economica* and the *Book of Minerals*. Among other translators of Greek philosophical texts, we should mention Qusta ibn Luqa (d. AH 300/AD 912), Abu 'Uthman al-Dimashqi (d. AH 298/AD 910), Ibn Zur'AH (d. AH 398/AD 1008) and Ibn al-Khammar (d. AH 408/AD 1017), as well as the already-mentioned Abu Bishr Matta (d. AH 328/AD 940) and his disciple Yahya Ibn 'Adi.

None of those translators made any significant or original contribution to Arabic philosophical literature, although they laid the groundwork for subsequent developments and served as the chief purveyors of Greek philosophy and science into the Islamic world. However, there were noteworthy exceptions, Abu Bishr Matta was a skilled logician, and the Jacobite Yahya ibn 'Adi stands out as the best-known writer on Christian theological questions and on ethics in Arabic. The Harranean Thabit ibn Qurra (d. AH 289/AD 901) was an outstanding mathematician and astronomer as well as a translator.

The Systematization of Philosophical Ideas

Al-Kindi, already mentioned in connection with the translation of Aristotle's *Metaphysics* and the apocryphal *Theologia Aristotalis*, should be regarded as the first genuine writer on philosophical subjects in Islam. He appears from bibliographical sources to have been a truly encyclopedic writer on every philosophical or scientific subject; his works total around three hundred, of which only a small number have survived in Arabic or Latin. He was profoundly interested in Greek thought as well as Indian religious ideas, and was a professional astrologer. His extant works, however, give the impression of eclectic and hasty composition, reflecting the influence of Socrates, Plato and Aristotle in an undefined manner.

We owe to him however the first treatise on philosophical terms and definitions, modelled on Aristotle's book *Delta of the Metaphysics,* which became in due course the model of almost all subsequent parallel treatises. The first genuine system-builder in Islam, however, was al-Farabi. He was the first outstanding logician of Islam, who commented on or paraphrased the six books of Aristotle's Organon, together with the *Rhetoric* and the *Poetics,* which formed part of the Organon in the Syriac-Arabic tradition and to which the *Isagog* of Porphyry, also paraphrased by al-Farabi, was added. He also wrote several original treatises on the analysis of logical terms, which had no parallels until modern times. He defended Aristotelian logic against the Arabic grammarians who regarded logic as a foreign importation, doubly superfluous and pernicious.

He also laid down the foundations of Arab-Islamic Neoplatonism in a series of writings, the best-known of which is *al-Madina al-fadila (Opinions of the Inhabitants of the Virtuous City).* This treatise is inspired by the same utopian ideal as Plato's *Republic,* but is essentially an exposition of the emanationist world-view of Plotinus to which a political dimension has been added. In that latter respect, it had hardly any impact on political developments in Islam, but it did inspire subsequent writers on political philosophy such as Ibn Bajja. Another great champion of the emanationist world-view was Abu 'Ali al-Husayn Ibn Sina (Avicenna), who was a confessed spiritual disciple of al-Farabi.

The only great Platonist of Islam was Abu Bakr al-Razi, the greatest medical author and practitioner of the third and fourth centuries AD (ninth and tenth century AD). Both in ethics and in metaphysics, al-Razi exhibits a profound veneration for Plato, 'the master of the philosophers and their leader', as well as to the great Alexandrian doctor and philosopher Galen, whose epitomes of Plato's *Dialogues,* as we have mentioned, formed the basis of the Arabic translations of Plato's works in the third century AH (ninth century AD). Although a Manichean or Harranean influence is discernible in his thought, the 'five eternal principles' which form the substance of al-Razi's metaphysics and cosmology, namely the Creator (*al-Bari'*), the soul, prime matter (*al-hayula, hyle*) space and time, can be shown to derive from Plato's *Timaeus* and his other dialogues. The other noteworthy Platonist, especially in the realms of ethics and psychology, was a fellow Persian philosopher, Ibn Miskawayh, the best known ethical philosopher of Islam.

The Legacy of Aristotle

As already mentioned, all the works of Aristotle were translated into Arabic with the exception of the *Politics,* which for some obscure reason remained unknown to the Arabs. In addition a large number of apocryphal writings, including the *Secret of Secrets*, the *Economica, De plantis, De mundo,* the *Theologia* and the *Liber de causis* were also attributed to Aristotle. Of these works, the Organon, *On the Soul*, the *Nicomachean Ethics*, the *Physics*, the *Metaphysics, On Generation and Corruption* and *On the Heavens* played a decisive role in the development of logical and metaphysical ideas in Islam.

However, chiefly due to the influence of the apocryphal *Theologia Aristotalis*, the tendency of early Muslim philosophers was to interpret Aristotle in Neoplatonic terms; a basic premise of this interpretation was the total agreement of Plato and Aristotle on all major issues alleged to separate them. (A famous treatise of al-Farabi entitled *al-Jam' bayn ra'yay al-hakimayn (The Reconciliation of Plato and Aristotle)*, probably modelled on Porphyry's lost work of the same title, illustrates this point.) The picture radically changed with the appearance on the philosophical scene of the greatest Arab Aristotelian, Ibn Rushd of Cordoba, known in Latin as Averroes. Ibn Rushd continued the tradition of commenting on Aristotle's works initiated in

Arab Spain by Ibn Bajja (Avempace) and in the East by al-Farabi. Ibn Rushd, however, produced the most extensive commentaries on all the works of Aristotle with the exception of the *Politics*, for which he substituted the *Republic* of Plato.

These commentaries, which have survived in Arabic, Hebrew or Latin, earned him in the Middle Ages the title of the Commentator, or as Dante put it in *Inferno* V. 144, 'che'l gran commento feo' (he who wrote the grand commentary). Ibn Rushd actually wrote three types of commentaries, known as the large, middle and short commentaries, on the major Aristotelian treatises, notably the *Physics*, the *Metaphysics*, the *Posterior Analytics, On the Soul* and *On the Heavens*. In addition, he defended Aristotle against the onslaughts of al-Ghazali, the famous Ash'arite theologian, in a great work of philosophical debate entitled the *Tahafut al-tahafut (Incoherence of the Incoherence)*, a rebuttal of al-Ghazali's *Tahafut al-falasifa (Incoherence of the Philosophers)*.

Presocratic and Post-Aristotelian Philosophers

The records of the early Greek philosophers in Arabic, such as al-Sijistani's *Siwan al-hikma (Vessel of Wisdom)* and al-Shahrastani's *al-Milal wa'l nihal*, usually begin with the Seven Sages, followed by a list of the Presocratics, including Thales, Anaxamines, Anaximander, Democritus, Pythagoras and Heraclitus, with very brief accounts of their views, which are invariably given a religious and mystical twist. This is particularly true of Empedocles and Pythagoras, who are said to have received 'wisdom' (*hikma*) from Semitic sources, notably Luqman and Solomon, and to have asserted as genuine Muslims *avant la lettre* the unity of God, the creation of the world and the resurrection.

Of the post-Aristotelian philosophers, Chrysippus is almost the only Stoic philosopher mentioned; Zeno of Citium is almost unknown, despite the significant influence of Stoicism both in logic and in ethics on the early philosophers and theologians. Diogenes the Cynic, often confused with Socrates, is represented as a key moral and ascetic figure, but of the latter Stoic philosophers such as Cicero, Epictetus and Marcus Aurelius, no mention is made in the classical Arabic sources. Of the materialists, only the names of Democritus and Epicurus are mentioned. The impression one gains from reading these sources is that Greek philosophy had, according to the authors, reached its zenith with Aristotle, who superseded his predecessors in such a way as to render them superfluous.

Ibn Bajja, for instance, in his paraphrase of the *Physics* of Aristotle, justifies his total omission of the views of the Presocratics on the grounds that Aristotle had refuted their 'dialectical' views and therefore it was unnecessary to dwell on them, a position which al-Ghazali had also adopted in his *Tahafut al-falasifa*. As his target, al-Ghazali chose Aristotle to the exclusion of all others, on the ground that 'he (Aristotle) had refuted all his predecessors, including his teacher, whom they nickname Plato the Divine. Then he excused himself for disagreeing with his teacher, saying, "Plato is a friend and the truth is a friend, but truth is a greater friend than Plato"' (an obvious paraphrase of *Nicomachean Ethics* I). Of Aristotle's Greek commentators, the Arab historians of ideas and philosophers refer frequently to, or quote from, the writings of Alexander of Aphrodisias, Themistius, Olympiodorus, Simplicius, Philoponus and Nicolaus of Damascus (first century BC). The earliest commentators, such as Theophrastus (d. 288 BC) and Strato (d. *c*.269 BC), were virtually unknown to the Arabs.

The chief historical significance of the Muslim-Spanish phase in the rise and development of Muslim philosophy is that it served as a major link in the transmission of Greek philosophy to Western Europe. The Muslims had been the custodians of that philosophy, which had been almost completely forgotten in Western Europe since the time of Boethius, who was responsible chiefly for translating the Aristotelian logic into Latin. By the end of the twelfth century, the translation of Arabic philosophical, scientific and medical works into Hebrew or Latin by such eminent scholars as Gerard of Cremona, Michael Scot and Herman the German had wrought a genuine intellectual revolution in learned circles. The most influential Muslim philosopher to leave a lasting impression on Western thought was Ibn Rushd (Averroes).

During the thirteenth century, philosophers and theologians split into two rival groups, the Latin Averroists with Siger of Brabant and Boethius of Dacia at their head, and the anti-Averroist group led by Albert the Great and Thomas Aquinas. The confrontation between these two groups became so violent that in the second half of the thirteenth century the Bishop of Paris, Étienne Tempier, had to intervene and in 1270 and 1277 issued ecclesiastical condemnations of a total of 219 propositions which were of Aristotelian or Averroist inspiration. It should be noted, however, that it was thanks to the Latin translations of Ibn Rushd's commentaries that the rediscovery of Aristotle in Western Europe and the concurrent emergence of Latin Scholasticism, one of the glories of late medieval thought, were made possible.

11

Concept of Philosophy in Islam

Nature and Origins of Islamic Philosophy

One of the interesting features of Islamic philosophy is that there is controversy as to what it actually is. Is it primarily the sort of philosophy produced by Muslims? This is unsatisfactory, since many Muslims who work as philosophers do not deal with Islamic issues in their philosophical work. Also, there are plenty of philosophers who are not Muslims and yet whose work is clearly in the area of Islamic philosophy. Could we call 'Islamic philosophy' philosophy which is written in Arabic? Certainly not, since a great deal of Islamic philosophy, perhaps the majority of it is written in other languages, in particular Persian. Is Islamic philosophy then philosophy which examine the conceptual features of specifically Islamic issues? Not necessarily, since there are many thinkers whose work on logic and grammar, for example, is part of Islamic philosophy, even though there is no direct religious relevance in their work.

Some commentators have tried to develop a central agenda which everyone who can be called an Islamic philosopher must share; they then have the difficulty of fitting everything in Islamic philosophy into that framework, a task which ultimately tends to fail. Perhaps the best way of specifying the nature of Islamic philosophy is to say that it is the tradition of philosophy which arose out of Islamic culture, with the latter term understood in its widest sense. When did Islamic philosophy start? This is also a difficult question to answer, since from the early years of Islam a whole variety of legal and theological problems arose which are clearly philosophical, or at least use philosophical arguments in their elucidation. For example, there were heated debates about the acceptability of anthropomorphic language to describe the deity, and about the roles of free will and determination in the lives of human beings. Philosophy in its fullest sense began in the third century of the *hijra*.

The supremacy of the Abbasids over the Umayyads had led to an eastward movement of the Islamic empire, with the capital moving from Damascus to Baghdad. By this time also, Islam dominated such areas as Egypt, Syria and Persia, all places which were thoroughly immersed in Greek culture. The new rulers sought to apply the learning which existed in the empire to their own purposes. Much of this knowledge was very practical, being based on medicine, astrology, astronomy, mathematics and engineering. The caliph al-Ma'mun founded in Baghdad the *bayt al-hikma*, the House of Wisdom, in AH 217/AD 832, which served as an observatory and, more importantly, as a library and centre for the translation of Greek texts into Arabic.

Many of the translators were Christians, who translated texts first from Greek into Syriac and then into Arabic. In addition to the influence of the many translations of Greek texts, there was also an important transmission of Indian and Persian literature into Arabic, which undoubtedly had an influence on the development of Islamic philosophy. It should not be thought that these translations were uncontroversial. Many Muslims questioned the necessity for Muslims to study philosophy at all. After all, Islam presents a complete practical and theoretical model of the nature of reality, and the 'first sciences' of the Greeks often seemed unnecessary and even opposed to Islam.

Muslims had not only the Qur'an to help them regulate their lives and theoretical queries; they had also the *hadith*, the traditional sayings of the Prophet and the righteous caliphs (his immediate successors and companions) and the *sunna*, the practices of the community. There was further the system of *fiqh*, Islamic law, which discussed particular problems concerning how Muslims ought to behave, and the science of grammar, which explained how the Arabic language ought to be understood. There was also by this time a well-developed system of *kalam*, theology, which dealt with the less obvious passages of the Qur'an, and which sought conceptual unity in apparent difficulties arising from the combinations of different canonical texts. What need was there then for the sort of philosophy which existed in Greek, which originated with non-Muslims and was initially transmitted into Arabic by non-Muslims?

This would not have been such a heated issue had philosophy not seemed to be so antagonistic to Islam on so many points. The philosophy that was transmitted into Arabic at this time was profoundly Neoplatonic; it tended to agree with Aristotle that the world is eternal, that there is a hierarchy of being with the intellect at the summit and the world of generation and corruption at the bottom, and recommended a rather ascetic system of ethics. Even more crucial was the criterion of validity which the philosophers used. This was based on reason, as opposed to revelation, and naturally brought into question the significance of religious revelation. Thus philosophy came to be seen not so much as an alternative formulation of religious truths but as a rival and competing system of thought, one which required opposition by Islam. Those Muslims who worked as philosophers had to justify themselves, and they did so in a number of ways.

The first philosopher of the Arabs, al-Kindi, tended to argue that there is no basic inconsistency between Islam and philosophy, just as there is no basic inconsistency between Plato and Aristotle. Philosophy helps the Muslim to understand the truth using different techniques from those directly provided through Islam. Once philosophy became better established, however, it managed to sever the link with religion altogether, as we can see from al-Farabi onwards. Religion is then taken to represent the route to truth available to the unsophisticated and simple believer; when compared to philosophy it is seen as a version of the truth, albeit perhaps of poorer conceptual quality. The most determined defender of this view is undoubtedly Ibn Rushd (Averroes), with whom this form of philosophy largely came to an end in the sixth century AH (twelfth century AD).

Falsafa and Hikma

Peripatetic philosophy in the Islamic world came to have considerable importance for a fairly limited period, from the third to sixth centuries AD (ninth to twelfth century AD). Sometimes the distinctness of this form of reasoning from traditional Islamic methodologies was emphasised by the use of the term *falsafa*, an Arabic neologism designed to represent the Greek *philosophia*. Often, however, the familiar Arabic term *hikma* was used. *Hikma* means 'wisdom', and has a much wider meaning than *falsafa*. A good deal of *kalam* (theology) would be classed as *hikma*, as would mysticism or Sufism. Whereas much *falsafa* is defined as the knowledge of existents, wider conceptions of the discipline tend to use the term *hikma*. Al-Suhrawardi, the creator of illuminationist philosophy, called it *hikmat al-ishraq*, a title which was taken up later by Mulla Sadra, and which is often translated in English as theosophy. This sort of philosophy involves study of reality which transforms the soul and is never really separated from spiritual purity and religious sanctity.

Philosophy as *hikma* has the advantage of referring to a wide range of conceptual issues within Islam. Philosophy can then deal both with the exoteric aspects of the Qur'anic revelation and the esoteric dimensions which lie at the heart of religion. Both the Qur'an and the universe are often viewed as aspects of divine revelation which require interpretation, and philosophy in its widest sense has a vital role here. Western commentators have tended to overemphasize the Greek background of Islamic philosophy, yet most of the major Islamic philosophers wrote extensively on the Qur'an and saw the role of philosophy as lying chiefly in the hermeneutic investigation of holy texts.

This is particularly the case with the philosophers in Persia and India, who continued the philosophical tradition after it largely, came to an end in its Peripatetic form. Islamic philosophy is then essentially 'prophetic philosophy', since it is based on the interpretation of a sacred text which is the result of revelation. It deals with human beings and their entelechy, with the One or Pure Being, and the grades of the universal hierarchy, with the universe and the final return of all things to God. An important aspect of this view is that it sees Islamic philosophy not as a transitory phenomenon but as a continuing tradition in the Islamic world, not as something largely imported from an alien culture but as an essential aspect of Islamic civilization.

A good example of this wider notion of philosophy lies in the controversy over the 'oriental philosophy' (*al-hikmat al-mashriqiyya*) of Ibn Sina (Avicenna). Ibn Sina is well known as a creator of a Peripatetic philosophical system, one which came to have considerable significance within both Islamic and Western philosophy. His book *Mantiq al-mashriqiyyin (Logic of the Orientals)* deals largely with logical differences between him and Aristotle, but also includes a reference to other of his own works in which he claims to have gone in an entirely different direction from that of the Peripatetic (*mashsha'i*) thinkers. This book is not extant; perhaps the *Mantiq* is the first part of it. From what we find in his surviving works, a picture of the 'oriental philosophy' can be constructed.

The Aristotelian universe becomes transformed, reason is linked to the intellect, the external universe becomes interiorized, facts become symbols and philosophy itself becomes a type of gnosis or *sophia*. The aim of philosophy is not only the theoretical knowledge of the substances and accidents of the universe, but also the experience of their presence and instantiation in such a way as to enable the soul to free itself from the confines of the universe. The universe is experienced not as something external to be understood but rather as a succession of stages along a path on which one is travelling. The notion of this 'oriental philosophy' has played an important part in the development of future illuminationist and Sufi forms of philosophy which not only seek to understand the universe rationally but also analyse the wonder we feel when we contemplate the divine mystery of that universe.

An advantage of seeing Islamic philosophy as broadly *hikma* rather than as the narrower *falsafa* is that it avoids the danger of regarding it as predominantly an unoriginal and transmitted form of thought. This has often been the form of interpretation favoured by Western commentators, who are interested in seeing how originally Greek (and sometimes Indian and Persian) ideas reach the Islamic world and then form part of alternative systems of philosophy. There is no doubt that an important part of Islamic philosophy does follow this path, and the study of it is perhaps more appropriately a part of the history of ideas than of philosophy.

Yet it should not be forgotten that by far the larger part of Islamic philosophy does not deal with the concerns of Peripatetic philosophy as such, but is firmly directed to the issues which arise within the context of an Islamic perspective on the nature of reality. Peripatetic philosophy, *falsafa,* may well enter this process, but it is far from the uncritical application of Greek ideas to Islamic issues. Although the central principles of *falsafa* have their origin in Greek philosophy, they were so radically transformed and developed within Islamic philosophy that there is no justification in thinking that the latter is merely a result of the transmission of ideas from outside Islam.

Heresy and the Decline of Peripatetic Philosophy

A highly influential attack on the role of philosophy as part of Islam was carried out by al-Ghazali in his Tahafut al-falasifa (The Incoherence of the Philosophers). According to al-Ghazali, the Peripatetic philosophers (he was thinking in particular of Ibn Sina) present as truths theses which are often either heretical (*kufr*) or innovatory (*bid'a*). One might have expected him to go on to argue that these philosophical theses are therefore unacceptable on those grounds alone, but he does not do so. Instead, al-Ghazali criticizes these theses because, he argues, they do not follow from the arguments which the philosophers themselves give. These arguments are philosophically weak, and so need not be accepted. It is a happy consequence of the failure of these arguments that the principles of Islam are seen to rest on solid rational principles, at least in the sense that their contraries are untrue.

Although al-Ghazali is often regarded as the archenemy of philosophy, it is evident on closer inspection of many of his texts that he himself seems to adhere to many of the leading principles of Ibn Sina's thought. Also, in common with many other opponents of philosophy, he had a high regard for logic (which was regarded as a tool of philosophy rather than a part of it) and insisted on the application of logic to organized thought about religion. Some opponents of philosophy such as Ibn Taymiyya even went so far as to criticize logic itself, but on the whole as the Peripatetic tradition of philosophy declined in the Sunni Islamic world it nonetheless entered other areas of Islamic life, such as theology and jurisprudence, and continued to have an influence until it was revived within the last century as part of the Islamic renaissance (*nahda*).

Philosophy persisted in the Shi'i world far more easily, and there has been a continuing tradition of respect for philosophy in Persia and other Shi'i communities up to today. Sunni Muslims tend to accept that the door to *ijtihad* (independent judgment) is now closed, and we must seek resolution of any theoretical and practical difficulties by referring to a series of canonical texts and to the consensus of the community. Shi'i Muslims appeal also to the authority of the imams, and especially in the case of some Shi'is to the 'hidden' or twelfth imam, as being in the continuing line of religious descent from the Prophet and from his son-in-law Imam 'Ali. Since the bases of religious authority are more fluid for the *shi'a*, it tends to be more receptive to philosophy than is the case with the Sunnis.

The legal definitions of what constitutes heresy and unbelief are sometimes much looser (as with the Isma'ilis, for example), and the openness to a diversity of ideas and approaches has marked many Shi'i communities and countries. While Peripatetic philosophy went into a sharp decline in the Sunni world after the sixth century AH/twelfth century AD, it continued as part of a variety of philosophical approaches in the Shi'i world, either on its own or combined with elements of illuminationist (*ishraqi*) philosophy, and developed into more and more complex theoretical systems. Of course, philosophy continued to flourish in both the Sunni and Shi'i worlds in the sense of mystical philosophy or Sufism, which has been a persistent aspect of Islamic philosophy throughout its life.

Reason and Revelation

Many Western commentators on Islamic philosophy take the conflict between reason and revelation as its central issue. This is often symbolized as the struggle between Athens and Jerusalem, or between philosophy and religion. While this is far too crude to be an accurate description, it does raise an important issue which has been discussed ever since Islamic philosophy began and which is still a live issue today in the Islamic world. If revelation tells believers everything they need to know, why bother to explore the same topics with reason? There are a number of answers to this question. First of all, the Qur'an itself speaks not only to Muslims, but to everyone who is able to read and understand it. It constantly urges the reader to consider rationally the evidences for Islam, and so places a high value on reason.

This is not to suggest that there is no role for faith, nor that faith will not be necessary at some stage in order to approach God, but the Qur'an does offer rational indications of the truth of what it is advocating in terms of signs and proofs. This is certainly not an argument for free enquiry in the modern sense of the term, but it is an approach which places high value on the notion of independent reason, which might be seen as sympathetic also to the practice of philosophy itself. According to Islam, the Prophet Muhammad is the last prophet. This implies that from that time on, no messenger can claim divine authority. We are reliant upon the correct interpretation of the *ayat* (signs) in both the Qur'an and in the universe.

The ending of prophecy means that God expects human beings to use their reason to seek to understand the nature of reality, albeit reason which is guided by the principles of Islam. As the Qu'ran has it, 'We will show them our signs in all the parts of the earth and in their own souls, until they clearly see what are true'. It is not as though there is competition between prophecy and philosophy, since the latter should be seen as supplementing and explaining the former. There are good grounds, then, for thinking that there is no basic incompatibility between the pursuit of reason and the pursuit of religion, at least not in Islam.

Epistemology in Islamic Philosophy

Nature of Knowledge

Muslim philosophers are primarily concerned with human happiness and its attainment. Regardless of what they consider this happiness to be, all agree that the only way to attain it is through knowledge. The theory of knowledge, epistemology, has therefore been their main preoccupation and appears chiefly in their logical and psychological writings. Epistemology concerns itself primarily with the possibility, nature and sources of knowledge. Taking the possibility of knowledge for granted, Muslim philosophers focused their epistemological effort on the study of the nature and sources of knowledge. Their intellectual inquiries, beginning with logic and ending with metaphysics and in some cases mysticism, were in the main directed towards helping to understand what knowledge is and how it comes about.

Following in the footsteps of the Greek philosophers, Muslim philosophers consider knowledge to be the grasping of the immaterial forms, natures, essences or realities of things. They are agreed that the forms of things are either material (that exists in matter) or immaterial (existing in them). While the latter can be known as such, the former cannot be known unless first detached from their materiality. Once in the mind, the pure forms act as the pillars of knowledge. The mind constructs objects from these forms, and with these objects it makes judgments. Thus Muslim philosophers, like Aristotle before them, divided knowledge in the human mind into conception (*tasawwur*), apprehension of an object with no judgment, and assent (*tasdiq*), apprehension of an object with a judgment, the latter being, according to them, a mental relation of correspondence between the concept and the object for which it stands.

Conceptions are the main pillars of assent; without conception, one cannot have a judgment. In itself, conception is not subject to truth and falsity, but assent is. However, it should be pointed out that *tasdiq* is a misleading term in Islamic philosophy. It is generally used in the sense of 'accepting truth or falsity', but also occasionally in the sense of 'accepting truth'. One must keep in mind, however, that when assent is said to be a form of knowledge, the word is then used, not in the broad sense to mean true or false judgment, but in the narrow sense to mean true judgment. In Islamic philosophy, conceptions are in the main divided into the known and the unknown. The former are grasped by the mind actually, the latter potentially. Known conceptions are either self-evident (that is, objects known to normal human minds with immediacy such as 'being', 'thing' and 'necessary') or acquired (that is, objects known through mediation, such as 'triangle').

With the exception of the self-evident conceptions, conceptions are known or unknown relative to individual minds. Similarly, Muslim philosophers divided assent into the known and the unknown, and the known assent into the self-evident and the acquired. The self-evident assent is exemplified by 'the whole is greater than the part' and the acquired by 'the world is composite'. In Kitab at-tanbih 'ala sabil as-sa'ada (The Book of Remarks Concerning the Path of Happiness), al-Farabi calls the self-evident objects: 'the customary, primary, well-known knowledge, which one may deny with one's tongue, but which one cannot deny with one's mind since it is impossible to think their contrary'. Of the objects of conception and assent, only the unknown ones are subject to inquiry. By reducing the number of unknown objects one can increase knowledge and provide the chance for happiness. But how does such reduction come about?

Sources of Knowledge

In Islamic philosophy there are two theories about the manner in which the number of unknown objects is reduced. One theory stresses that this reduction is brought about by moving from known objects to unknown ones, the other that it is merely the result of direct illumination given by the divine world. The former is the upward or philosophical way, the second the downward or prophetic one. According to the former theory, movement from the known objects of conception to the unknown ones can be effected chiefly through the explanatory phrase (*al-qawl ash-sharih*). The proof (*al-burhan*) is the method for moving from the known objects of assent to the unknown ones.

The explanatory phrase and proof can be either valid or invalid, the former leads to certitude, the latter to falsehood. The validity and invalidity of the explanatory phrase and proof can be determined by logic, which is a set of rules for such determination. Ibn Sina points out that logic is a necessary key to knowledge and cannot be replaced except by God's guidance, as opposed to other types of rules such as grammar for discourse (which can be replaced by a good natural mind) and metre for poetry (which can be replaced by good taste).

By distinguishing the valid from the invalid explanatory phrase and proof, logic serves a higher purpose, namely that of disclosing the natures or essences of things. It does this because conceptions reflect the realities or natures of things and are the cornerstones of the explanatory phrase and proof. Because logic deals only with expressions that correspond to conceptions, when it distinguishes the valid from the invalid it distinguishes at the same time the realities or natures of things from their opposites. Thus logic is described as the key to the knowledge of the natures of things. This knowledge is described as the key to happiness; hence the special status of logic in Islamic philosophy.

Logic and knowledge

We are told that because logic deals only with the known and unknown, it cannot deal with anything outside the mind. Because it is a linguistic instrument (foreign in nature to the realities of things), it cannot deal with such realities directly, whether they exist in the mind or outside it, or are external to these two realms of existence. It can only deal with the states or accidents of such realities, these states comprising links among the realities and intermediaries between the realities and language. Logic therefore deals with the states of such realities, as they exist in the mind. Such states are exemplified by 'subject' or 'predicate', 'universality' or 'particularity', 'essentiality' or 'accidentality'. In other words, logic can deal with realities only in that these realities are subjects or predicates, universal or particular, essential or accidental and so on.

Because the ultimate human objective is the understanding of the realities, essences or natures of things, and because the ultimate logical objective is the understanding of conceptions, logicians must focus on the understanding of those conceptions that lead to the understanding of the essences if they intend to serve humanity. Ibn Sina points out that since the essences are universal; such expressions are also universal in the sense of representing universal conceptions such as 'human being', not in the sense of being universal only in expression, such as 'Zayd'. A universal expression can be applied to more than one thing, as the last two examples show, but one must keep in mind Ibn Sina's distinction between these two types of universal expressions, the former represents reality, although indirectly, the latter does not. It is only the former with which the logician should be concerned.

Considering that the discussion of universals occupies a central place in Arabic logic, it is important to focus briefly on this subject to ensure understanding of the proper objects of the knowledge of the natures of things. Muslim philosophers divide universal expressions into five types, known together as the five predicables, genus, species, difference, property and common accident. Genus refers to the common nature of all the species that fall under it, such as 'animality' for 'human being', 'dog', 'cat' and so on. As such, it tells us what the general nature of a thing is. Species refers to the common nature of all the individuals that fall under it, such as 'human being' for 'John', 'George' and 'Dorothy'. As such, it tells us what the specific nature of a thing is.

Difference refers to that which differentiates the members of the genus, such as 'rational', which differentiates the species of being human from other animal species; it tells us which thing a being is. These three universals are essential to a thing; that is, without them the essence will not be what it is. Property and common accident are accidental, in that they attach to the thing but are not part of its essence. Property refers to something that necessarily attaches to one universal only, such as 'capacity for laughter' for 'human being'. Common accident refers to a quality that attaches to more than one universal, either in an inseparable manner, such as 'black' for 'crow', or in a separable manner, such as 'black' for 'human being'. The inseparability of the common accident, however, is only in existence.

Only the first three of the above universals constitute the essences of things. If one is to understand the essence of a thing, one must first understand its genus, species and difference or differences. The understanding of these three universals takes place through the explanatory phrase and proof, of which these universals are simple elements. The explanatory phrase is either definition or description. The definition is a phrase which mirrors the essence of a thing by indicating its general and specific essential qualities, that is, its genus, species and difference; the description is like the definition except that it indicates the property instead of the difference. Thus the description does not give a complete picture of the essence of a thing as does the definition. The proof is a set of propositions, which consist of conceptions joined or separated by particles. The proof that helps in the understanding of the essences of things is that which moves from known universal judgments to an unknown universal one.

The important question that concerned Muslim philosophers is how the universals or forms that are essential to the natures of things arrive at the human mind before it has the chance to employ the explanatory phrase and proof to compose known conceptions and known judgments from them. In order to answer this question, Muslim philosophers first discussed the structure of the human soul and then the steps through which the universals pass on their way to the place of knowledge. As stated above, conceptions come to the mind through either the philosophical way or the prophetic way. The philosophical way requires one first to use one's external senses to grasp the universals as they exist in the external world, mixed with matter. Then the internal senses, which like the external senses are a part of the animal soul, take in these universals and purify them of matter as much as possible. The imagination is the highest internal sense, in which these universals settle until the next cognitive move. It is from this point to the next step in the philosophical journey that the details seem particularly unclear.

The Role of the Mind

All Muslim philosophers believe that above the senses there is the rational soul. This has two parts, the practical and theoretical intellects. The theoretical intellect is responsible for knowledge; the practical intellect concerns itself only with the proper management of the body through apprehension of particular things so that it can do the good and avoid the bad. All the major Muslim philosophers, beginning with al-Kindi, wrote treatises on the nature and function of the theoretical intellect, which may be referred to as the house of knowledge.

In addition to the senses and the theoretical intellect, Muslim philosophers include in their discussion of the instruments of knowledge a third factor. They teach that the divine world contains, among other things, intelligences, the lowest of which is what al-Kindi calls the First Intellect (*al-'aql al-awwal*), better known in Arabic philosophy as the 'agent intellect' (*al-'aql al-fa''al*), the name given to it by al-Farabi, or 'the giver of forms' (*wahib as-suwar*). They contend that the world around us is necessary for the attainment of philosophical knowledge. Some, such as Ibn Bajja, Ibn Rushd and occasionally Ibn Sina, say that the mixed universals in the imagination that have been derived from the outside world through the senses are eventually purified completely by the light of the agent intellect, and are then reflected onto the theoretical intellect.

Al-Farabi's and Ibn Sina's general view, however, is that these imagined universals only prepare the theoretical intellect for the reception of the universals from the agent intellect that already contains them. While expressing the view, Ibn Sina states that it is not the universals imagination in themselves that are transmitted to the theoretical intellect but their shadow, which is created when the light of the agent intellect is shed on these universals. This is similar, he says, to the shadow of an object which is reflected on the eye when sunlight is cast on that object.

While the manner in which the universals in the imagination can prepare the theoretical intellect for knowledge is in general unclear, it is vaguely remarked by al-Farabi and Ibn Sina that this preparation is due to the similarity of these universals to the pure universals, and to the familiarity of the theoretical intellect with the imagined universals owing to its proximity to the imagination. In other words, the familiarity of this intellect with what resembles its proper objects prepares it for the reception of these objects from the agent intellect.

Philosophical and Prophetic Knowledge

The prophetic way is a much easier and simpler path. One need not take any action to receive the divinely given universals; the only requirement seems to be the possession of a strong soul capable of receiving them. While the philosophical way moves from the imagination upward to the theoretical intellect, the prophetic way takes the reverse path, from the theoretical intellect to the imagination. For this reason, knowledge of philosophy is knowledge of the natures of things themselves, while knowledge of prophecy is knowledge of the natures of things as wrapped up in symbols, the shadows of the imagination.

Philosophical and prophetic truth is the same, but it is attained and expressed differently. Ibn Tufayl's Hayy Ibn Yaqzan is the best illustration of the harmony of philosophy and religion. The so-called double truth theory wrongly views these two paths to knowledge as two types of truth, thus attributing to Ibn Rushd a view foreign to Islamic philosophy. One of the most important contributions of Islamic philosophy is the attempt to reconcile Greek philosophy and Islam by accepting the philosophical and prophetic paths as leading to the same truth.

Muslim philosophers agree that knowledge in the theoretical intellect passes through stages. It moves from potentiality to actuality and from actuality to reflection on actuality, thus giving the theoretical intellect the respective names of potential intellect, actual intellect and acquired intellect. Some Muslim philosophers explain that the last is called 'acquired' because its knowledge comes to it from the outside, and so it can be said to acquire it. The acquired intellect is the highest human achievement, a holy state that conjoins the human and the divine realms by conjoining the theoretical and agent intellects.

Following in the footsteps of Alexander of Aphrodisias, al-Farabi, Ibn Bajja and Ibn Rushd believe that the theoretical intellect is potential by nature, and therefore disintegrates unless it grasps the eternal objects, the essential universals, for the known and the knower are one. Ibn Sina rejects the view that the theoretical intellect is potential by nature. He argues instead that it is eternal by nature because unless it is, it cannot grasp the eternal objects. For him, happiness is achieved by this intellect's grasping of the eternal objects, for such grasping perfects the soul. Muslim philosophers who believe that eternity is attained only through knowledge also agree with Ibn Sina that knowledge is perfection and perfection is happiness.

Ethics in Islamic Philosophy

Theological Preludes

The earliest ethical discussions in the seventh and eighth centuries appear to have centred on the question of *qadar*, which could equally mean 'capacity', as predicated of man, or 'predetermination', as predicated of God. The early so-called Qadarites of Damascus raised the question of *qadar* in the context of the moral responsibilities of the Umayyad caliphs, who justified their most oppressive policies on the ground that they were part of the divine decree (*qada' wa qadar*). Subsequently, the Mu'tazilite theologians of Basra and Baghdad refined upon the speculation of their Qadarite predecessors and attempted for the first time to give an adequate definition of right and wrong and its bearing on God's justice and his decrees in the world. This definition was expressed in essentially rationalist and deontological terms and was received with disapproval by their traditionalist and conservative rivals, who adhered to a voluntarist thesis according to which right is by definition what God commands and wrong is what he prohibits.

Other instances of Mu'tazilite rationalism include the espousal of the absolute identity of God's essence and his attributes, the irreversibility of his decrees and the freedom of the will as a precondition of moral responsibility. Mu'tazilite theologians also stressed God's wisdom and goodness and exonerated him of the responsibility for evil in the world, which was 'created' by humankind. The degree to which Mu'tazilite theological ethics was influenced by Greek philosophy cannot be fully determined from our present knowledge of the early sources, since the translation of philosophical texts had not been started by the time the founder of the school, Wasil ibn 'Ata, launched this radical theological movement in the second century AH (eighth century AD). However, contact with Christian theologians, such as John of Damascus and his disciple Theodore Abu Qurrah, was definitely a factor in initiating the Qadarite theologians, the forerunners of the Mu'tazila, into the scholastic methods of discourse that Syriac-speaking Christian scholars had been applying to theological questions prior to the Arab conquest of Syria, Egypt and Iraq.

Early Socratic and Stoic Trends

Al-Kindi, the first genuine philosopher of Islam, was also the first writer on philosophical ethics, and it is significant that he was in sympathy with Mu'tazilite theology during the heyday of that movement. However, unlike his Mu'tazilite contemporaries, whose starting-point was the Qur'an and the Traditions (*hadith*) of Muhammad, al-Kindi's starting point was Greek philosophy. He is reported by the classical bibliographers to have written a number of ethical treatises reflecting a profound interest in

Socratic thought. Thus, in addition to a treatise on *Ethics*, he is credited with a work on *Paving the Way to Virtue*, as well as an extant tract, Fi al-hila li-daf' al-ahzan (On the Art of Dispelling Sorrows). Of his Socratic writings, a tract on the *Excellence of Socrates, A Dialogue between Socrates and Aschines* and a short collection, *Alfaz Sugrat (Socratic Utterances)*, which has survived, are mentioned in the classical sources.

It is noteworthy, however, that in the last-mentioned collection the personalities of Socrates and Diogenes the Cynic are fused and both emerge as paragons of virtue and asceticism. However, in the more discursive Fi al-hila li-daf' al-ahzan the Stoic ideal of *apatheia* (freedom from passion) and the consequent indifference to the vicissitudes of fortune are set out in eloquent terms. The antidote of sorrow, which al-Kindi argues in Stoic fashion is inseparable from humanity's ephemeral condition in this world of generation and corruption, is to consider that sorrow results either from our actions or from the actions of others. In the first case, it is our duty as rational agents to refrain from doing that which is the cause of sorrow.

In the second case, averting the sorrow which results from the actions of others is either in our power or it is not. If it is in our power, we ought certainly to avert it; if it is not in our power, we should not grieve at the prospect of injury in the hope that it might somehow be turned away. However, should we nevertheless be afflicted by sorrow resulting from actions over which we have no control, it is our duty as rational beings to bear this with fortitude. This view, and the exhortation to shun material possessions as temporary acquisitions of which we are mere borrowers and not real owners, reflect clearly the influences of the great second-century Stoic teacher Epictetus and appear to derive from his famous *Enchiridion*.

However, it was Socrates and his disciple Plato who were at the centre of the moral-ascetic speculation of the early Muslim ethical philosophers. Abu Bakr al-Razi, in his ethical treatise al-Tibb al-ruhani (The Spiritual Physic), refers to Plato as 'the master of the Philosophers and their leader', and to his teacher Socrates as 'the ascetic and godly' sage. He speaks of the three Platonic parts of the soul as the rational or divine, the irascible or animal and the concupiscent or vegetative souls, as these parts are designated by the Alexandrian physician-philosopher Galen in a treatise on ethics (which has survived in Arabic translation only). He then proceeds to summarize Plato's teaching on the manner in which each of the parts or 'souls' should be 'managed' through reasoning and demonstration, a process which he labels 'spiritual physic' or therapy.

Another Socratic-Platonic theme which recurs in al-Razi's writings is the folly of the hedonistic life which turns man into a slave or a beast. Because so many of our pleasures are either ephemeral or unattainable, we are assailed by anxiety or grief. But the true philosopher will not succumb to grief, because he understands that nothing in this world of generation and corruption is ever permanent and that whatever cannot be turned away should be ignored or disregarded, since it is often the product of passion and not of reason: 'For reason summons us only to what is susceptible of bringing about profit sooner or later; grief does not bring any advantage.... That is why the perfectly rational man will only follow the summons of reason...and will never follow the summons of passion or allow himself to be led by it or get close to it' (*Rasa'il al-Razi al-falsafiya*: 69).

Like Socrates and Plato, al-Razi believed that the soul on leaving the body will return to its original abode in the intelligible world, after passing through an endless cycle of purifications. That, he argues, is why the fear of death is irrational, and like al-Kindi and other moral philosophers he admonishes the truly reasonable man to resign himself to the prospect of death as a logical consequence of our being human. As al-Kindi had written, 'Since the definition of man is that he is a living, dying, rational being, then if there was no death, there would be no man' (*al-Hila li-daf' al-ahzan*: 45), death being an essential part of the very definition of man.

However, al-Razi adds to this argument another argument which appears to derive from Epicurus, namely that death is the privation of sensation; in death, man is stripped of the sensations of pleasure or pain and thus is in a better condition than the living who are constantly subjected to pain, let alone the fact that pleasure sought by our concupiscent nature is really nothing but 'relief from pain' or return to the natural condition (as Plato has taught in the *Philebus*). Therefore, 'according to the judgment of reason the condition of death is better than the condition of life' (*Rasa'il al-Razi al-falsafiya*: 93).

The Advent of Aristotle

The first systematic writer on philosophical questions in Islam was al-Farabi, who had also contributed to ethical discussions. He is reported in the classical sources to have written a commentary on 'parts' of the *Nicomachean Ethics*, translated into Arabic by Ishaq ibn Hunayn. This commentary is lost, but judging from an extant collection of Fusul muntaza'ah (Excerpts on Ethics),which he is established as having written, he appears to have followed Aristotle's lead in dividing the virtues into moral (practical) and intellectual. The former, he says, are the virtues or perfections of the concupiscent part or faculty of the soul; they include temperance, courage, liberality and justice. The latter are the perfections of the intellectual part and include practical reasoning, good judgment, sagacity and sound understanding.

In his discussion of justice, al-Farabi also follows Aristotle's lead, arguing that justice consists in the equitable distribution of 'common goods' in the city or the state.

These goods include security, wealth, dignity and public office, of which every member of the city or state is entitled to a share. Another more general meaning of justice is given as 'man's exercise of virtuous actions in himself and in relation to others, whatever such a virtue might be'. An interesting feature of al-Farabi's ethics which has no Aristotelian parallel is the discussion of evil. He starts in Neoplatonic fashion by asserting that 'evil has no existence as such in anything found in these worlds; that is generally in whatever does not exist through human volition. Everything therein is good'.

Evil, then, is a predicate of human action, not of physical occurrences. However, al-Farabi disagrees with traditional Neoplatonists who identified being with the good and not-being with evil pure and simple, on the ground that 'being is good only when it is in conformity with justice (or merit); not-being is evil when it is not in conformity with justice'. This appears to reflect Heraclitus' concept of *dike* as chaos. Al-Farabi's successor and spiritual disciple Ibn Sina (Avicenna) is the author of a very short tract on ethics which follows closely the Platonic model in psychology. Ibn Sina divides the soul into the rational, irascible and concupiscent, to which correspond the virtues of wisdom, courage and temperance respectively, and with justice being the 'summation' of all three. To ensure the enforcement of justice within the state, argues Ibn Sina, the existence of the caliph, as conceived of by the Shi'ites, is necessary as the sovereign of the world and God's vicegerent on earth.

More explicitly than al-Farabi, Ibn Sina develops in his psychological writings a theory of conjunction (*ittisal*) of the soul with the active intellect, that supermundane agency which according to the Muslim Neoplatonists governs the sublunary world. With this conjunction, he argues, is bound up the ultimate perfection of the soul which has attained the highest degree of wisdom and virtue, becoming thereby a replica or a mirror of the higher intelligible world. Therein lays man's ultimate happiness while his soul is still in the body. Ibn Rushd, the great Aristotelian philosopher and commentator, is known from the bibliographical sources to have written a paraphrase and a middle commentary on the *Nicomachean Ethics*, which have survived only in Hebrew and Latin, together with a paraphrase of Plato's *Republic* which is also relevant to his ethical theory.

The principal virtues, according to Ibn Rushd, correspond to the perfection of the three parts of the soul, the rational, the irascible and the concupiscent. Justice is then described along Platonic lines as the 'harmony' of the three corresponding virtues of wisdom, courage and temperance; but it has, as Aristotle stated in the *Nicomachean Ethics*, two subdivisions which Ibn Rushd calls common or universal, corresponding to 'perfect virtue', and particular, whose further subdivisions are distributive and rectificatory. Contrary to expectations, however, Ibn Rushd does not identify happiness with the contemplative life, as Aristotle had done, but rather with conjunction (*ittisal*) with the active intellect, which the Muslim Neoplatonists - with whom he was at loggerheads - had regarded as man's ultimate goal.

Ibn Miskawayh and the Persian Writers on Ethics

The most important writer on ethics in Islam, however, was an eclectic who inclined to Platonism, Ahmad ibn Muhammad Ibn Miskawayh. He laid down in his Tahdhib al-akhlaq (The Cultivation of Morals) and other ethical writings the groundwork for a whole tradition of Persian ethical writing, the chief representatives of which were Nasir-i Khusraw, Nasir al-Din al-Tusi, Jalal al-Din al-Dawani, Hussain Kashifi, Mulla Ahmad Nuraqi among others. The psychological basis of Ibn Miskawayh's ethics is clearly Platonic, as was generally the case in Islamic philosophical circles. Onto Plato's threefold division of the soul, as modified by Galen, he grafts a threefold division of virtue into wisdom, corresponding to the rational part of the soul; courage, corresponding to the irascible part; and temperance, corresponding to the concupiscent part. Justice, which Ibn Miskawayh describes as a form of moderation (*i'tidal*) or proportion (*nisba*), arises when the three powers or parts of the soul are in harmony.

This virtue is not part of virtue, but virtue entire, as Aristotle had argued. Its subdivisions, according to Aristotle as interpreted probably by Porphyry, are then given as three, our duties to God, to our superiors or equals, and finally to our ancestors. Ibn Miskawayh, however, refers to the genuine Aristotelian twofold subdivisions of justice into distributive and rectificatory and predicates the exercise of this supreme virtue on submission to the holy law (*shari'a*), which emanates from God. He then assigns to the 'just imam' or caliph the function of warding off the different forms of violating justice. Ibn Miskawayh even attributes to Aristotle, quoting an apocryphal Aristotelian source in Arabic translation, the view that justice stipulates rendering God the kind of worship due to him as our beneficent creator.

However, the Neoplatonic element in Ibn Miskawayh's ethics is nowhere more pronounced than in his analysis of happiness. Its two subdivisions, according to him, are practical and theoretical. The latter consists in 'conjunction' with the active intellect, whereby man is able to join the 'higher intellectual' realm. However, Ibn Miskawayh recognizes beyond this intellectual perfection a 'divine' or supernatural condition whereby man partakes of divine perfection or achieves a condition of self-divinization which goes far beyond his worldly conditions. This 'divine condition' is also alleged to derive from an Aristotelian fragment *On the Virtues of the Soul*, which Ibn Miskawayh quotes in Arabic translation, but which is clearly different from the apocryphal tract of the Aristotelian corpus known as *De virtutibus et vitiis*.

Ibn Miskawayh's two best-known Persian followers are Nasir al-Din al-Tusi, author of Akhlaq-i Nasiri (Nasirean Ethics), and Jalal al-Din al-Dawani, author of *Lawami al-ishraq fi makarim al-akhlaq (Flashes of Illumination on the Nobility of Character)*, known also as *Akhlaq-i Jalali*. Both al-Tusi and al-Dawani follow closely the lead of Ibn Miskawayh in the Tahdhib al-akhlaq. A fundamental difference between Ibn Miskawayh and the latter two authors is the addition of 'household management' and politics to the purely ethical part of their work by both al-Tusi and al-Dawwani. This may be viewed as a broadening, in Aristotelian fashion, of the scope of practical philosophy, which Ibn Miskawayh had tended to confine to ethical discourse only.

In the political section, inspired chiefly by al-Farabi, al-Tusi argues that orderly association is an essential precondition of the good life. Of the three forms of government, the monarchical, the tyrannical and the democratic (which he attributes to Aristotle), he favours the monarchical, identified like Plato's with the 'rule of the virtuous' or aristocrats. However, the true monarch is assisted by divine inspiration but is subordinate to the imam, who according to Shi'ite doctrine is in 'temporary concealment'. This monarch acts accordingly in a vicarious or interim capacity to ensure the administration of justice in the absence of the true head of the community or 'hidden imam'.

Al-Dawani's ethical treatise follows essentially al-Tusi's lead, but in genuine Shi'ite fashion he stresses more than his predecessor the position of humans as God's vicegerent (*khalifa*) on earth. In mystical fashion, he then goes on to argue that people reflect in their capacity as God's vicegerent the dual character of the divine nature, the outer and the inner, the spiritual and the corporeal, and more than any other creatures, including the angels, can be described as the 'image' of God. The foremost duty of the ruler, he argues, is to preserve the ordinances of the divine law (*shari'a*) and to conduct the affairs of state in accordance with universal principles and the requirements of the times. The ruler is for that reason God's 'shadow' and the vicar of the Prophet.

Philosophical and Religious Ethics

A specific blend of philosophical and religious ethics is characteristic of the writings of some late authors, including al-Raghib al-Isfahani, Abu Hamid al-Ghazali, Fakhr al-Din al-Razi and others. Al-Ghazali is the foremost representative of this group, who in both his ethical treatise *Mizan al-amal (The Balance of Action)* and his religious summa, *al-Ihya' 'ulum al-din (The Revival of the Religious Sciences)*, has developed an ethical theory in which Platonic psychology serves as the groundwork of an essentially Islamic and mystical worldview. In this theory, the table of the four cardinal virtues accords with the Platonic virtues but admits of a series of subdivisions or ramifications analogous to those of his predecessors.

A good example of the combination of religious and philosophical ideas in al-Ghazali is the manner in which happiness can be achieved. Happiness, as the chief good, admits of two subdivisions, the worldly and the otherworldly. Otherworldly happiness, which is our ultimate goal, cannot be achieved without certain worldly goods. These include the four cardinal virtues of wisdom, courage, temperance and justice, the bodily virtues of health, strength, good fortune and a long life, the external virtues of wealth, kin, social position and noble birth, and finally the 'divine virtues' of guidance, good counsel, direction and divine support. Those virtues are referred to in the Qur'an and the *hadith*, al-Ghazali says, and the final virtue, 'divine support', is identified with the Holy Spirit.

The road to moral and spiritual perfection is described as the 'quest for God'. The seekers after God must satisfy two conditions, their actions must be governed by the prescriptions or ordinances of the 'divine law' (*al-shar'*), and they must ensure that God is constantly present in their hearts. By this presence al-Ghazali means genuine contrition, adoration and submission, born of the seeker's awareness of the beauty and majesty of God which al-Ghazali, like other Muslim mystics or Sufis, regards as analogous to human passion or love (*'ishq*).

Logic in Islamic Philosophy

The Subject Matter and Aims of Logic

As was their custom in discussing all the branches of philosophy, the Islamic philosophers' devoted considerable attention to identifying the subject matter studied by logic and the aims at which logical studies are directed. Al-Farabi's logical and linguistic writings comprise the majority of his philosophical output, epitomizes the approach to logic that is characteristic of Islamic Aristotelianism. In his Ihsa' al-'ulum (Enumeration of the Sciences), he defines logic as an instrumental, rule-based science aimed at directing the intellect towards the truth and safeguarding it from error in its acts of reasoning. He defends the need for such a science of reasoning on the grounds that it is possible for the mind to err in at least some of its acts, for example, in those in which the intelligibles sought are not innate, but are rather attained discursively and empirically 'through reflection and contemplation'.

Al-Farabi compares logic to tools such as rulers and compasses, which are used to ensure exactness when we measure physical objects subject to the errors of sensation. Like these tools, logical measures can be employed by their users to verify both their own acts of reasoning and the arguments of others. Indeed, logic is especially useful and important to guide the intellect when it is faced with the need to adjudicate between opposed and conflicting opinions and authorities.

Al-Farabi's view of logic as a rule-based science which governs the mind's operations over intelligibles is repeated in many of his introductory logical works, and it formed the foundation for Ibn Sina's later refinements. In the opening chapters of his al-Madkhal, the first logical book of his encyclopaedic work *al-Shifa' (Healing)*, Ibn Sina describes the purpose of logic as one of enabling the intellect to acquire 'knowledge of the unknown from the known'. Like al-Farabi, he defends the need for logic by arguing that the innate capacities of reasoning are insufficient to ensure the attainment of this purpose, and thus they require the aid of an art.

While there may be some cases in which innate intelligence is sufficient to ensure the attainment of true knowledge, such cases are haphazard at best; he compares them to someone who manages to hit a target on occasion without being a true marksman. The most important and influential innovation that Ibn Sina introduces into the characterization of logic is his identification of its subject matter as 'second intentions' or 'secondary concepts', in contrast to 'first intentions'. This distinction is closely linked in Ibn Sina's philosophy to his important metaphysical claim that essence or quiddity can be distinguished from existence, and that existence in turn can be considered in either of its two modes, existence in concrete, singular things in the external world; or conceptual existence in one of the soul's sensible or intellectual faculties.

In al-Madkhal, Ibn Sina argues that logic differs from the other sciences because it considers not conceptual existence as such (this would be psychology), but rather the accidents or properties that belong to any quiddity by virtue of its being conceptualized by the mind. These properties, according to Ibn Sina, include such things as essential and accidental predication, being a subject or being a predicate, and being a premise or a syllogism. It is these properties that allow the mind to connect concepts together in order to acquire knowledge of the unknown; they provide the foundation for the rules of reasoning and inference that logic studies. They are moreover formal properties in the sense that, as properties belonging to all concepts in virtue of their mental mode of existence, they are entirely independent of the content of the thought itself; they are indifferent to the intrinsic natures of the quiddities which they serve to link together.

In the Ilahiyyat (*Metaphysics*) of *al-Shifa'*, Ibn Sina introduces the terminology of first and second 'intentions' or concepts in order to express the relation between the concepts of these quiddities themselves - which are studied in the theoretical sciences - and the concepts of the states and accidents of their mental existence which logic studies: 'As you know, the subject matter of logical science is second, intelligible intentions (*al-ma'ani al-ma'qula al-thaniyya*) which are dependent upon the primary intelligible intentions with respect to some property by which they lead from the known to the unknown'.

For example, the second intentions of 'being a subject' and 'being a predicate' are studied in logic independently of whatever first intentions function as the subject and predicate terms in a given proposition, for example, 'human being' and 'rational animal' in the proposition 'a human being is a rational animal'. The logical second intentions depend upon the first intentions because the first intentions are the conceptual building blocks of the new knowledge which second intentions link together: but logic studies the second intentions in abstraction from whatever particular first intentions the logical relations depend upon in any given case.

Logic, Language and Grammar

The attention that Ibn Sina and al-Farabi devote to the proper characterization of the subject matter of logic stems in part from a concern to distinguish logic from grammar. In the ancient and medieval traditions, the study of logic was closely tied to the philosophical consideration of language, and for this reason many Arabic grammarians - whose linguistic theories were developed to a high degree of complexity and sophistication - were contemptuous of the philosophers for importing Greek logic, which they saw as a foreign linguistic tradition, into the Arabic milieu.

This attitude toward Greek logic is epitomized in a famous debate reported to have taken place in Baghdad in 932 between the grammarian Abu Sa'id al-Sirafi and Abu Bishr Matta, a Syriac Christian who translated some of Aristotle's works into Arabic and is purported to have been one of al-Farabi's teachers. The extant account of the debate is heavily biased towards al-Sirafi, who attacks logical formalism and denies the ability of logic to act as a measure of reasoning over and above the innate capacities of the intellect itself. His principal claims are that philosophical logic is nothing but Greek grammar warmed over, that it is inextricably tied to the idiom of the Greek language and that it has nothing to offer speakers of another language such as Arabic.

It is against the background of such attacks that the discussions of the relations between logic, language and grammar by al-Farabi, Ibn Sina and al-Farabi's pupil Yahya ibn 'Adi (also a Syriac Christian and translator), are to be understood. Al-Farabi and Yahya both present essentially the same perspective on the relations between logic and language, a moderate perspective which Ibn Sina later rejects. In the Ihsa' al-'ulum, al-Farabi argues that logic and grammar both have some legitimate interest in language, but whereas grammatical rules primarily govern the use of language, logical rules primarily govern the use of intelligibles:

And this art [of logic] is analogous to the art of grammar, in that the relation of the art of logic to the intellect and the intelligibles is like the relation of the art of grammar to language and expressions. That is, to every rule for expressions which the science of grammar provides us, there is a corresponding [rule] for intelligibles which the science of logic provides us.

More precisely, al-Farabi explains that although grammar and logic share a mutual concern with expressions, grammar provides rules that govern the correct use of expressions in a given language, but logic provides rules that govern the use of any language whatsoever in so far as it signifies intelligibles. Thus, logic will have some of the characteristics of a universal grammar, attending to the common features of all languages that reflect their underlying intelligible content. Some linguistic features will be studied in both logic and grammar, but logic will study them as they are common and grammar in so far as they are idiomatic. On the basis of this comparison with grammar, then, al-Farabi is able to complete his characterization of the subject matter of logic as follows: 'The subject-matters of logic are the things for which [logic] provides the rules, namely, intelligibles in so far as they are signified by expressions, and expressions in so far as they signify intelligibles'.

Like al-Farabi, Yahya ibn 'Adi, in a treatise entitled Maqala fi tabyin al-fasl bayna sina'atay al-mantiq al-falsafi wa-al-nahw al-'arab (On the Difference Between Philosophical Logic and Arabic Grammar), makes his case for the independence of logic from grammar based upon the differences between the grammar of a particular nation and the universal science of logic. He argues that the subject matter of grammar is mere expressions (*al-alfaz*), which it studies from the limited perspective of their correct articulation and vocalization according to Arabic conventions. The grammarian is especially concerned with language as an oral phenomenon; the logician alone is properly concerned with 'expressions in so far as they signify meanings' (*al-alfaz al-dalla 'ala al-ma'ani*).

To support this claim, Yahya points out those changing

grammatical inflections do not affect the basic signification of a word: if in one sentence a word occurs in the nominative case, with the appropriate vocalization, its signification remains unchanged when it is used in another sentence in the accusative case and with a different vocal ending. In Ibn Sina's view, however, such accounts of the logician's interest in language and its differences from that of the grammarian did not go far enough. In keeping with his own understanding of logic as the science which studies second intentions, Ibn Sina criticized such earlier attempts to introduce linguistic concerns into the subject matter of logic.

In al-Madkhal, Ibn Sina labels as 'stupid' those who say that 'the subject matter of logic is speculation concerning expressions in so far as they signify meanings (*ma'ani*)'. However, Ibn Sina does not deny that the logician is sometimes or even often required to consider linguistic matters; his objection is to the inclusion of language as an essential constituent of the subject matter of logic. The logician is only incidentally concerned with language because of the constraints of human thought and the practical exigencies of learning and communication. Ibn Sina goes so far as to claim that, 'if logic could be learned through pure thought so that meanings alone could be attended to in it, then it would dispense entirely with expressions'; but since this is not in fact possible, 'the art of logic is compelled to have some of its parts come to consider the states of expressions'. For Ibn Sina, then, logic is a purely rational art whose purpose is entirely captured by its goal of leading the mind from the known to the unknown; only accidentally and secondarily can it be considered a linguistic art.

Conceptualization and Assent

While the close links between logic and linguistic studies emerge in the Islamic philosophers' consideration of the subject matter of logic, the links between logic and epistemology come to the fore in the consideration of the divisions within logic and the order of the books within Aristotle's Organon. All the principal Islamic Aristotelians organize their understanding of the divisions of logic around the epistemological couplet of *tasawwur* (conceptualization), and *tasdiq* (assent), which constitute for them the two states of knowledge that logic aims to produce in the intellect.

Conceptualization is the act of the mind by which it grasps singular (though not necessarily simple) essences or quiddities, such as the concept of 'human being'. Assent, by contrast, is the act of the intellect whereby it makes a determinate judgment to which a truth-value can be assigned; in fact, conceptualization is defined in Islamic philosophy principally by contrast with assent. Thus, any act of knowledge that does not entail the assignment of a truth-value to the proposition that corresponds to it will be an act of conceptualization alone, not assent. More specifically, the Islamic philosophers link assent to the affirmation or denial of the existence of the thing conceived, or to the judgment that it exists in a certain state, with certain properties. Thus, assent presupposes some prior act of conceptualization, although conceptualization does not presuppose assent.

One of the purposes of including a consideration of the *tasawwur-tasdiq* dichotomy in introductory discussions of the purpose of logic is to provide an epistemological foundation for the two focal points of Aristotelian logic, the definition and the syllogism. The purpose of the definition is identified as the production of an act of conceptualization, and the purpose of the syllogism is identified as causing assent to the truth of a proposition. However, since the definition and the syllogism are both considered in the *Prior* and *Posterior Analytics* and the works that come after them in the Organon, the study of the ways of producing conceptualization and assent presupposes as its foundation the study of single terms and propositions in the *Categories* and *De interpretatione.*

Predicables, Categories and Propositions

In keeping with the ancient Greek tradition, the Islamic philosophers considered the books of the Organon to be an ordered series which begins with the study of the signification of simple terms in the *Categories* and then proceeds to the study of propositions in the *De interpretatione.* In addition to these two Aristotelian texts, a work of the Neoplatonist Porphyry, known as the *Isagog,* was appended to the beginning of this series as an introduction to the study of the *Categories.* It was concerned with the five predicables, genus, species, difference, property and accident.

While all of the Islamic Aristotelians wrote commentaries on the *Isagog* and utilized its grouping of the predicables, not all were convinced of its utility as an introduction to Aristotle. Ibn Rushd openly expresses such doubts in the introduction to his Talkhis kitab al-maqulat (Middle Commentary on the Categories), where he indicates that his original intention was to omit the *Isagog* entirely from his series of middle commentaries on the Organon. At the end of his work on the *Isagog* itself, he explains bluntly that he does not believe that Porphyry's text is a helpful introduction to the study of logic and questions whether it is really a logical text at all. His sole reason for completing the commentary, he tells us, was to comply with a request made by his friends.

The logical character of the *Categories* presented a related problem for other Islamic philosophers. In the introduction to his Sharh al-'ibarah (Great Commentary on the De interpretatione), al-Farabi rehearses some of the controversies inherited from the Greek tradition over the relations between the *Categories* and the *De interpretatione.* As al-Farabi points out, the *De interpretatione* can be understood quite well without a prior knowledge of the *Categories*, and the former work makes no explicit references to the latter. Moreover, the *De interpretatione* is principally concerned with the formal relations amongst propositions, such as contradiction and contrariety, whereas the *Categories* is concerned with the signification or meaning of terms as such. Furthermore, in its opening chapters, the *De interpretatione* considers in formal terms the simple parts of which propositions are composed, that is, the noun and the verb.

Despite these concerns, however, al-Farabi opts for the traditional ordering of these books on the grounds that the *Categories* is relevant to the whole of logic, since it studies 'the simplest of the subject matters in which logic actualizes itself'. In his Falsafa Aristutalis, al-Farabi opts for a similar solution to the logical status of the Categories, explaining that it comprises an investigation and classification of 'the instances of being from which the first premises are compounded', which are 'the primary significations of the expressions generally accepted by all'. Al-Farabi's misgivings in both of these texts stem from the largely ontological focus of the Aristotelian *Categories*, which calls into question its placement within the Organon.

This concern was echoed later by Ibn Sina, who points out that many of the discussions in the *Categories* would be better placed in metaphysics or psychology, since they pertain to the study of expressions as directly signifying external or mental beings, in other words, to first rather than to second intentions. But since the *Categories* is useful in instructing us how to formulate definitions - which is one of the principal goals of logic - its placement in the Organon can be justified on practical grounds. Islamic philosophers viewed *De interpretatione* as a study of the composition and truth-values of categorical propositions.

Thus al-Farabi, in his great commentary on this text, explains that the term 'interpretation' used in the title of the work means 'complete statement' (*al-qawl al-tamm*). A complete statement, according to al-Farabi, must be one which causes a complete understanding in the mind; in other words, one in which assent occurs along with conceptualization. This is achieved principally by a simple, predicative, categorical statement (*al-qawl al-jazim al-hamli al-basit*) which affirms or denies a predicate of its subject.

Theory of Argumentation

For the entire Islamic tradition, the crowning glory of Aristotelian logic is the syllogistic theory outlined in the *Prior* and *Posterior Analytics*, especially the latter. The purpose of logic is to provide the means whereby knowledge is to be acquired, and the most valuable type of knowledge is that which is certain and necessary, that is, knowledge gained according to the paradigm of demonstrative science laid out in the *Posterior Analytics*. This part of logic, in the words of al-Farabi's Ihsa' al-'ulum, is 'the strongest and pre-eminent in dignity and authority. Logic seeks its primary aim in this part alone, and the rest of its parts are only for its sake'. Even the formal study of the syllogism itself is primarily undertaken for the sake of its employment in demonstrations.

In their formal syllogistic theory, the Islamic Aristotelians mainly follow Aristotle's *Prior Analytics*. While they are aware of the fourth figure traditionally ascribed to Galen, the tendency is to dismiss this figure as superfluous and intuitively implausible, as Ibn Sina does in the seventh method of his al-Isharat wa-'l-tanbihat (Remarks and Admonitions); or to ignore it entirely, as al-Farabi does in his *Kitab al-qiyas*. Similarly, the Arabic philosophers knew of the alternative propositional logic of the Stoics and incorporated elements of it in their discussions of conditional or hypothetical (*shartiyyah*) syllogisms.

However, they did not accept the Stoic inference schemata, nor did they treat conditional connectives as truth-functional, since they did not consider the parts of conditional statements to be complete propositions in their own right. Moreover, for the Islamic logicians 'conditional' was a generic term which included both 'conjunctive' (*al-muttasilat*) conditionals (of the form, 'if... then') and 'disjunctive' (*al-munfasilat*) conditionals (of the form, 'either... or'). Conditional syllogisms of both sorts were viewed as relying upon a process of 'reiteration' or 'repetition' (*istithna'*), a term which referred to the repetition of the antecedent or the consequent, or one of the two disjuncts, in so far as it formed the second premise of a syllogism. Thus in the conjunctive conditional syllogism, 'If it is daytime, then it is light; but it is daytime, therefore it is light', 'it is daytime' would be labelled the *mustathna'* or reiterated premise, since it is by its restatement that the syllogism reaches its conclusion.

When we turn up to the specific application of syllogistic theory to particular types of argumentation, the epistemological concerns of Islamic logic surface once more. In particular, the Islamic philosophers explained the primacy of demonstration, and the ancillary role of dialectical, rhetorical, poetic and sophistical syllogisms, by reference to the epistemic status of the premises used in each type of syllogism, and the type of assent they could produce to the conclusion of the syllogisms in which they were employed.

The classification of syllogisms and their premises according to the nature of their assent is found in the logical writings of all the major Islamic philosophers, but the most complete and systematic classification of premises occurs in three of Ibn Sina's works, *al-Burhan (Demonstration)*, in *al-Shifa'*, *al-Najah (Deliverance)* and al-Isharat wa-'l-tanbihat (Remarks and Admonitions). Although these three accounts differ somewhat in the number and variety of the premises listed in each, generally they present a single and consistent theory. Demonstrative syllogisms are composed of premises which necessitate assent and include self-evident first principles as well as sensible, empirically evident propositions. Dialectical syllogisms are based upon generally accepted beliefs (*al-mashhurat*), which are equivalent to the *endoxa* of Aristotle's Topics; on premises granted for the purposes of dialectical debate; and in general, on all premises assented to because they are universally accepted by all people, or by people deemed authoritative.

Rhetorical syllogisms are similar to dialectical ones, except that they are accepted unreflectively and on the basis of a more limited authority, relative, for example, to a particular group or sect; as such, they are only supposed or presumed to be 'generally-accepted beliefs'. Sophistical premises are those accepted because of some misleading resemblance to another type of premise, and poetic premises are those that produce a motion in the faculty of imagination (*al-takhyil*), not an act of intellectual assent.

The inclusion of rhetorical and poetical syllogisms in this enumeration reflects a common assumption among Islamic philosophers that Aristotle's *Rhetoric* and *Poetics* are parts of his logical Organon. This assumption was inherited by the Islamic tradition from the Greek commentators, and it was used by them in part to account for the differences between philosophical and popular modes of discourse and argumentation, particularly in the context of discussions of the relations between philosophy and religion. The Islamic philosophers held that whereas philosophers rely principally upon demonstrative and dialectical syllogisms, religious leaders and theologians generally use rhetorical and poetical syllogisms to persuade the general populace. Religion is thus viewed as an image or reflection of philosophical, demonstrative truth propounded in language and argument-forms that can be easily understood by the mass of humanity.

The place of dialectic within the theory of argumentation is perhaps the most ambivalent in Islamic logic. While dialectic is seen as inferior to demonstration, its importance for philosophy is none the less recognized. A good example of this is found in al-Farabi's enumeration in his *Kitab al-jadal* of the ways in which dialectic serves philosophers. According to al-Farabi, dialectic hones argumentative skills, introduces the principles of the special demonstrative sciences, alerts the mind to the self-evident principles of demonstration, helps to develop communicative skills and provides the means for refuting sophistry. Of these five uses, only the fourth is external to the proper aims of philosophy and closer to the tasks usually reserved to theology and religion. The other four pertain to the learning or acquisition of truly philosophical skills, even if they lie outside the strictly demonstrative aims that are the ultimate end of philosophy.

In the case of the theory of demonstration itself, Islamic logicians organized their commentaries on the *Posterior Analytics* around the definition and the demonstrative syllogism as the means by which both conceptualization and assent are most perfectly attained. Al-Farabi's Kitab al-burhan offers an excellent summary of the standard approach taken by Islamic philosophers to theory of demonstration and its epistemological aims. Just as he identified the categorical statement as the embodiment of perfect assent on the propositional level, here al-Farabi identifies demonstrative certitude as complete or perfect assent on the level of syllogistic inference. Moreover, certitude is defined by al-Farabi in terms of what we would now label 'second-order' knowledge:

> Certitude is for us to believe, concerning the truth to which we have assented, that it is not possible at all for what we believe about this matter to be different from what we believe it to be; and in addition to this for us to believe, concerning our belief, that another belief is not possible - in the sense that whenever some belief about the first belief is formed, it is impossible for it to be otherwise, and so on *ad infinitum*.

Certitude requires not just knowledge of a conclusion, *p*, but knowing that we know *p*. This sort of certitude al-Farabi calls 'necessary certitude'. However, he also allows for non-necessary certitude, which holds 'only at a particular time', and thus can be applied to propositions about merely contingent beings: 'Necessary certitude and necessary existence are convertible in entailment, for what is verified as necessarily certain is necessarily existent'. While al-Farabi recognizes both of these varieties of certitude to be forms of perfect assent, in his view necessary certitude alone fulfils the strict conditions of Aristotelian demonstration, since it alone will pertain to objects which cannot be other than they are.

Al-Farabi's remarks on the utility of dialectic, combined with his extension of the notion of perfect assent beyond the confines of strict and necessary demonstration, illustrate the overall breadth of the Islamic philosophers' theories of argumentation. Despite their professions of the primacy of the demonstrative paradigm within philosophy, the Islamic Aristotelians recognized a broad range of legitimate and useful argument forms and acknowledged their importance as philosophical tools leading to knowledge of the unknown.

Meaning in Islamic Philosophy

Religious Context

Since the Qur'an was transmitted in Arabic, an understanding of the nature of that language is a vital aspect to an understanding of the text itself. Those brought up within the traditions of jurisprudence, grammar and theology were of the opinion that they were the best positioned to pronounce on the meaning of the text. All scriptures require interpretation, and a wide diversity of views arose within the Islamic community over the correct reading of much of the Qur'an, with the creation of different schools of thought based upon political and religious divisions such as those between the Sunni and the Shi'i communities and between the Ash'arites and the Mu'tazilites.

It was accepted quite early on that while some parts of the Qur'an are clear, others are less easy to grasp and so require more complex interpretations. Some passages are *zahir* (exoteric) while others are *batin* (esoteric), and naturally the commentators disagreed on occasion over which texts fell into which category and how the esoteric texts were to be read. In a religious text, of course, even the apparently plain and commonplace can be given a richer and deeper interpretation, and different interpreters produced different interpretations. None of these was arbitrary. All were based upon argument and a variety of Islamic sources, but this hermeneutic process was capable of arriving at a variety of conclusions.

Language versus Logic

The arrival of Greek logic in the Islamic world caused great controversy in the fourth century ah/tenth century ad. It brought with it the view that logic is superior to language since the latter deals only with the contingent and conventional, while logic encompasses the necessary and the universal. Language deals only with *alfaz* (utterances), while logic gets to the heart of the matter by analysing *ma'ani* (concepts) themselves. This controversy was explored in the celebrated debate between the grammarian Abu Sa'id al-Sirafi and the logician Abu Bishr Matta in Baghdad in AH 320/AD 932.

Matta argued that logic was more important than language since the meanings which are embedded in a particular language are analysable without reference to that particular language. Those meanings could exist in a whole variety of languages. Logic is the only rigorous tool for judging when language is used correctly or otherwise, and the logician is the best qualified to adjudicate on such issues.

This was a very important debate, since if Matta were to carry the day it would imply that the traditional approach to Islamic texts rests on an error. Only logic, as understood by the Greeks and a non-Muslim such as Matta, is a sound vehicle for the understanding of texts. Al-Sirafi was clear on the significance of the debate, and he argued that it is impossible to separate language and logic in the way Matta wants. Although logic is useful at one level in dealing with concepts, it is far from comprehensive and is better suited to analysing the Greek language than the Arabic. Problems in understanding Arabic texts can only be answered by a good understanding of the Arabic language and the culture which surrounds it. Logic by itself is not sufficient.

This sort of debate continued in the Islamic world for some time, albeit in a more sophisticated form. The debate is highly significant, since it is really about the appropriate notion of meaning to be employed. Must that notion of meaning be taken from the context in which the text to be analysed has itself originated, or can it come from elsewhere? How one answers this question has radical implications for the way in which Islamic philosophy is to be pursued, and the protagonists of the argument are well aware of this.

Ambiguity, Equivocation and Analogy

There are two main theories of meaning in Islamic philosophy, one broadly Neoplatonic and adopted by Ibn Sina (Avicenna) and al-Ghazali, and one broadly Aristotelian and defended by Ibn Rushd (Averroes). On the former account, the definition of *x* does not include the existence of *x*, so that something else is required to move *x* from the realm of possibility to the realm of actuality if it is to be instantiated. For Ibn Sina the mover is another thing, ultimately God, which causally necessitates the change, while for al-Ghazali it is God who directly established quite arbitrary rules for the behaviour of contingent phenomena.

This means that for al-Ghazali it is possible to think of something happening without its customary explanation, that is, without a natural explanation. God could always have brought it about that people on occasion write philosophy books without possessing a head, or that straw does not burn when in contact with fire. Ibn Rushd operates with a different concept of meaning, in accordance with which the cause of an event is part of its definition or essence. If headless people were to start composing philosophical books we should need to construct an entirely novel conceptual scheme for such a possibility to make sense.

Al-Ghazali, by contrast, argues that we can conceive of such changes to our conceptual scheme by using our imagination, and failure to approve the possibility of such changes is merely a result of intellectual laziness, not the flouting of necessity. It is possible, then, for God to do anything he wishes so long as it is logically possible. God can resurrect the dead, he can intervene in the natural world, he can be aware of events in the world, he can create that world at any time he wishes out of nothing. These are all actions which Ibn Rushd argued are not possible even for God, if what is meant when talking about such actions is similar to what we mean when we talk about what we do.

Al-Ghazali suggests that any analysis of the properties of God which interprets them as equivocal, ambiguous or metaphorical is a subtle attack upon the notion of God in its religious sense. It involves pretending to make God part of one's metaphysics but changing the way in which one talks about him to such an extent that he no longer is equivalent to the God of Islam. For Ibn Rushd, there are serious problems in talking about God using the same sort of language we use about ourselves. God cannot be defined in terms of a genus or species since he cannot consist of a plurality of qualities as we do. Rather, he is the exemplar of all things, and we must work towards a conception of him by thinking analogically about the things in the world of which we have experience.

The way in which al-Ghazali talks about God seems to be in line with religion, but really it involves treating the deity as someone much like ourselves but more so, and as a plurality of predicates rather than a complete unity. Ibn Rushd goes along with Aristotle's argument that there can be no priority or posteriority within the same genus, and so develops a theory of meaning which is based upon the *pros hen* notion of equivocation rather than the genus-species relation. We can use the same language about God as we use about ourselves, but we should realize that the latter type of use is derivative upon the former, since the latter concepts are aspects of the paradigm which is to be found when we talk about God. When we use the same concept to refer to God and to ourselves we are speaking not univocally but equivocally, acknowledging the very real difference which exists between the level of the human and the level of the divine.

The Main Debate

In al-Ghazali's concept of meaning, the appropriate people to interpret religious texts are those professionally involved in the religion, such as theologians, jurisprudents and so on. They need to understand the religious context of the text and apply the terms univocally to God and to his creatures. The correct way to think analytically is to adopt the methodology of the thought-experiment, holding ideas together in the imagination to see if they can be combined without contradiction. If we can imagine dead people being resurrected and leaving their graves to continue a physical existence somewhere else, in hell or paradise, then there is nothing impossible about that idea and there is no need to suggest that it is a metaphorical or equivocal reference to something else.

If the Qur'an refers to physical resurrection, and if we can think about physical resurrection without contradiction, then why not just accept that what is meant by physical resurrection is what we would normally understand by that miraculous event? It follows from Ibn Rushd's approach that the best people to interpret difficult theological passages are not the theologians but the philosophers, since only the latter are skilled in understanding analytical and demonstrative thought. The philosopher can understand how a religious text may embody a whole range of meanings, some intended for a more sophisticated audience and some designed for a more naïve and practically-oriented audience.

The latter might understand by physical resurrection that the consequences of what we do outlive us, and the moral status of what we do affects us in this life and others after we are dead. They might find this easier to understand if they can think of themselves, or something like themselves, surviving their death. The more sophisticated audience would understand by the religious text what the philosophers understand by it, what it really means. This sort of audience does not require the rhetorical and poetic language which is capable of moving the largest section of the community to action. Only philosophers are capable of resolving the meaning of a text once and for all.

The other theoreticians who work within the Islamic sciences, such as theology and jurisprudence, will constantly disagree about the appropriate meaning, and as a result they will sow discord in the community. The role of the philosopher is to resolve the meaning of the text and then communicate that meaning to different kinds of audiences in different kinds of ways, each suited to the limitations of the audience to understand the real point of the text. It can thus be seen that the issue of meaning in Islamic philosophy concerns not only the philosophy of language but also politics. It is linked to the question as to who is entitled to derive the meanings of a text and how that meaning may be communicated to others. Although the focus of discussion is generally on the relationship between ordinary language and language about God, it has far broader implications, and leads to a diversity of views on how to do philosophy itself.

Aesthetics in Islamic Philosophy

Plotinus' *Ennead* V.8, 'On Intelligible Beauty', was the basis for the fourth chapter of the Arabic compilation known as the *Theology of Aristotle*. Against the background of the discussion of beauty in this text, Islamic philosophers developed the theme of the differences between sensible and intelligible beauty; and the love and pleasure associated with each. The notion of intelligible beauty is included in the discussion of the names and attributes of God contained in al-Farabi's al-Madina al-fadila (The Virtuous City). Among the divine names al-Farabi lists 'beauty' (*al-jamal*), 'brilliance' (*al-baha'*), and 'splendour' (*al-zina*).

Although the connotations of these terms are principally visual and hence sensible, al-Farabi argues that beauty in all things is primarily ontological, the more any being attains its final perfection, the more beautiful it is. From this he reasons that God, whose existence is most excellent, is the most beautiful of beings. Moreover, God's beauty surpasses all other beauty because it is essential, not accidental, the source of God's beauty is his own substance as defined by his self-contemplation, whereas created beauty derives from accidental and corporeal qualities that are not one with their own substances.

Finally, al-Farabi argues that pleasure and beauty are intimately related, and that consequently God's pleasure, like his beauty, is beyond our comprehension. Pleasure is attendant upon the perception or apprehension (*idrak*) of beauty, and it increases in proportion to the beauty of what is perceived. Since God is the most beautiful of beings, and since his proper activity consists in an act of self-contemplation in which knower and known are completely one, the intensity and certitude of God's perception of his own beauty, al-Farabi reasons, must yield a pleasure of equal intensity. Moreover, since God's perception of his own beauty is the function of an eternal and uninterrupted act of contemplation, his pleasure, unlike ours, is continual rather than intermittent.

While al-Farabi's treatment of beauty in this context is principally an extension of his general account of divine transcendence and perfection along standard Neoplatonic lines, the development of the connection between beauty, perception and pleasure introduces a more properly aesthetic element into his account. Beauty in God, like beauty in the sublunar world, is found principally in things in so far as they achieve their proper perfection; when that beauty, be it sensible or intelligible, becomes an object of contemplation, it becomes in turn a source of pleasure for the one beholding it.

The contrast between sensible and intelligible beauty and the affective pleasures proper to each is developed in more detail in the Risala fi al-'ishq (Treatise on Love) by Ibn Sina. Ibn Sina discusses the youthful love of external, bodily beauty. He opens his discussion of the love of beauty with a consideration of four principles, three of which pertain to the psychology of the human soul. The first is based upon Ibn Sina's characteristic view of the soul as a single substantial unity comprising a hierarchy of distinct powers. Either these powers can work together in harmony, in which case the lower will be ennobled by their cooperation with the highest faculty that of reason or the lower powers can rebel.

These two possibilities are especially evident in the relations between reason and imagination (*al-takhayyul*) and the desires attendant upon them. The second principle is an elabouration upon the first, there are some human actions which pertain only to the bodily, 'animal' faculties within this hierarchy, including sensation, imagination, sexual intercourse, desire and aggression. Either these actions can be pursued in a purely animal fashion, or thev can be transformed into something uniquely human under the guidance of reason.

Ibn Sina's third principle is that everything ordained by God has its own proper goodness and hence is the object of some legitimate desire; nonetheless, the lower desires can interfere with the higher, and thus their unlimited pursuit is to be avoided. Finally, Ibn Sina's fourth principle presents his definition of beauty in so far as it is the object of love for both the rational and animal souls: beauty (*al-husn*) consists in order (*al-nazm*), composition, (*al-ta'lif*) and symmetry (*al-i'tidal*). In the animal soul, this love of beauty is purely natural, arising either from instinct or from the simple pleasure of sensible perceptions. In the rational soul, however, love of beauty is more reflective, ultimately resting upon the recognition of the proximity of the beloved object to God, the First Beloved.

In applying these principles, Ibn Sina argues that there is what we might call an innate aesthetic sense implanted in every intellectual being (*al-'aqil*) which kindles in it a passionate desire for what is beautiful to behold (*al-manzar al-husn*). Despite the overall orientation of his discussion to the desire for the supra-sensible and purely intelligible beauty of God, Ibn Sina's remark here clearly pertains to the realm of sensible judgments. In fact, Ibn Sina even argues that such a desire for sensible beauty on the part of an intellectual being can be a noble thing, so long as the purely animal aspects of the desire are subordinated and the intelligible allowed to influence the sensible, such a purified aesthetic desire, according to Ibn Sina, results in a partnership (*al-shirka*) between the animal and rational souls.

As evidence of this more general claim, Ibn Sina notes that even the most wise of humans can be preoccupied by a 'beautiful human form', and he implies that such a preoccupation is justified not only by the intrinsic aesthetic principles he has outlined, but also on the assumption that internal and external beauty and harmony mirror one another, unless the external beauty has been accidentally harmed or the internal character has been altered (for better or worse) by habituation. Finally, Ibn Sina also defends the desire for some sort of physical union with such a beloved, through kissing and caressing, although the expression of such an aesthetic impulse through sexual union is considered inappropriate except for the purpose of procreation, and where sanctioned by religious law.

Rhetoric and Poetics

Most discussions of aesthetic themes by Islamic philosophers occur in the context of their considerations of the arts or rhetoric and poetics and the Aristotelian treatises devoted to these topics. Following a practice established by the sixth-century Greek commentators on Aristotle, these treatises were classified by the Islamic philosophers as parts of Aristotle's logical corpus, the Organon. Thus the approach to these arts was not primarily aesthetic, but was focused on linguistic issues and the cognitive functions of rhetorical and poetic language. Rhetoric and poetics were classified as popular methods of instruction which produced less than certain states of belief in their audiences, who were assumed to be incapable of grasping the finer points of truly philosophical demonstration.

The Islamic philosophers did not explicitly limit the use of rhetoric and poetics to the spheres of religious discourse and political communication, however, and in their commentaries on Aristotle's *Poetics* some effort was spent on explaining the linguistic mechanisms whereby speech becomes figurative and metaphorical. Ibn Rushd in particular attempted to apply his understanding of Aristotle's views on poetics to the interpretation and criticism of Arabic poetry, and his Talkhis kitab al-shi'r (Middle Commentary on the *Poetics)* is full of citations of the works of well-known Arabic poets.

Nonetheless, most of the interest taken by the Islamic philosophers in the arts of rhetoric and poetics stemmed from the foundations provided by these arts for explaining the relationship between philosophy and religion. The central books of al-Farabi's Kitab al-huruf, along with Ibn Rushd's Fasl al-maqal, are devoted to this theme, which is nicely summed up in the following passage from al-Farabi.

And since religion only teaches theoretical things by evoking imaginings and by persuasion, and its followers are acquainted with these two modes of instruction alone, it is clear that the art of theology which follows religion is not aware of anything that is not persuasive, and it does not verify anything at all except by persuasive methods and statements.

The use of the language of 'imaginings' and 'persuasions' indicates a reference to the cognitive aims that the Islamic philosophers traditionally ascribed to the arts of rhetoric and poetics. Religion is a reflection of and handmaiden to philosophy, dependent upon philosophy as a copy is dependent upon its original. In understanding religion as an imitation of philosophy, the Islamic philosophers were consciously evoking the background of Aristotle's *Poetics* and Plato's *Republic* and the aesthetic theories which they developed through a creative blending of the respective views of their two ancient sources on the nature of imitation.

Imitation and Imagination

Ibn Sina's Risala fi al-'ishq, discussed in §1, contains elements of a theory of aesthetic judgment that is also developed, from a somewhat different perspective, in his discussions of the psychological underpinnings of the art of poetics. In these discussions, aesthetic judgments are attributed to the faculty of imagination (*al-mutakhayyila*) and the related internal sense faculties that formed a part of the Islamic Aristotelians' development of the concept of imagination (*phantasia*) found in Aristotle's *On the Soul* and *Parva naturalia*. In turn the notion of imitation or *mimsis,* as found in Plato's *Republic* as well as in Aristotle's *Poetics,* was interpreted in terms of the functions of the imaginative faculty.

Al-Farabi, Ibn Sina and Ibn Rushd all identify the imagination as the faculty by which a poet produces the figurative discourses proper to their art, and to which they appeal in their audience. These authors all contrast this use of and appeal to the imagination with the strictly intellectual and rational aim proper to all other modes of discourse and forms of reasoning. Al-Farabi's Ihsa' al-'ulum provides one of the most extensive descriptions of the character of poetic imagination. Two aspects of poetic statements are emphasized by al-Farabi, their representation of their subjects in terms 'more noble or more debased' than they actually are, and their ability to bring about an appetitive, as well as a cognitive, movement in the audience. That is, by depicting a subject in terms of images that evoke a loathsome object, the poet is able to make the hearers feel aversion to the thing depicted, 'even if we are certain that it is not in fact as we imagine it to be'.

The reason for this aversion is directly linked to the poet's appeal to the imaginative faculty, 'for the actions of a human being frequently follow his imagination, more than they follow his opinion and his knowledge, because often his opinion or his knowledge are contrary to his imagination, whereas his doing of something is proportional to his imagining of it, and not to his knowledge or his opinion about it'.

A similar point is made by Ibn Sina in a number of texts. Ibn Sina frequently contrasts poetics with other modes of discourse by distinguishing the poet's attempt to produce an act of imagination (*takhyil*) in the audience with the more intellectual goal of seeking to produce an act of assent (*tasdiq*) to the truth or falsity of some claim. Ibn Sina, like al-Farabi, emphasizes the fact that such acts of imagination may often be contrary to what we know or believe to be the case, and he has a favourite example to illustrate this point: if someone tells us that 'honey is vomited bile', we are likely to lose our appetite for the honey before us, even if we are quite certain that the metaphor is literally false. Ibn Sina also echoes al-Farabi's claim that this ability of the imagination to affect our action is owing to the close link between the imaginative faculty and the appetitive motions of the soul.

The emphasis upon the imagination's ability to intervene in the soul's intellectual assent appears to have been directly linked by the Islamic philosophers to the theme of imitation. Al-Farabi, for example, appears to have made this connection in his Ihsa' al-'ulum, since he concludes his remarks on the poetic statement's ability to influence behaviour with the observation that this is 'what happens when we see likenesses imitative of the thing, or things resembling something else'.

By the same token, throughout his Talkhis kitab al-shi'r, Ibn Rushd consistently interprets the Arabic term for *mimsis* (*muhaka*) as equivalent to *takhyil*, the evoking of an image. And in several passages, Ibn Sina contrasts imaginative utterances which 'imitate one thing by another' with imaginative utterances that happen to be literally true as well. Generally, then, for the Islamic philosophers 'imitation' appears to refer to those specific acts of imaginative representation in which the object is depicted in terms not proper to it, or more specifically, which portray it as better or worse than its actual state. In this way, imitation is linked not only or even principally to Aristotelian *mimsis*, but rather to Plato's notion of imitation as it relates to the theory of the Forms found in the *Republic*.

This emerges clearly from a discussion in a little treatise by al-Farabi known simply as the Kitab al-shi'r (Book on Poetics). In this treatise, al-Farabi identifies imitation, along with metric composition, as constitutive of the very substance of poetry, with imitation the most crucial of the two elements. In order to explain the nature of poetic imitation, which occurs through language, al-Farabi draws heavily upon its similarities to imitation through action, for example, in the making of statues or in performative imitations. Here too imitation is said to have as its end to 'cause an imagining' of the imitated object, either directly or indirectly. The difference between direct and indirect imitation refers to the distance that separates the representation of the object from the reality itself, as illustrated in the example of a statue. For if an artist wished to imitate a person named Zayd:

> ... He might make a statue which resembles him, and along with this make a mirror in which he sees the statue of Zayd. And it might be that we would not see the statue itself, but rather the form of his statue in the mirror. And then we would know him through what imitates an imitation of him, and thus be two degrees removed from him in reality.

The possibility of degrees of removal from the original is highly evocative of Plato's description of the possible states of removal from the Forms in the myth of the cave. Al-Farabi believes this possibility holds not only for artistic imitation, but also for linguistic imitation in poetry. While these associations are sometimes viewed pejoratively by the Islamic philosophers, as one might expect in the light of their Platonic resonances, this attitude is not universal. Al-Farabi himself reports noncommittally that many people consider the more remote imitation to be the more perfect and artistic, and here as in his other works he admits the power of imitative utterances for inciting humans to actions to which intellectual opinion or knowledge fail to move them.

It is Ibn Sina, however, who goes furthest in eliminating the negative overtones of these descriptions of poetic speech. In all but his most youthful writings, Ibn Sina emphasizes that the poet's concern with the imagination requires that his work be judged on its own terms and not on the level of intellectual judgments. Strictly speaking, poetic imaginings are neither true nor false; but in so far as poetic statements may imply corresponding intelligible propositions, they may possess a truth-value incidentally and secondarily. For this reason, although many will remain literally false, this need not be universally the case:

> And in general poetic [syllogisms] are composed of premises which evoke images... be they true or false. Generally they are composed of premises to the extent that they possess a figure and a composition which the soul receives by means of what is in them of imitation and even of truth; for nothing prevents this [that is, their being true].

By the same token, Ibn Sina also allows for the use of poetic and imaginative discourse that is ethically neutral, seeking neither to ennoble nor to debase what is imitated, but rather merely aiming to 'provoke wonder through the beauty of the comparison' and thus to fulfil what could be termed a purely aesthetic end.

Platonism in Islamic Philosophy

Plato's influence on Islamic philosophy can be observed most clearly in ethics and political philosophy, given the works available to Islamic thinkers. However, his role lay more in creating an environment hospitable to philosophical reflection than in contributing to the formation of specific philosophical doctrines (where the influence of Aristotle was stronger). He was referred to as 'the sublime and divine Plato', no doubt because his writings seemed to lead one more directly than any other Greek philosopher to reflect on human actions in the light of transcendent goals.

At this level of inspiration, collections of sayings attributed to Plato, notably on the adverse relation of knowledge to wealth and power, helped to set a stage on which philosophy could play a propaedeutic role for Muslims seeking truth as they followed the 'straight path' laid out in the Qur'an. At the same time 'philosophy' so practised could present itself as an encompassing way of life, so competing with observant Islam. Here a discussion inspired by Plato regarding the relative weight of logic and grammar is relevant, since Arabic had tended to legislate semantic conflicts by recourse to grammar, while Greek philosophical texts (they originating in another language) extolled logic as a norm for rational discourse, transcending the peculiarities of a single tongue and the grammar proper to it.

This potential conflict came to the fore in considering the qualities required for a just ruler of a Muslim polity, specifically regarding the relative merits of 'prophecy' (the generic Islamic term for the deliverances of revelation) and philosophical reason. The *locus classicus* for such considerations is Plato's *Republic,* which offered an ideal paradigm for a just ruler that was adopted in lieu of Aristotle's more legislative treatment in the *Politics* - the only text of Aristotle's not translated into Arabic. Al-Farabi's treatise on the 'perfect state' (al-Madina al-fadila (The Virtuous City)) presents a didactic Neoplatonic version of Plato's *Republic,* one in which 'the Good' is transmuted into 'the First' in such manner that the ordering proper to cosmos and the microcosmic ideal polity emanates from the ever-fruitful One.

Al-Farabi states unequivocally that philosophical reason outstrips prophecy as a requisite for the wise and just ruler, but the pattern established in his treatise was able to be adapted by those who weighed their relative merits otherwise. What was severely contested, however, was the relevance of Plato's ideal scenario (or its adaptation by al-Farabi) to the actual ruling of an Islamic polity. Rulers themselves took issue with it, speaking from experience, as did intellectuals (such as al-'Amiri) who assimilated Plato's lofty philosophical ideals to Sufi ascetic practices. In the Plato's dictum that philosophers are prevented from attaining wisdom by the mores of the city in which they live, and spoke their own experiences more directly.

Plato's teaching on the human soul as 'an incorporeal substance that moves the body' seemed to offer a philosophical teaching conducive to Islam, even though Ibn Sina's way of adopting this teaching would put 'philosophy' in conflict with Qur'anic faith in resurrection of the body. Ethical thinkers like Ibn Miskawayh adopted Plato's tripartite division of the soul, however, in elabourating an ethical teaching relating Islam to a wider humanist culture, relying on extant sayings which quoted Plato, 'whoever rules his reason is called wise; whoever rules his anger is called courageous; and whoever rules his passion is called temperate.' The influence of sayings of this sort would permit a wise ruler like Ibn al-'Amid to say that he considered himself a 'member of the following [*shi'a*] of Plato, Socrates and Aristotle'. In this manner, Plato contributed anthropology to Islamic thought which could be used to elabourate the 'straight path' of the Qur'an as well as bring it into contact with a wider humanist civilization.

Modern Islamic Philosophy

Reactions to the West

There has been a tendency in the Islamic world since the late nineteenth century to explore the issue of the relative decline or decadence of Arabic intellectual thought and science as compared with its Western equivalent. During the Christian medieval period the Islamic world was in its cultural and political ascendancy, and was at the centre of theoretical work in both science and philosophy. However, by the nineteenth century an enormous gap had opened between the Islamic world and the West. A wide variety of explanations for this decline have since been sought.

The realization that this gap existed led to the *Nahda* (rebirth or renaissance) movement between 1850 and 1914. Beginning in Syria but developed largely in Egypt, the movement sought to incorporate the main achievements of modern European civilization while at the same time reviving classical Islamic culture which predated imperialism and the centuries of decadence. The main problem facing the *Nahda* thinkers had was how to interpret the Islamic cultural tradition, including philosophy, in an environment dominated by the West.

Jamal al-Din al-Afghani and Muhammad 'Abduh both argued that Islam is inherently rational and need not be abandoned in the face of the encroachment of Western forms of scientific and cultural thought. Mustafa 'Abd al-Raziq argued, that it is possible to demonstrate the authenticity of the traditional Islamic philosophical works and its modern relevance within Islamic society. He posits an inseparable link connecting rationalism and revelation in Islam, and he defends the traditional Islamic sciences as compatible with science and rationality. In this he constitutes what might be thought of as a more conservative position than his predecessor 'Abduh, who was more dubious about the values of some of the Islamic schools of thought, in particular of Sufism.

Muhammad 'Abid al-Jabiri suggests that a viable Arab future can only come about through a deconstruction and critique of the reasons for the decline of the Arab world. He criticizes the dichotomy between the Islamicists, who hark back to a Golden Age in the past, and the liberal Westernizers, who praise the principles of the European Renaissance from which colonialism originated. The solution he offers is the freeing of modern Arabic thought from both the language and the theological limitations of the past. The Arab mind has become very much part and parcel of traditional ways of exploring the world, and is restricted in its potential if it remains too closely wedded to its Islamic heritage.

Fu'ad Zakariyya' argued that the Arab world declined due to its inability to historicize the past and its dependence on tradition, while Zaki Najib Mahmud brought out the importance of philosophy in taking us from the known to the unknown, and was critical of the ability of religion to interfere with this movement in thought. Hasan Hanafi presents a form of phenomenology which argues that a new concept of *tawhid* (divine unity) should be developed which will involve a principle of unity and equality for all people. Hanafi also throws the charge of decadence back at the West, suggesting that the West is now entering a period of decadence and will require an infusion of ideas and energy from the East. He uses the language of liberation theology, which holds that revelation is adaptable to the language of each age.

The original revelation was suited to the time and place of the Prophet and not necessarily of the current world. Modern Muslims should reinterpret revelation in modern language and in accordance with present demands; fossilized conservatism is a misinterpretation of the true dynamic and dialectical spirit of Islam. Fazlur Rahman also contends that Islamic conservatism contradicts the essence of Islam. Islam's aims are economic reform and the establishment of a just social order. According to the Qur'an, he argues, moral and economic decline are related events. Therefore Islamic societies should turn away from petrified conservatism and educate their children in the new technologies. Islam should not be limited to communities of the faithful, but should seek a prominent place in the new ethical and social world order.

Another movement in Islamic political philosophy depicts Muslims not as the antagonists of Western culture, but rather as being in the vanguard of the globalization of peace and social justice. The most popular thinker of this school in the USA is Malcolm X, who began his career as an isolationist minister for the Nation of Islam movement. At first he used Islam to separate African-Americans from white people, but later he preached an internationalized Islam that reaches beyond racial and national differences.

An important African thinker in this tradition is Ali

Mazrui, who tries to harmonize several interdependent factors in Islamic theology with current global realities. Mazrui proposes a marriage between the Islamic monotheistic *jihad* (universal struggle), Islam's anti-racist and humanist agenda, and the need for global economic cooperation; he employs culture as a vehicle for social change through his integration of multiculturalism, the politics of pan-Islamicism and the need for globalism. He takes Islam to be the first Protestant revolution in Christianity. Moreover, he suggests that Islam's economic message turns monotheism from isolated spirituality to communitarian humanism - in the form of a Muslim world order among a community of faithful (*umma*) - through global economic cooperation, social justice and the brotherhood of all.

The essence of a multicultural perspective implies the acknowledgement that cultures project their own biases onto their perceptions of other societies. In a world which demands global economic policy-making and increasing interdependency, Mazrui believes that Muslims should see their religion of 'all is Godism' as a type of globalism. His innovation (*ijtihad*) interprets the Islamic *jihad* as an agenda of global peace and justice, thereby transforming what is taken to be a negative image of Islam into a signal for economic unity and world peace.

The Persian Approach to Philosophy

The area of the Islamic world which continued most forcefully the Islamic tradition in philosophy after the decline of Peripateticism is undoubtedly Persia. Interestingly, one of the staunchest advocates of the form of thought which might be called neo-Illuminationism, and which stems from the *ishraqi* principles of al-Suhrawardi, is Henry Corbin, a French philosopher who worked in Iran. Corbin was active in translating and interpreting post-Avicennan Islamic philosophy with an emphasis on shi'ism, *ishraqi* thought and the mysticism of Ibn al-'Arabi. He posited the existence of a perennial school of philosophical wisdom, which can be detected through the recurrence of archetypal symbols such as the icon of light. Such icons exist in the works of Shihab al-Din al-Suhrawardi in the early twelfth century ad, and have their source in Eastern (*ishraqi*) traditions such as Zoroastrianism, Hermeticism and Manicheism. (The term *ishraq*, which signifies 'light', also means 'East' or 'Orient'.)

For Corbin, '*ishraq*' designates not only a static spatial direction but a prescriptive invitation for a hermeneutic reorientation, whereby persons scrutinize their spiritual needs and points of return to archetypal origins. Corbin also discusses the role of the imagination, a faculty which exists between the senses and the intellect. While the senses perceive discrete data and the intellect categorizes, imagination is concerned with the world of archetypes (*'alam at-mithal*). For example, the notion of the perfect person (*al-insan al-kamil*) is an icon for the psychic centre. This centre signifies peace and the perfection of the self-realization process. Corbin asserts that by means of a series of epistemic states - which include revelation (*kashf*) and recollection (or archetypal memory) (*dhikr*) - one may return to the eternal origin. This process describes a cycle, thereby reasserting the Islamic theme of the unity of being (*al-wahdat al-wujud*).

Corbin's followers, such as Hermann Landolt, William Chittick and Seyyed Hossein Nasr, have developed his ideas in a variety of different ways. The latter is the best known contemporary Islamic philosopher. According to him, people share a spiritual component that cannot be actualized by either descriptive or pragmatic accounts of nature. Nasr's world perspective includes a normative element which integrates people in the same way as earlier religions and cosmologies. In the past, everyone considered their religion to be the true religion; today, however, we are confronted with a plurality of religions. How can a Muslim attain a workable relation with the sacred in such an environment? Nasr employs Sufism to refer to the archetypal dimensions common to all religions; it is through the realm of mysticism that different forms of spirituality meet.

The contemporary world creates the need for followers of different creeds and cultures to communicate. Islam must coexist with the Western world, but this does not imply an Islamic surrender to all the practices of Western society. Nasr's views on Western scientific progress show his dissatisfaction with many Western perspectives. Citing the ecological disasters of overpopulation and pollution, Nasr criticizes the value of Western technological advances. According to him, the fault lies in the mistaken metascientific presupposition that an innate nature exists which is disconnected from humanity and can be investigated separately and controlled. Moreover, the increasingly pervasive quantitative perspective supplied by units of measurement - like that by which the size of a building might be described - is an incomplete outlook because it does not articulate the qualitative effects of what it describes on the surrounding environment.

By contrast, Nasr holds that Islamic and Eastern perspectives on science and technology are integrative and harmonious. They stress unity in their studies of nature, thereby acknowledging the long-term ecological significance of development. Unless religious and spiritual values are embedded in a technological agenda, ecological disasters as well as a general lack of a sense of meaning in life are inevitable. Western science and its technological consequences are of ecological import to modern civilization. Consequently, neither science nor technology can consider itself irrelevant to environmental ethics. Philosophy along Neoplatonic lines should be pursued, since only this form of analysis does justice to the spiritual wholeness of humanity.

The main emphasis in recent Persian philosophy has been on the thought of Mulla Sadra and al-Suhrawardi.

Islamic philosophy has moved from the *madrasa* (traditional school) system and became an important part of the university curriculum. One of the most interesting thinkers is Mahdi Ha'iri Yazdi, whose work on knowledge by presence (*'ilm al-huduri*) provides an example of the fruitful combination of ideas from Western analytical philosophy and the *ishraqi* tradition in order to elucidate metaphysical and epistemological problems. Recent Shi'ite theologians, as students of the work of Mulla Sadra, were versed in the dialectics of time and change.

Ali Shari'ati, another student of Corbin, is an important social thinker whose work advocates a social process of Islamization. He rejects both the Peripatetic philosophers and the mystical thinkers, claiming that the existential being of each person contains a determination formed through mutual trust and compassion between them and God as their essence. This presumption is the ground for each person's being and the very core of each subject's potential for therapeutic unity (*tawhid*); its purpose is justice in both the providential and the social contexts. Islamization is achieved through an existential empathy and a phenomenological assimilation of exemplary people - such as the Imam Hossein (the Prophet's grandson) or Fatima - into archetypal memory.

The martyrdom of 'Ali or Hossein is a paradigmatic message, not for sorrow but for the assimilation of their characters into the self. Further, Shari'ati depicts history as a dialectical process which does not exclude economic and material realities, Islam as a practical religion or people as potential agents of justice. He replaces the Platonic theory of epistemic recollection with a theory of normative archetypal recollection. One may gain normative knowledge through the archetypal recollection of a religion's most exemplary mythical figures. Religion provides social ideals, and yet it demands not a withdrawal to a secret realm but a social revolution in the everyday world.

A creative commentary on Mulla Sadra was produced by Ruhollah Khomeini, who argues that people are primarily social as well as private citizens. Thus religious teachings relate not only to the personal morality of individuals but also to their social responsibilities and political actions. In practice, these ideas imply a theocracy that does not distinguish between politics and religion. Bringing such a dominion into existence, he claims, requires an internal revolution from the masses directed against the existing ruling class, but this revolution must be guided by the directives of the religious authorities. He modifies Islamic theology with the notion of the religious jurist-ruler's guardianship (*velayat-e-faqih*), whose role is to guide the community of faithful in their universal struggle (*jihad*). This *jihad* is not essentially military, but is largely educational and seeks the expansion of monotheistic (that is, Islamic) ethics.

Khomeini was a member of the School of Qom, based on the college in that city, which also produced Muhammad Hossein Tabataba'i, Murtaza Mutahheri and Muhammad Taqi Misbah Yazdi, all of whom have directed their influential thought at confronting the challenge to Islamic philosophy coming from the West. It should not be thought that this is an essentially reactionary strategy, however; Misbah has encouraged many of his students to study in the West and to take seriously scientific and logical thought as practised in the West. Also, although much of Misbah's work has been on Mulla Sadra, he has been far from uncritical of the latter. In particular, he criticizes the notion of prime matter, which Mulla Sadra identifies as the pure potentiality for existents. He questions the principle that a potentiality for existents exists prior to existents themselves; after all, there is nothing but existents.

Misbah argues further that many relations are not truly essences. For example, in the mind-dependent realm, we may ascribe 'below' as a relation between a table and book, but this subject-directed ascription does not imply that below is an essence in the actual world. An interesting and quite recent controversy in Persian philosophy has been that between Abdul Soroush on the one hand, and the philosophers of the school of Qom, as well as those influenced by the Corbin school, on the other. Soroush introduced a number of concepts from Western philosophy into Iran, in particular the leading ideas of Popper, Moore, Berlin and Wittgenstein. This led him to suggest that we should use a notion like that of collective reason to understand and interpret religious ideas.

Collective reason is the best way of dealing with theoretical and practical problems, and is preferable to relying solely on solutions attainable through the efforts of the jurisprudents and religious authorities. Not surprisingly, this aroused the ire of the school of Qom philosophers, and their representative Sadiq Larijani engaged Soroush in a debate which largely dealt with the correct interpretation of thinkers such as Popper, Watkins and Stalnaker, and in particular Hempel's paradoxes of confirmation. Soroush was also attacked by the Corbin circle, whose basic philosophical approach relies very much on Heidegger along with traditional Islamic philosophy, and who was quite out of sympathy with the analytical nature of Soroush's books. This controversy is interesting in that it brings out the fact that philosophers in Iran are generally familiar now not only with traditional forms of Islamic philosophy but also with the current philosophical ideas of the West. Modern philosophers do not entirely reject Western views, but neither is they completely taken over by the West; they are prepared to examine Western views with a critical sympathy.

Modern Trends

A very vibrant area in Islamic philosophy is the history of philosophy, in particular the Greek tradition in Islamic philosophy. There exists both in the West and in the Islamic world a large number of scholars who have developed accounts of this close relationship and who continue to edit, translate and work on important texts in order to get some idea of the nature of the philosophical material which was produced in the early centuries of Islam. In addition, many philosophers in the Islamic world have adapted Western philosophy so as to make sense of the philosophical problems in which they are interested. C.A. Qadir in Pakistan developed an account of Islamic philosophy which he thought was in line with logical positivism, while 'Abd al-Rahman Badawi applied existentialism to Arab society. Zaki Najib Mahmud followed William James in presenting a pragmatic account of philosophy.

Some thinkers applied particular techniques in the Islamic tradition to philosophy, so that 'Ali Sami al-Nashshar for example based his work on Ash'arite theology, while Muhammad 'Aziz Lahbabi (1954) used Hegelianism to develop a theory of being which is quite unusual within the context of Islamic ontology. Hichem Djait (1986) combines Hegelianism with existentialism. He argues that only dialectical epistemology can be used to understand the modern situation of the Arab world, and that the apparent opposites of decadence/renaissance, Arab/non-Arab, orthodox/heterodox, tradition/modernity needs to be transcended if we are to understand the present nature of Islamic culture. Abdallah Laroui (1976) and Muhammad Arkoun (1985) both stress the contrast between Islam and modernity, and the former advocates the adoption of Westernization as the appropriate strategy for the Islamic world. In his approach to the Qur'an, Arkoun uses the semiotic ideas current in modern French literature to argue that Islam has always been changing and developing, so that there is no point in referring to a particular constant orthodoxy.

While many of these thinkers are hostile to mysticism and its Islamic form, Sufism, there can be little doubt that the latter represents a very potent framework for a good deal of present Islamic philosophy. The tradition of Sufism presents both a way of life which avoids many of the rigidities of traditional Islam and also a complex conceptual system which enables the philosopher to develop ideas and arguments which are intellectually satisfying. Modern Islamic philosophy employs a wide variety of different techniques and approaches to the subject.

Mystical Philosophy in Islam

Islamic Philosophy

It is important at the outset to ask what is meant by mystical philosophy in the context of the Islamic philosophical tradition. The term in Arabic closest to the phrase 'mystical philosophy' would perhaps be *al-hikmat al-dhawqiyya*, literally 'tasted philosophy or wisdom', which etymologically corresponds exactly to sapience from the Latin root *sapere*, meaning to taste. As understood in English, however, the term 'mystical philosophy' would include other types of thought in the Islamic context, although *al-hikmat al-dhawqiyya* was at its heart. *Al-hikmat al-dhawqiyya* is usually contrasted with discursive philosophy, or *al-hikmat al-bahthiyya*.

Mystical philosophy in Islam would have to include all intellectual perspectives, which consider not only reason but also the heart-intellect, in fact primarily the latter as the main instrument for the gaining of knowledge. If this definition is accepted, then most schools of Islamic philosophy had a mystical element, for there was rarely a rationalistic philosophy developed in Islam which remained impervious to the distinction between reason and the intellect (as *nous* or *intellectus*) and the primacy of the latter while rejecting altogether the role of the heart-intellect in gaining knowledge.

This entry concentrates on those schools which not only include but emphasize *noesis* and the role of the heart-intellect or illumination in the attainment of knowledge. We shall therefore leave aside the Peripatetic school, despite the mystical elements in certain works of al-Farabi, the 'oriental philosophy' of Ibn Sina (Nasr 1996b) and the doctrine of the intellect adopted by the Muslim Peripatetics (*mashsha'un*) in general. Instead, the discussion will concentrate primarily upon the Isma'ili philosophy so closely connected with Hermetic, Pythagorean and Neoplatonic teachings, the school of Illumination (*ishraq*) of al-Suhrawardi and his followers, certain strands of Islamic philosophy in Spain and later Islamic philosophy in Persia and India. However, it would also have to include the doctrinal formulations of Sufism and its metaphysics from al-Ghazali and Ibn al-'Arabi to the present.

Isma'ili and Hermetic Philosophy

Isma'ili philosophy was among the earliest to be formulated in Islam going back to the *Umm al-kitab (The Mother of Books)* composed in the second century AH (eighth century AD). It expanded in the fourth century AH (tenth century AD) with Abu Hatim al-Razi and Hamid al-Din Kirmani and culminated with Nasir-i Khusraw. By nature this whole philosophical tradition was esoteric in character and identified philosophy itself with the inner, esoteric and therefore mystical dimension of religion. It was concerned with the hermeneutic interpretation (*ta'wil*) of sacred scripture and saw authentic philosophy as a wisdom which issues from the instructions of the Imam (who is identified on a certain level with the heart-intellect), the figure who is able to actualize the potentialities of the human intellect and enable it to gain divine knowledge.

The cosmology, psychology and eschatology of Isma'ilism are inextricably connected with its Imamology and the role of the Imam in initiation into the divine mysteries. All the different schools of Isma'ili philosophy, therefore, must be considered as mystical philosophy despite notable distinctions between them, especially, following the downfall of the Fatimids, between the interpretations of those who followed the Yemeni school of Isma'ilism and those who accepted Hasan al-Sabbah and 'The Resurrection of Alamut' in the seventh century AD (thirteenth century AD).

Two of the notable philosophical elements associated with Shi'ism in general and Isma'ilism in particular during the early centuries of Islamic history are Hermetism and Pythagoreanism, the presence of which is already evident in that vast corpus of writings associated with Jabir ibn Hayyan, who was at once alchemist and philosopher. The philosophical dimension of the Jabirian corpus is certainly of a mystical nature, having incorporated much of Hermeticism into itself, as are later works of Islamic alchemy which in fact acted as channels for the transmission of Hermetic philosophy to the medieval West. When one thinks of the central role of Hermeticism in Western mystical philosophy, one must not forget the immediate Islamic origin of such fundamental texts as the *Emerald Tablet* and the *Turba Philosophorum*, and therefore the significance of such works as texts of Islamic mystical philosophy.

Obviously, therefore, one could not speak of Islamic mystical philosophy without mentioning at least the hermetical texts integrated into Islamic thought by alchemists as well as philosophers and Sufis, and also Hermetic texts written by Muslim authors themselves. It should be recalled in this context in fact that the philosopher Ibn Sina had knowledge of certain Hermetic texts such as *Poimandres* and the Sufi Ibn al-'Arabi displays vast knowledge of Hermeticism in his *al-Futuhat al-makkiyya (The Meccan Illuminations)* and many other works.

As for Pythagoreanism, although elements of it are seen in the Jabirian corpus, it was primarily in the *Rasa'il* (Epistles) of the Ikhwan al-Safa' in the fourth century AH (tenth century AD), who came from a Shi'ite background and whose work was wholly adopted by later Isma'ilism, that one sees the full development of an Islamic Pythagoreanism based upon the symbolic and mystical understanding of numbers and geometric forms (Netton 1982). What is called Pythagorean number mysticism in the West had a full development in the Islamic world, and was in fact more easily integrated into the general Islamic intellectual framework than into that of Western Christianity?

Illuminationist Philosophy

Perhaps the most enduring and influential school of mystical philosophy in Islam came into being in the sixth century AH (twelfth century AD) with Shihab al-Din al-Suhrawardi, who founded the school of *ishraq* or Illumination. Al-Suhrawardi's basic premise was that knowledge is available to man not through ratiocination alone but also, and above all, through illumination resulting from the purification of one's inner being. He founded a school of philosophy which some have called theosophy in its original sense, that is, mystical philosophy through and through but without being against logic or the use of reason. In fact, al-Suhrawardi criticized Aristotle and the Muslim Peripatetics on logical grounds before setting about expounding the doctrine of *ishraq*. This doctrine is based not on the refutation of logic, but of transcending its categories through an illuminationist knowledge based on immediacy and presence, or what al-Suhrawardi himself called 'knowledge by presence' (*al-'ilm al-huduri*), in contrast to conceptual knowledge (*al-'ilm al-husuli*) which is our ordinary method of knowing based on concepts.

In his masterpiece Hikmat al-ishraq (The Philosophy of Illumination), translated by the foremost Western student of al-Suhrawardi, Henry Corbin, as *Le Livre de la Sagesse Orientale*, the Master of Illumination presents an exposition of a form of mystical philosophy which has had a following up to the present day. Based upon the primacy of illumination by the angelic lights as the primary means of attaining authentic knowledge, the school of *ishraq* in fact was instrumental in bestowing a mystical character upon nearly all later Islamic philosophy, which drew even closer to Islamic esotericism or Sufism than in the earlier centuries of Islamic history without ever ceasing to be philosophy.

Although the wedding between philosophy and mysticism in Islam is due most of all to the gnostic and sapiential nature of Islamic spirituality itself, on the formal level it is most of all the school of Illumination or *ishraq* which was instrumental in actualizing this wedding, as eight centuries of later Islamic philosophy bears witness.

Philosophy in the Maghrib and Spain

The rise of intellectual activity in the Maghrib and, especially, Andalusia was associated from the beginning with an intellectual form of Sufism in which Ibn Masarra was to play a central role. Most of the later Islamic philosophers of this region possessed a mystical dimension, including even the Peripatetics Ibn Bajja and Ibn Tufayl. The former's *Tadbir al-mutawahhid (Regimen of the Solitary)*, far from being a political treatise, deals in reality with man's inner being. Ibn Tufayl's *Hayy ibn Yaqzan (Living Son of the Awake)*, interpreted by many in the West in naturalistic and rationalistic terms, is a symbolic account of the wedding between the partial and universal intellect within the human being, a wedding which results consequently in the confirmation of revelation that is also received through the archangel of revelation, who is none other than the objective embodiment of the universal intellect.

Moreover, this mystical tendency is to be seen in its fullness in less well-known figures such as Ibn al-Sid of Badajoz who, like the Ikhwan al-Safa', was devoted to mathematical mysticism, and especially the Sufi Ibn Sab'in, the last of the Andalusian philosophers of the seventh century AH (thirteenth century AD), who developed one of the most extreme forms of mystical philosophy in Islam based upon the doctrine of the transcendent unity of being (*wahdat al-wujud*) (Taftazani and Leaman 1996). Andalusia was also the home of the greatest expositor of Sufi metaphysics, Ibn al-'Arabi.

Illuminationist Thought in the East

In eastern lands of the Islamic world and especially Persia, which was the main theatre for the flourishing of Islamic philosophy from the seventh century ah (thirteenth century AD) onward, primarily mystical philosophy was dominant during later centuries despite the revival of the discursive philosophy of the *mashsha'is*, such as Ibn Sina, by Khwajah Nasir al-Din al-Tusi and others. It was in the East in the seventh and eighth centuries ah (thirteenth and fourteenth centuries AD) that the doctrines of *ishraq* with its emphasis on inner vision and illumination were revived by al-Suhrawardi's major commentators, Shams al-Din al-Shahrazuri and Qutb al-Din al-Shirazi, who was also a master of Ibn Sinan philosophy.

The next three centuries saw mystical ideas and doctrines become ever more combined with the philosophical theses of the earlier schools, and figures such as Ibn Turkah Isfahani sought consciously to combine the teachings of Ibn Sina, al-Suhrawardi and Ibn al-'Arabi. This tendency culminated in the tenth century AH (sixteenth century ad) with the establishment of the School of Isfahan by Mir Damad and the foremost metaphysician of later Islamic thought, Mulla Sadra, in whom the blending of ratiocination, inner illumination and revelation became complete. In this school the most rigorous logical discourse is combined with illumination and direct experience of ultimate reality, as seen so amply in Mulla Sadra's masterpiece *al-Asfar al-arba'ah (The Four Journeys)*.

This later Islamic philosophy is certainly mystical philosophy, relying as it does on 'experiential' knowledge and direct vision of ultimate reality and the angelic worlds, a vision that is associated with the eye of the heart (*'ayn al-qalb* or *chism-i dil*). However, it is also a philosophy in which the categories of logic are themselves seen as ladders for ascent to the world of numinous reality in accordance with the Islamic perspective, in which what would be called Islamic mysticism from a Christian perspective is of a gnostic (*'irfani*) and sapiental nature, Islamic mysticism being essentially a path of knowledge of which love is the consort, rather than a way of love exclusive of knowledge.

In any case it was this type of philosophy, associated especially with the name of Mulla Sadra, that has dominated the philosophical scene in Persia during the past few centuries and produced major figures such as Hajji Mulla Hadi al-Sabzawari and Mulla 'Ali Zunuzi in the thirteenth century AH (nineteenth century AD), both of whom were philosophers as well as mystics. It is also this type of philosophy that continues to this day and has in fact been revived during the past few decades. Nearly all philosophers in Persia associated with the school of Mulla Sadra, which is also known as *al-hikmat al-muta'aliya* (literally the 'transcendent theosophy'), have been and remain at once philosophers and mystics.

In India likewise, Islamic philosophy began to spread only after al-Suhrawardi and during the past seven centuries most Islamic philosophers in that land have been also what in the West would be called mystics. It is not accidental that the school of Mulla Sadra spread rapidly after him in India and has had expositors there to this day. Perhaps the most famous of Muslim intellectual figures in India, Shah Waliullah of Delhi, exemplifies this reality. He was a philosopher and Sufi as well as a theologian, and his many writings attest to the blending of philosophy and mysticism. It can in fact be said that Islamic philosophy in India is essentially mystical philosophy, despite the attention paid by the Islamic philosophers there to logic and in some cases to natural philosophy and medicine.

Sufism and the Akbarian Tradition

No treatment of mystical philosophy in Islam would be complete without a discussion of doctrinal Sufism and Sufi metaphysics, although technically speaking in Islamic civilization a clear distinction has always been made between philosophy (*al-falsafa* or *al-hikma*) and Sufi metaphysics and gnosis (*al-ma'rifah, 'irfan*). However, as the term 'mystical philosophy' is understood in English, it would certainly include Sufi metaphysical and cosmological doctrines which were not explicitly formulated until the sixth and seventh centuries ah (twelfth and thirteenth centuries ad) although their roots are to be found in the Qur'an and hadith and the sayings and writings of the early Sufis.

The first Sufi authors who turned to an explicit formulation of Sufi metaphysical doctrines were Abu Hamid Muhammad al-Ghazali in his later esoteric treatise such as *Mishkat al-anwar (The Niche of Lights)* and *al-Risalat al-laduniyya (Treatise on Divine Knowledge)*, and 'Ayn al-Qudat Hamadani who followed a generation after him. The writings of these great masters were, however, a prelude for the vast expositions of the master of Islamic gnosis Muhyi al-Din Ibn al-'Arabi, perhaps the most influential Islamic intellectual figure of the past seven hundred years. Not only did he profoundly influence many currents of Sufism and establish an 'Akbarian tradition' identified with such later masters as Sadr al-Din Qunawi, 'Abd al-Rahman Jami and, in the last century, Amir 'Abd al-Qadir and Shaykh Ahmad al-'Alawi. He and his school also influenced formal philosophy to such an extent that a figure such as Mulla Sadra would not be conceivable without him.

The Ibn al-'Arabian doctrines of the transcendent unity of being, the universal man, the imaginal world and eschatological realities are not only esoteric and mystical doctrines of the greatest significance in themselves for the understanding of the inner teachings of Islam, but are also sources of philosophical meditation for generations of Islamic philosophers to the present day, who have cultivated diverse and rich schools of mystical philosophy during the past eight centuries and brought into being currents of philosophical thought that are still alive in the Islamic world. One need only think of such fourteenth century ah (twentieth century ad) figures as 'Alalamah Tabataba'i in Persia and 'Abd al-Halim Mahmud in Egypt to realize the significance of the wedding between philosophy and mysticism in the Islamic intellectual tradition, not only over the ages, but as part of the contemporary Islamic intellectual scene.

Bibliography

Abraham, A. J. *Islamic Fundamentalism and the Doctrine of Jihad*. Lima, OH: Wyndham Hall Press, 2002.

Abu Khalil, As'ad. *Bin Laden, Islam, and America's New 'War on Terrorism'*. Open Media Pamphlet Series. New York: Seven Stories Press, 2002.

Ahmed, Nafeez Mosaddwq. *The War on Truth: 9/11, Disinformation and the Anatomy of Terrorism*. Northampton, MA: Olive Branch Press, 2005.

Aho, James. *Politics of Righteousness: Idaho Christian Patriotism*. Seattle, WA: University of Washington Press, 1995.

Alexander, Yonah. *European Terrorism Today & Tomorrow*. Brassey's Terrorism Library. Washington, DC: Brassey's, 1992.

Alexander, Yonah. *Middle East Terrorism: Current Threats and Future Prospects*. International Library of Terrorism; New York: G.K. Hall & Co., 1994.

Alexander, Yonah. *Middle East Terrorism: Selected Group Profiles*. Washington, DC: Jewish Institute for National Security Affairs, 1994.

Alexander, Yonah. *Palestinian Religious Terrorism: Hamas and Islamic Jihad*. New York: Transnational, 2002.

Alexander, Yonah. *Palestinian Secular Terrorism: Profiles of Fatah, Popular Front for the Liberation of Palestine, Popular Front for the Liberation of Palestine-General Command, and Democratic Front for the Liberation of Palestine*. New York: Transnational, 2003.

Alexander, Yonah. *Terrorism in Europe*. New York: St. Martin's Press, 1982.

Alexander, Yonah. *Usama bin Laden's al-Qaida: Profile of a Terrorist Network*. Ardsley, NY: Transnational Publishers, 2001.

Alexander, Yonah; Latter, Richard, editors, *Terrorism and the Media: Dilemmas for Government, Journalists and the Public*. Washington, DC: Brassey's, 1990.

Al-Khattar, Aref M. *Religion and Terrorism: An Interfaith Perspective*. Westport, CT: Praeger, 2003.

Anderson, Chris. *The Billy Boy: The Life and Death of LVF Leader Billy Wright*. Edinburgh: Mainstream, 2002.

Anderson, Sean. *Terrorism: Assassins to Zealots*. Lanham, MD: Scarecrow Press, 2003.

Anti-Defamation League, *Extremism in the Name of Religion: The Violent Record of the Kahane Movement and Its Offshoots*. New York: ADL, 1995.

Anti-Defamation League, *Extremism in the Name of Religion: The Violent Legacy of Meir Kahane and Its Offshoots*. Update. New York: ADL, 1995.

Anti-Defamation League, *Extremism on the Right: A Handbook*. New York: Anti-Defamation League, 1988.

Appleby, R. Scott. *Ambivalence of the Sacred: Religion, Violence, and Reconciliation*. Lanham, MD: Rowman & Littlefield Publishers, 2000.

Arostegui, Martin C. *Twilight Warriors: Inside the World's Special Forces*. London: Bloomsbury Publishing, 1995.

Ateneo Center for Asian Studies, *Before and After September 11, 2001: An Asian Perspective*. Quezon City: Ateneo de Manila University Press, 2005.

Avruch, Kevin. *Culture and Conflict Resolution*. Washington, DC: United States Institute of Peace, 1998.

Bar, Shmuel. *Warrant for Terror: Fatwas of Radical*

Islam and the Duty of Jihad. Hoover Studies in Politics, Economics, and Society. Lanham, MD: Rowman & Littlefield, 2006.

Bartholomeusz, Tessa J. *Buddhist Fundamentalism and Minority Identities in Sri Lanka*. New York: State University of New York Press, 1998.

Barton, Greg. *Indonesia's Struggle: Jemaah Islamiyah and the Soul of Islam*. Sydney, Australia: University of New South Wales Press, 2004.

Cateura, Linda Brandi. *Voices of American Muslims: 23 Profiles*. New York: Hippocrene Books, 2005.

Catholic Institute for International Relations, *Guatemala, Never Again*. Maryknoll, NY: Orbis Books, 1999.

Davies, Barry. *Terrorism: Inside a World Phenomenon*. London: Virgin Books, 2003.

Devji, Faisal. *Landscapes of the Jihad: Militancy, Morality, Modernity*. Ithaca, NY: Cornell University Press, 2005.

Devji, Mantoshe Singh. *The Mad Messiah: Osama bin Laden and the Seeds of Terror*. Scottsdale, AZ: Inkwell Productions, 2002. Emerson, Steven. *American Jihad: The Terrorists Living Among Us*. New York: Free Press, 2002.

Emerson, Steven. *Worldwide Jihad Movement: Militant Islam's Target the West*. Jerusalem, Israel: Institute of the World Jewish Congress, 1995.

Eriksson, Tore. *11th March 2004 Madrid Terrorist Attacks: Observation Report*. Karlstad, Sweden: Swedish Rescue Services Agency, 2006.

Ernst, Carl W. *Following Muhammad: Rethinking Islam in the Contemporary World*. Chapel Hill, NC: University of North Carolina Press, 2003.

Esposito, John L. *Islam: The Straight Path*. 3rd edition. New York: Oxford University Press, 1998.

Esposito, John L. *The Islamic Threat: Myth or Reality?*. New York: Oxford University Press, 1992.

Esposito, John L. *The Oxford Dictionary of Islam*. New York: Oxford University Press, 2003.

Esposito, John L. *Unholy War: Terror in the Name of Islam*. New York: Oxford University Press, 2002.

Etzioni, Amitai. *How Patriotic is the Patriot Act? Freedom Versus Security in the Age of Terrorism*. New York: Routledge, 2004.

Fandy, Mamoun. *Saudi Arabia and the Politics of Dissent*. New York: Palgrave, 2001.

Farah, Douglas. *Blood From Stones: The Secret Financial Network of Terror*. New York: Broadway Books, 2004.

Gardell, Mattias. *Gods of the Blood: The Pagan Revival and White Separatism*. Durham, NC: Duke University Press, 2003.

Gerges, Fawaz A. *The Far Enemy: Why Jihad Went Global*. New York: Cambridge University Press, 2005.

Habeck, Mary R. *Knowing the Enemy: Jihadist Ideology and the War on Terror*. New Haven, NY: Yale University Press, 2006.

Han, Henry H., editor. *Terrorism & Political Violence: Limits & Possibilities of Legal Control*. Terrorism (Oceana Publications, inc.) ; 2nd series. New York: Oceana, 1993.

Hiro, Dilip. *War Without End: The Rise of Islamist Terrorism and Global Response*. New York: Routledge, 2002.

Hoffman, Bruce. *Holy terror: The Implications of Terrorism Motivated by a Religious Imperative*. Santa Monica, CA: RAND, 1993.

Howard, Russell D. *Defeating Terrorism: Shaping the New Security Environment*. Guilford, CT: McGraw-Hill, 2004.

Huband, Mark. *Warriors of the Prophet: the Struggle*

for Islam. Boulder, CO: Westview Press, 1999.

Hudson, Rex A. *Who Becomes a Terrorist and Why: The 1999 Government Report on Profiling Terrorists*. Guilford, CT: Lyon Press, 2002.

Jaber, Hala. *Hezbollah: Born with a Vengeance*. New York: Columbia University Press, 1997.

Jacquard, Roland. *In the Name of Osama bin Laden: Global Terrorism & the bin Laden Brotherhood*. Durham, NC: Duke University Press, 2002.

Jaimoukha, Amjad M. *The Chechens: A Handbook*. New York: Routledge Curzon, 2005.

Karawan, Ibrahim. *Islamic Impasse*. New York: Oxford University Press, 1997.

MacArthur, John. *Terrorism, Jihad, and the Bible: A Response to the Terrorist Attacks*. Nashville, TN: W Publishing Group, 2001.

Lutz, James M. *Global Terrorism*. New York: Routledge, 2004.

Maley, William. *Fundamentalism Reborn?: Afghanistan and the Taliban*. New York: New York University Press, 2001.

Miniter, Richard. *Losing Bin Laden: How Bill Clinton's Failures Unleashed Global Terror*. Washington, DC: Regnery, 2003.

Mishal, Shaul. *The Palestinian Hamas: Vision, Violence, and Coexistence*. New York: Columbia University Press, 2000.

Napoleoni, Loretta. *Modern Jihad: Tracing the Dollars Behind the Terror Networks*. Sterling, VA: Pluto Press, 2003.

Noorani, A. G. *Islam & Jihad: Prejudice versus Reality*. New York: Zed Books, 2002.

Nusse, Andrea. *Muslim Palestine: The Ideology of Hamas*. Amsterdam: Harwood Academic Publishers, 1998.

O'Ballance, Edgar. *Islamic Fundamentalist Terrorism,*

1979-95: The Iranian Connection. Washington Square, NY: New York University Press, 1997.

O'Ballance, Edgar. *Islamic Fundamentalist Terrorism: 1979-95*. Basingstoke: Macmillan, 1997.

Ojeda, Auriana. *Islamic Fundamentalism*. San Diego, CA: Greenhaven Press, 2003.

O'Kane, Rosemary. *Revolutionary Reign of Terror: the Role of Violence in Political Change*. Brookfield, VT: Elgar, 1991.

Rana, Muhammad Amir. *A to Z of Jehadi Organizations in Pakistan*. Lahore: Mashal Books, 2004.

Randal, Jonathan C. *Osama: The Making of a Terrorist*. New York: Knopf, 2004.

Rapoport, David C. *The Rationalization of Terrorism*. Frederick, MD: University Publications of America, 1982.

Scheuer, Michael. *Through Our Enemies Eyes: Osama bin Laden, Radical Islam, and the Future of America*. Rev. ed., 2nd ed., Washington, DC: Potomac Books, 2006.

Taheri, Amir. *Holy Terror: Inside the World of Islamic Terrorism*. Bethesda, MD: Adler & Adler, 1987.

Venske, Ben. *The al-Qaeda Threat: An Analytical Guide to al-Qaeda's Tactics & Targets*. Alexandria, VA: Tempest Publishing, 2003.

Waardenburg, Jacques. *Muslims and Others: Relations in Context*. New York: Walter de Gruyter, 2003.

Wiktorowicz, Quintan. *Global Jihad: Understanding September 11*. Falls Church, VA: 2002.

Zacharias, Ravi K. *Light in the Shadow of Jihad*. Sisters, OR: Multnomah Publishers, 2002.

Index

R

S

T

V

W